NEEDED TRUTH

A Magazine for the Teaching

of the Word of God

(First published 1888)

VOLUME 128
2021-2022

*If you abide in My word, you are
My disciples indeed.
And you shall know the truth,
and the truth shall make you. free.
(John 8:31,32 NKJV)*

PUBLISHED BY:
HAYES PRESS
The Barn, Flaxlands,
Royal Wootton Bassett,
Wiltshire, U.K., SN4 8DY

From the Editors' desk

Issue 1 2021

We leave a year behind us that will surely live long in the memory; will this one we are now entering be any less memorable? It seems as though the new U.S. Administration carries more existentialist threat towards Israel, and that perhaps means that the shadows are shortening still more ahead of our Lord's return for His Church.

I was recently thinking of how the Day of the Lord (cf. 2 Thess.2:2) is a recurring theme of major and minor prophets alike in the Old Testament. They announced it as a day of darkness and wrath and judgement, with blessing for Israel lying beyond when peacefully back in her land. The prophetic vista scoped out stretches far beyond the discipline and then return of the Exiles from the 6th century BC onward. The full expression of 'Jacob's trouble' (Jer.30:7 KJV) lies ahead for Israel and the surrounding nations mentioned back then.

Where do we today find hope in all this? It is from the fact that the Church the Body was hidden in the Old Testament. This is the plainest way to see that the Church is 'not appointed for wrath' (1 Thess.5:9), having no direct or immediate textual connection with the Day of the Lord there. But to what extent are current global trends part of the build-up? Facing up to such things as the worldwide scourge in our time, there are those, principally those without God, who seem overwhelmed by a sense of life's apparent meaninglessness; while those whose lifestyles show that they truly know God can always find dignity in living as God's imagers. This should be the goal of all who have been bought out of the human slave market of sin. It's always good to hear of this happening to more and more people. In one sense, none of this is new in a fallen world where generation after generation has met with triumph and disaster, but hopefully with the help of more accurate, biblical counsel from our friends than Job received, we can overcome the various temptations which those two imposters present us with.

Have a blessed New Year.
Brian

Who endures, wins

Jones Goodson Mankhwazi, Chilomoni, Malawi

Temptation is part of Christian life. As a true born-again believer, you cannot live in this world without facing temptations. We face them daily, when we overcome them our genuine faith is manifested before God and men. Some Christians, when tempted, question God and ask: "Why me, Lord?" They ask due to a lack of knowledge and understanding of Christian principle.

Our Saviour, Jesus Christ, who is our master, faced the same challenge. He was tempted by Satan in the wilderness: *"Then Jesus was led up by the Spirit into the wilderness to be tempted by the devil."*[1] Spiritual victory is often followed by testing. Jesus, in His response to all three temptations, quoted the Word of God, demonstrating the power of scripture in battling the Evil One.

There was nothing morally wrong with turning stones to bread, but Satan was tempting Jesus to do a miracle outside of the Father's will. This explains why Jesus quotes Deuteronomy 8:3. Bread alone does not sustain life; ultimately God is the one who sustains all life. It is our responsibility to trust God and remain in God's will. There are many types of temptations and challenges in life. During His time on earth, Jesus demonstrated to us how to overcome in the midst of temptations. He is our great teacher when it comes to learning how to overcome temptations.

Life is tough even at the start for some of us. Perhaps you come from a very poor family, or it was difficult for you to finish your education. Jesus knows what it feels like to have a difficult situation. He faced many challenges, but that did not stop Him from knowing His relationship to His heavenly Father and being committed to God's purpose. No matter what your problem is, your relationship with God in heaven will help you to overcome your difficult circumstances and to achieve your spiritual goal.

Three spiritual elements that can help us to overcome temptations:

Persistence
Jesus Christ succeeded in His mission by finishing the work the Father had sent Him to do when He faced all the trials in life. Jesus was able to remain composed through all those trials because what He had in His heart was greater than all the threats, accusations and insults He faced.

He knew how to persevere. You will never be successful unless you have the spirit of persistence. Fight until you feel the joy of victory.

It is obvious that God wants us to be fighters because the Bible calls us soldiers:[2] we are more than conquerors,[3] we are warriors, we are a people who battle. Stay in the fight until you win.

Prayer

"But they who wait for the LORD shall renew their strength; they shall mount up with wings like eagles;they shall run and not be weary; they shall walk and not faint."[4]

Prayer is where you receive the ability to continue the fight. A Christian must have a daily dynamic personal prayer life with God. Prayer helps you to have a continual communication and fellowship with God. You achieve nothing for the Lord without prayer. If you are always in touch with the Father, you will always be nourished in your life. Sometimes when you are serving God you might be criticised, pressed, opposed and become weak in faith. This is the time that we must kneel down, pray to God and cast our burdens before Him. He will see us through, if our prayer is based on the Word of God. In prayer, we find comfort, encouragement and spiritual refreshment.

Patience

"Therefore do not throw away your confidence, which has a great reward. For you have need of endurance, so that when you have done the will of God you may receive what is promised."[5]

Whoever endures, wins. We are not omniscient as God is; that's why we need to be patient and rely on God who gives guidance according to His purpose. When we are patient in the time of trials, we are able to be calm in the midst of challenges and keep moving, having a good relationship with God. Patience is the key to attaining the highest level. It's scriptural to say that the patient man is stronger than a mighty warrior.[6] Patience brings wisdom that helps us to tackle trials.

References: [1]Matt.4:1-11 [2]2 Tim.2:3-4 [3]Rom.8:37 [4]Isa.40:31 [5]Heb.10:35-36 [6]Prov.16:32
Bible quotations from the ESV.

Knowing God

Social justice

Andy Seddon, Swindon, England

God created humans to know Him, and so pursuing this knowledge has got to be the greatest possible pursuit of our life both now and for all eternity. When Jesus was praying for His disciples in the hours leading up to His crucifixion, He defined 'eternal life' like this: *"that they know you, the only true God, and Jesus Christ whom you have sent."*[1] So knowing God involves more than just an academic knowledge, but encompasses a living, emotional relationship with God that changes our lives. J.I. Packer makes a distinction between 'knowing' and 'knowing about' God, and warns that 'one can know a great deal about God without much knowledge of Him'.[2] Many Jews and religious leaders in Jesus' day were proof of this.[3]

True knowledge of God

How do we show that we truly know God? What will our lives increasingly look like if we have this knowledge of Him? That is what this series of articles seeks to explore based on some key scriptural texts. Our text on this occasion is taken from Jeremiah 22:15-17:

"Do you think you are a king because you compete in cedar? Did not your father eat and drink and do justice and righteousness? Then it was well with him. He judged the cause of the poor and needy; then it was well. Is not this to know me? declares the LORD. But you have eyes and heart only for your dishonest gain, for shedding innocent blood, and for practicing oppression and violence."

Jeremiah is writing about (and to) Jehoiakim, a wicked son of the famously good King Josiah. Jehoiakim reigned in Judah between 609-598 B.C. not long before the eventual Babylonian captivity and exile of Judah. Egypt oppressed Judah at this time, and Jehoiakim was appointed as king by the Pharaoh (Neco) who imposed a hefty tax on the land of a hundred talents of silver and a talent of gold.[4] Jehoiakim obtained this money by taxing his own people[5] which no doubt created additional hardship and poverty throughout the land, and this was whilst he lived comfortably in his 'cedar' palace, probably built or maintained financially by the same taxes.

Jeremiah condemns Jehoiakim's 'dishonest gain' (v.17) and self-indulgence and contrasts him with his good father Josiah who did 'justice and righteousness' (v.15), and who 'judged the cause of the poor and needy' (v.16), and then he asks rhetorically, *"Is that not what it means to know me?"* (v.16 NIV).

That Jehoiakim did not truly know the God of Israel is evidenced further by his arrogant and fearless disregard for God's Word and God's prophet which you can read about in Jeremiah 26:24. So our knowledge of God is evidenced in our treatment of others; this applies to people both in and outside the community of God's people. In the New Testament Paul writes: *"So then, as we have opportunity, let us do good to everyone, and especially to those who are of the household of faith."*[6] Our treatment of others is born out of our love, which in turn is evidence of our knowledge of God, as the apostle John writes: *"*Anyone *who does not love does not know God, because God is love."*[7]

The focus on the vulnerable and needy
Throughout the Bible we are repeatedly drawn to God's special concern for the most needy and vulnerable in society. For example, the LORD Almighty, speaking through Zechariah, commands: *"Administer true justice; show mercy and compassion to one another. Do not oppress the widow or the fatherless, the foreigner or the poor"*.[8] This quartet of 'widows, orphans, immigrants and the poor', represents those who were the most economically and socially powerless in society; it is not so different these days. In the New Testament, James echoes Zechariah's words: *"Religion that is pure and undefiled before God the Father is this: to visit orphans and widows in their affliction, and to keep oneself unstained from the world."*[9] The latter part of this verse reminds us that our personal moral purity is greatly important, but of equal importance to God is our pro-social care and concern for the needy and vulnerable.

Knowledge of God's character
Our attitude to others reflects our grasp of God's character, and this should lead to us increasingly growing to learn to love what He loves and to hate what He hates. The Lord discourages worldly boasting on the basis of 'wisdom', 'might' or 'riches', but says: *"let him who boasts boast in this, that he understands and knows me, that I am the LORD, who practices steadfast love, justice, and righteousness in the earth. For in these things I delight, declares the LORD."*[10] And so those who know their God should do likewise, as Micah emphasises: *"He has told you, O man, what is good; and what does the LORD require of you but to do*

justice, and to love kindness, and to walk humbly with your God?"[11]

Knowledge of God's love for our neighbour

Our attitude towards others reflects the level of our appreciation of how God feels about others. The wise man writes: *"Whoever oppresses a poor man insults his Maker, but he who is generous to the needy honors him."*[12] The Psalmist also writes at length that it is the God of Jacob *"who executes justice for the oppressed, who gives food to the hungry. The LORD sets the prisoners free; the LORD opens the eyes of the blind. The LORD lifts up those who are bowed down;... The LORD watches over the sojourners; he upholds the widow and the fatherless ..."*[13] So should our attitude and behaviour be, as far as we have opportunity.

Knowledge of God's love for His children

Our attitude towards our brothers and sisters in Christ reflects our grasp of God's deep love and identification with them. Jesus in Matthew 25 spoke of a future day when He would return as the glorified Son of Man and would separate out the 'sheep' from the 'goats'. Many who believed they belonged to Jesus will be shocked on that day to discover they never did. The evidence is found in the way they treated others who belonged to Christ.

The 'righteous' (or 'sheep') will say to Him: *"'Lord, when did we see you hungry and feed you, or thirsty and give you drink? And when did we see you a stranger and welcome you, or naked and clothe you? And when did we see you sick or in prison and visit you?' And the King will answer them, 'Truly, I say to you, as you did it to one of the least of these my brothers, you did it to me.'"*[14] Conversely, Jesus, when warning His disciples of the persecution and hatred they were going to face from enemies after his departure, explains: *"all these things they will do to you on account of My name, because they do not know Him who sent me."*[15]

Another instructive passage for church life is in 1 Corinthians 8 when Paul explores the behaviour of church members concerning a matter of personal conscience (eating food that has been offered to idols). Paul stresses the harm of doing something that offends a brother or sister with a weaker conscience (due to their different cultural background) just because their own conscience may allow it. Paul says: *"knowledge puffs up, but love builds up"*, and then immediately adds: *"if anyone imagines he knows something, he does not yet know as he ought to know."* Paul warns therefore against destroying the brother *"for whom Christ died."*[16]

Knowledge of God's grace towards us

New York pastor Tim Keller writes: 'there is a direct relationship between a person's grasp and experience of God's grace, and his or her heart for justice and the poor.'[17] We see this in the reaction of Zaccheus the tax collector after he experienced the grace of Jesus towards him.[18] Jesus commanded His disciples as He sent them out with the message of the kingdom of heaven, to *"heal the sick, raise the dead, cleanse those who have leprosy, drive out demons. Freely you have received; freely give."*[19] We may not have the same miraculous gifts that were given to the disciples on that occasion, but we have the same responsibility to show God's love to others freely and generously. By doing so, we show that we truly know God.

References:
[1]Jn 17:3 [2]Packer, J.I. Knowing God,1973 [3]See for e.g. Jn 5:39 [4]2 Chron.36:3 [5]2 Kgs.23:35 [6]Gal.6:10 [7]1 Jn 4:8 [8]Zech.7:9-10 NIV [9]Jas.1:27 [10]Jer.9:23-24 [11]Mic.6:8 [12]Prov.14:31 [13]Ps.146:7-9 [14]Matt.25:37-40 [15]Jn 15:21 [16]1 Cor.8:1-2,11 [17]Keller, T. Generous Justice, 2010 [18]Lk.19:8 [19]Matt.10:7-8 NIV
Bible quotations from the ESV unless stated otherwise.

Ecclesiastes

The march of time
Martin Jones, Hamilton, Canada

I've recently been enjoying the flurry of activity in the Churches of God Archives Facebook group. One picture featured John Swift, my great-great-great-grandfather. Sadly, I know next to nothing about him – and that's only a few generations back; if we estimate a generation to be about 20-25 years, there have perhaps been 80-100 generations since the birth of Christ. The arithmetic tells me that I've got millions more ancestors whom I know nothing of – and so do you! Just think of all the triumphs and tragedies, the toil and the tears, the dreams and the decisions that have been lost to us in the mists of history.

Those mists remind me of what the Teacher (generally thought to be king Solomon) had to say in the Bible book of Ecclesiastes. Thirty-eight times, he uses the Hebrew word *'hevel'* or *'hebel'* – which is usually translated as 'meaningless,' 'vanity' or 'futile'; that seems confusing – after all, if everything really *is* meaningless, then such a statement itself must be meaningless! But the root of the word has the thought of a mist or a vapour, like the breath on a cold winter's day, which is there one minute and gone the next without a trace – rather like our ancestors.[1]

The same Hebrew word is used by David in Psalm 39:5 – *"You have made my days a mere handbreadth; the span of my years is as nothing before you. Everyone is but a breath, even those who seem secure."* This introduces another element to us – not only is a vapour ephemeral,[2] but it's enigmatic.[3] Older UK readers will remember 'pea-soupers' where you couldn't see your hand in front of your face. Paths that seemed safe and secure were made scary by a seemingly impenetrable fog. Isn't life a bit like that? The hymnwriter vividly describes his life's journey as 'groping in my misty way.'[4] That's as true today as when he wrote it well over a century ago, and it's always been true to human experience.

A good deal of people's lives seems geared to systems, security and stability in an uncertain world. Perhaps that's why decluttering and home organisation TV shows are all the rage, why there's a desire to have a detailed financial plan, budget and will, and why scientists are so busy doing complex models to predict the spread of Covid-19. We like to feel we're on top of things.

But the Teacher is asking us to accept that, just as we think we've got it all figured out and nailed down, we'll find that our goal, like that ethereal fog, is beyond our grasp. As much as we'd like to, we'll never be able to eliminate unpredictability 'under the sun' – we've as much chance of catching the wind.[5] But we shouldn't confuse this with the futility of atheism that says that, ultimately, everything really *is* meaningless and has no higher purpose – we're not simply locked into an endless and repetitive life cycle that's dictated by the laws of nature.

For the atheist, 'under the sun' is all there is. But at the end of Ecclesiastes, Solomon urges us to look beyond the sun, to the Creator above: *"Remember also your Creator in the days of your youth."*[6] And rather than invest our time in trying to answer the unanswerable existential questions of life,[7] we would be much better off focusing on what God expects us to do: *"Fear God and keep his commandments, for this is the whole duty of man."*[8] Why? *"For God will bring every deed into judgment."*[9]

What is fleeting and forgotten to humanity is being filed away by God for a future day – whether the Great White Throne for unbelievers[10] or the Judgement Seat of Christ for believers.[11] So we need to be sure that whatever we're doing now isn't simply growing attractive-looking grass that will one day be burned in the fire[12] rather than earning an eternal crown – that really would be futile!

References:
[1]Eccles.1:11 [2]lasting only for a short time [3]something that is mysterious or difficult to understand [4]John Parker, PHSS 190 [5]Eccles.1:14 [6]Eccles.12:1 [7]Eccles.1:17; 12:12 [8]Eccles.12:13 [9]Eccles.12:14 [10]Rev.20:11 [11]2 Cor.5:10 [12]Lk.12:28
Bible quotations from the NIV.

Image-bearing

Made in God's image
David Viles, Hayes, England

It was just a small silver coin, and Jesus' question was simple: *"Whose image and inscription is this?"* His rejoinder astonished His hearers: *"Render... to Caesar the things that are Caesar's, and to God the things that are God's."*[1] – a wonderfully concise, meaningful definition of the balanced and accountable Christian life.

The coin showed Caesar in profile, wearing the laurel wreath of victory. If the image was of emperor Tiberius, the inscription, too, was flattering – 'son of the divine Augustus'. Clearly, projecting an image was important to Roman emperors – nothing new then, even in today's image-conscious world, where people can hire an 'image consultant' to enhance their persona; or, for those less pretentious, purchase the products of the styling and beauty industry.[2]

Stamped with the likeness of God
So people in general are – and always have been – image conscious. We need not be surprised about this, because God Himself – in whose image every human being is created – is Himself very conscious of His image: *"My glory I will not give to another, nor My praise to carved images."*[3] To be created in the image of God, then, is to be a very exalted and privileged being indeed. The Genesis account differentiates the creation of human beings from the rest of God's wonderful creation as uniquely the considered, self-communing, deliberate effort of the Trinity – *"Let Us make man..."*[4] – the highest point of the divine creative work. Every human being is made *"a little lower than the angels ... crowned ... with glory and honor."*[5] To take a life made in God's image therefore has dire consequences; the dignity of all human beings must be taken most seriously.[6]

The Hebrew words for image and likeness are different but synonymous – an example of the common Hebrew device of stating something in two different ways. In essence, they signify the glorious thought that every human is stamped with the likeness and ownership of God, is responsible to Him and, marvellously, possesses the potential to relate to Him. It is notable that the same words – image and likeness – are used in relation to Adam and his son Seth.[7] We all like to look for resemblances between a parent and their child, but we recognise that they are similar yet different people; so it is on a higher level in relation to God and humanity.

Therefore, each person on this earth is in some sense like his or her Maker. But in what sense is this marvellous creature 'created in the image of God'? Much ink has been devoted to this question over the centuries and we must be careful to avoid speculation. Scripture provides one clear answer in terms of the divinely appointed destiny of humanity to rule over God's earthly creation.[8] Just as God is the master of all He surveys, so humanity – made in His image – has authority to 'subdue' (a strong word) earthly creation. We may infer that this includes the means of doing so – not just physical strength, but also the ability to reason, to plan, to design and build, to act and think creatively and to work constructively together. The fact that God is, for example, the creator of indescribable beauty or awesome natural phenomena explains how human beings on a lower, delegated level possess the ability to create beautiful art or impressive architecture, or amazing feats of scientific and technological endeavour.

Tarnishing and burnishing
Then came the Fall. According to one cynic, 'God made man in His own image, and man returned the favour'.[9] The devastating outcome was the tarnishing of God's image in human beings. That image – the image and glory of God[10] – remained, but the divine spark was obscured, sullied by sin. Praise be, then, to God – bending all His effort to burnish, restore and immeasurably enhance His image in redeemed humanity, predestined to be conformed to the image of His Son.[11]

References:
[1]Matt.22:20-21 [2]Worth in 2019 a staggering US$532 billion. Bethany Biron, Business Insider, 9 July 2019. [3]Isa.42:8 [4]Gen.1:26 [5]Ps.8:5 [6]Gen.9:6. Note that this exalted status continues to be the case, even after the Fall. [7]Gen.5:3
[8]Gen.1:28-30 [9]Frank Wedekind, 1864-1918, in effect paraphrasing
Rom.1:20-32 [10]1 Cor.11:7 [11]Rom.8:29
Bible quotations from the NKJV.

The Atonement

The market place: redemption

Stephen McCabe, Belfast, N.Ireland

Our English word 'atonement' comes from a Middle English word that means to be 'at one' (at-one) or in harmony with someone. The word that is usually translated as 'atone' in our Old Testament can mean to 'wipe clean' or 'appease'.

Scholars debate as to whether the root meaning of the word is 'to cover', 'to ransom', or 'to wipe clean'. An early, and helpful, use of the word (demonstrating some of these nuances) is seen in Genesis 32, where Jacob seeks to make peace with Esau (after having provoked his anger many years before). He says, *"I will appease him with the present that goes before me. Then afterward I will see his face; perhaps he will accept me."*[1] The thought is that the gift that Jacob sends ahead of him will atone for his previous wrongs before Esau; that Esau's anger will be appeased; that the gift will 'wipe clean' the anger on Esau's face; that the gift will purchase acceptance with Esau (we would say that Jacob is trying to 'redeem himself' in Esau's eyes); that there will be satisfaction for previous wrongs – and the result of all of this will be a reconciliation between the two estranged brothers. A rich picture of atonement in Genesis!

Scripture gives us different pictures that help us explore what God has done for us through the atoning work of Christ. One of those pictures is the market place – using the language of redemption or purchasing. The verb translated 'to redeem' in our Old Testament involves the idea of ransom – the exchange of money, or an object of value, to buy something back.

Redemption in Exodus

The language of redemption is used to describe God's work to bring the Israelites *"out of the land of Egypt, out of the house of slavery"*.[2] The Lord declares to Moses, *"I will bring you out from under the burdens of the Egyptians, and I will deliver you from their bondage. I will also redeem you with an outstretched arm and with great judgements."*[3] Moses, after their flight from Egypt, in his song of Exodus 15, says, *"In Your lovingkindness You have led the people whom You have redeemed."*[4]

How did that redemption work? The Lord said it was by *"an outstretched arm and with great judgements"*. The ultimate judgement in the liberation of Israel from Egypt, following the judgements that afflicted the land in various ways, was the death of the firstborn males in Egypt. The price of redemption in the Exodus account is ultimately seen in the forfeiting of the lives of Egypt's firstborn. The firstborn males in Israel were delivered from this judgement through the blood of the Passover Lamb as a sign on the houses where they lived so that, when the Lord saw the blood, He passed over them. As a result of this fearful judgement, and Egypt's reaction to it, God's people were bought back for Him.

In Exodus 13 (following the account of their departure from Egypt), the Lord then claims ownership of every firstborn man or beast among the Israelites.[5] Firstborn males in Israel were given to God perpetually in recognition of the redemption from Egypt, and when these sons would ask about this, Israelite families were to point them back to the Exodus, and the death of the firstborn in Egypt.

Rather than the death of all the firstborn animals and sons in sacrifice to the Lord (the latter explicitly forbidden in the Law[6]), the Israelites redeemed their firstborn sons for a price.[7] Israel were redeemed from the burden and bondage of Egypt. Israel could not have redeemed themselves from the oppression they were under in Egypt. They had no means to buy or negotiate their own way out. It was God who 'heard', 'remembered', 'saw', and 'took notice' of them[8] – it was God who acted to secure their redemption from slavery. It's also helpful to note what they were redeemed for. In simple terms, the purpose of Israel's liberation from Egypt is described by the Lord in Exodus: *"Let My people go, that they may serve Me."*[9] That service would be something wonderful – they were to be a people set apart for God, serving Him and enjoying His love, with an inheritance (the land which was promised to the patriarchs) and a future. God viewed them, and they were to consider themselves, as His *"own possession"* or *"special treasure"*[10] as a result of the redemption.

New Testament perspectives
The language of redemption as seen in Exodus (redeemed from slavery, redeemed for the service of God) sets the tone for what follows in Scripture, and is picked up strongly in the New Testament. Paul takes us through a remarkable re-framing of the 'exodus' journey from Romans 6 to 8. In Romans 6 those who are in Christ are freed from slavery to sin – *"when you were slaves of sin, you were free in regard*

to righteousness. Therefore what benefit were you then deriving from the things of which you are now ashamed. For the outcome of those things is death. But now having been freed from sin and enslaved to God, you derive your benefit, resulting in sanctification, and the outcome, eternal life."[11]

Paul is emphasising that slavery to sin and slavery to righteousness cannot co-exist. The outcome of being enslaved to sin is death (and separation from God). The outcome of slavery to God is holy living and eternal life in Christ. This redemption which liberates us from slavery to sin is not something we could have done ourselves, but is *"the free gift of God."*[12]

Romans 7 points us to Sinai, but emphasises our freedom from the Law (as per Galatians 4, where, in what would have been shocking to Jewish readers, Paul describes Sinai as bearing children who are to be slaves[13]) through the death and resurrection of the Lord Jesus (and our unity with Him)[14], demonstrating the superiority of the New Covenant over the Old. Romans 8 then brings us to a place of sonship and inheritance (*"…you have received a spirit of adoption as sons by which we cry out, "Abba! Father!" The Spirit Himself testifies with our spirit that we are children of God, and if children, heirs also, heirs of God and fellow heirs with Christ"*[15]) and even the ultimate completion of our redemption – *"having the first fruits of the Spirit, even we ourselves groan within ourselves, waiting eagerly for our adoption as sons, the redemption of our body."*[16]

So we quickly move from slavery to adoption as sons, and sharing the inheritance of God (all things) with the rightful heir Himself! (With a completion of that redemption still to come – discussed below.) In Roman society, for a slave to make the journey to being freed, adopted by his master, and gaining an equal inheritance with his biological/natural sons was a very rare thing (though not unheard of) – but what God has done for us in redeeming us for Himself is something of immeasurably more value.

This is the spiritual reality of our redemption experience here and now. In the language of Paul, this is how we are to 'reckon ourselves'[17] – and that should change how we live. We are often encouraged to 'be our own person' today. But see what Paul says: *"do you not know that your body is a temple of the Holy Spirit who is in you, whom you have from God, and that you are not your own? For you have been bought with a price: therefore glorify God in your body."*[18] Doesn't that run against the grain of the world? You are not your own – you belong to someone else, because you have been purchased at a very high price. And that's key to the thought of redemption – that a price has been paid. What was the price? Peter tells us: *"you were not redeemed with perishable things like silver or gold... but with precious blood, as of a lamb unblemished and spotless, the blood of Christ."*[19]

The song sung to the slain Lamb in Revelation 5 declares the purpose of our redemption: *"You were slain, and purchased for God with Your blood men from every tribe and tongue and people and nation. You have made them to be a kingdom and priests to our God, and they will reign upon the earth."*[20]

Our full redemption
We live in the 'now' and 'not yet' with God. We have our redemption right now, but we await with certain hope the redemption of our bodies. John speaks about it beautifully in his first letter – *"Beloved, now we are children of God, and it has not appeared as yet what we will be. We know that when He appears, we will be like Him, because we will see Him just as He is. And everyone who has this hope fixed on Him purifies himself, just as He is pure."*[21] We are children of God right now – but we can't even grasp what we will be when the full redemption of our bodies comes! We do know that we will appear glorious, as He is revealed in glory.[22] Everyone who has this hope purifies himself. This is our future – so 'reckon yourself' to be so now.

References:
[1]Gen.32:20 [2]Ex.20:2 [3]Ex.6:6 [4]Ex.15:13 [5]See Ex.13:1-16 [6]Deut.18:10 [7]Num.18:14-16 [8]Ex.2:24-25 [9]Ex.8:1 [10]Ex.19:5 NASB/NKJV [11]Rom.6:20-22 [12]Rom.6:23 [13]Gal.4:24 [14]Rom.7:4-6 [15]Rom.8:15-17 [16]Rom.8:23 [17]Rom.6:11 NKJV [18]1 Cor.6:19-20 [19]1 Pet.1:18-19 [20]Rev.5:9-10 [21]1 Jn 3:2-3 [22]Col.3:4 23 https://commons.wikimedia.org/wiki/File:Gor%C3%A9e-MaisonEsclaves1.jpg.
Bible quotations from the NASB.

A worldwide scourge

Peter Hickling, Cromer, England

This page in the magazine is intended to look at current worldwide problems from a Christian point of view, to encourage those of us who are Christians in our faith, and to try to answer the questions of those who are not. Few of our readers in any country of the world would doubt what the main worldwide problem is; at the time of writing, the Covid-19 virus has led to tens of millions of illnesses and over a million deaths. It has disrupted the economies of many countries, particularly the most advanced ones, and more hardships are still to come – many will lose their jobs, and perhaps their homes.

If you believe that there is a God, what sort of a god is he?

The Bible is quite unequivocal about this; it says that *"God is love."*[1] A statement like this cannot stand on its own; it must be authenticated by actions. This is true on a human level; if I say that I am honest, and you know that I tell lies, you will doubt anything that I say. The words and actions of Jesus Christ, the Son of God, supported all His claims. Scripture tells us that *"God so loved the world that he gave his only Son."*[2] The Gospels give detailed records of all that Jesus did and said, supporting His claims to be God in human form. For instance, He said, *"I and the Father are one."*[3] There are many references to the actions and words of Christ in the Gospels which authenticate His person and nature; they are summed up by the apostle John, when he wrote: *"Jesus did many other signs in the presence of the disciples, which are not written in this book; but these are written so that you may believe that Jesus is the Christ, the Son of God, and that by believing you may have life in his name."*[4]

Why does a loving God let this pandemic happen?

God loves His children, just as you love yours. Does that mean that He always gives them what they want? Do you? You must have read many stories of people who had deprived childhoods and were stronger in their adult lives than they would have been if they had had everything easy. The expression is not so often used today, but we used to often hear it said that someone had many 'trials' in his life. Like so many expressions in the English language this came from Scripture: James wrote, *"Count it all joy, my brothers, when you meet trials of various kinds."*[5] A 'trial' in this sense is not merely a problem, as we might say "S/he's a trial to me," but a test.

An outstanding example of this in the Bible is that of Job. He was rich, with extensive flocks and herds, and seemed to have everything he might want. God said to Satan, *"Have you considered my servant Job, that there is none like him on the earth, a blameless and upright man, who fears God and turns away from evil?"*[6]

Cynical Satan answered the LORD and said, *"Does Job fear God for no reason? Have you not put a hedge around him and his house and all that he has, on every side? You have blessed the work of his hands, and his possessions have increased in the land. But stretch out your hand and touch all that he has, and he will curse you to your face."*[7] God gave Satan permission to take away all Job's possessions, but Job passed the test. Even though his wife said, *"Curse God and die,"*[8] Job's response was "he *arose and tore his robe and shaved his head and fell on the ground and worshiped. And he said, 'Naked I came from my mother's womb, and naked shall I return. The LORD gave, and the LORD has taken away; blessed be the name of the LORD.' In all this Job did not sin or charge God with wrong."*[7]

Is it hard to suggest that this pandemic may be a trial? That God may have permitted it so that people will turn to Him, rather than to possessions? Most of us in the developed world are rich compared with our brothers and sisters in Africa and Asia: perhaps the possibility of danger to our lives might make us, our friends and our neighbours reassess our priorities.

References:
[1]1 Jn 4:8 [2]Jn 3:16 [3]Jn 10:30 [4]Jn 20:30-31 [5]Jas.1:2 [6]Job 1:8 [7]Job 1:9-11 [8]Job 2:9 [9]Job 1:20-22
Bible quotations from the ESV.

Job

The three friends

David Webster, Liverpool, England

The Bible book of Job addresses one of the great world issues: the problem of suffering and how a good God can allow people to suffer. However, those wanting a neat answer to this age-old problem will be disappointed. What we get is a reminder that (a) God is sovereign and in ultimate control (b) there is evil and sadness in our world (c) there is a great adversary, Satan.

Is all Scripture truth?
The Bible is God's Word and all of it came from God and is both accurate and useful for instruction![1] But that doesn't mean we can take any text from God's Word and assume the words are true. We need to interpret Scripture correctly and be aware that, sometimes, words are spoken which are neither true nor from God. The context of every Bible verse and passage is important. Job is one of the wisdom books of the Bible. And some of the words in Job are not true! 'The reader of the book of Job learns what is simply the world's wisdom, seemingly logical but actually wrong, and what constitutes God's wisdom and what builds confidence in God's sovereignty and righteousness.'[2] The books of Job and Ecclesiastes are good examples of where we need to be very careful of taking a text at face value!

Jumping to conclusions
We are looking at Job's three friends who *"set out from their homes and met together by agreement to go and sympathise with him and comfort him"*[3] after he had experienced terrible loss. The expression 'a Job's comforter' has come to mean 'a person who under the guise of giving comfort aggravates distress'.[4] This is probably to misrepresent the friends. They saw how Job's life was in ruins, his health was broken and his peace of mind was destroyed. For a full week they sat with him in respectful silence showing that they cared, doing what the Christians in Rome were later encouraged to do: *"weep with those who weep."*[5]

Because he is suffering, Eliphaz concludes that Job must have done something wrong and should now submit to the discipline of the Almighty.[6] Bildad seems to suggest that Job is receiving justice from the hand of God. Not only must Job have sinned but his family as well: *"Does God pervert justice? Does the Almighty pervert what is right? When your children sinned against him, he gave them over to the penalty of their sin."*[7] He assumes that Job has turned away from God and he and his children deserve the disasters that have come upon them. Zophar is convinced that Job has sinned and in a big way – he is the most condemnatory of the 'friends'!

God *"recognises deceivers; and when he sees evil, does he not take note?"*[8] He accuses Job, by insinuation,[9] of oppressing the poor, leaving them destitute, seizing houses and getting rich by dishonourable means. The implication of 11:6 is that Job deserves even worse than he got!

"Suffering means God is punishing you!"

"Who, being innocent, has ever perished?" asked Eliphaz[10] and the three friends spent a lot of energy trying to convince Job of this. But God vindicated Job[11] and the Lord Jesus explicitly refuted the idea that pain and suffering is necessarily the result of wrongdoing. Speaking about a local disaster the Lord said: *"Or those eighteen who died when the tower in Siloam fell on them – do you think they were more guilty than all the others living in Jerusalem? I tell you, no!"*[12] And of the blind man: *"Neither this man nor his parents sinned,"* said Jesus, *"but this happened so that the works of God might be displayed in him."*[13]

We do suffer as a consequence of our foolish actions and God does, of course, discipline us[14] but let's not make the same error of judgment that Job's friends made when we see difficulties and suffering coming into the lives of God's people by assuming they must have done something bad.

References:
[1]See 2 Tim.3:16-17 [2]Fee & Stuart, How to Read the Bible for All its Worth (Second Edition), Scripture Union [3]Job 2:11 [4]Concise Oxford Dictionary [5]Rom.12:15 ESV [6]Job 5:17 [7]Job 8:3-4 [8]Job 11:11 [9]Job 20:6-19 [10]Job 4:7 [11]Job 42:7-9 [12]Lk.13:4-5a [13]Jn 9:3 [14]Heb.12:5-11
Bible quotations from the NIV unless otherwise stated.

100 years in Africa

Missionary profiles

Eric Sampou, Port Harcourt, Nigeria

Early Impressions

From the African viewpoint, the brethren to be introduced below displayed a high standard of holiness and godliness. They were men of humility, usefulness and reliability. In spite of the rigours and strains of Africa, they had come to point us to Christ and to teach us truths about the kingdom of God. What visions they had! Yet could they have imagined that there would later be churches of God in Ghana, Liberia, Malawi, Kenya, Mozambique and Zimbabwe also?

They came into Nigeria and discovered that we had so many tribes and that we spoke 500 languages. English became our *lingua franca*. They experienced emotional upset and depression in a strange land, but the Lord stood with them. So many were ill due to the tropical climate with its unwanted warmth and oppressive heat. Our lives were primitive. We lived in huts of mud, bamboo or wood and corrugated iron with thatched roofs, and certainly not without mosquitoes, cockroaches and ants. Yet from the ranks of the idolaters whom they had come to work among, some were chosen, elect of God and came to be found among those worshipping God in His holiness and glory.

Thomas Wallace (1887-1925) was born in Barrow-in-Furness, a town in Cumbria, north-west England. In 1881, his parents, John Wallace and Ann Stewart had moved to Barrow, though married in Dundee in Scotland. In 1915, Tom secured a job of 'national importance' with Elder Dempster & Co. at the Nigerian Dry Dock & Engineering Co. on the Forcados River near Warri, Delta State, Nigeria. He saw this as an opening from God for gospel outreach work there. Some years later, in 1921, he was commended to work full-time on behalf of the Churches of God; he resigned his post at the Dry Dock Co. and his wife and two sons joined him in Ibadan to work now for the Lord alongside Edwin Matthew. Tom Wallace's early interest in evangelism remained strong.

Emily, his wife, became ill and had to return to England with their children. By this time, the Lord was working in several ways to bring about a developing evangelical work in Nigeria, but the Churches of God's missionary work there had really begun with Tom Wallace from Barrow. Tragically, Tom was 'called home' on 7 December 1925 at the age of 38 and his grave is in Ibadan, Nigeria.

Edwin Matthew (1865-1924) was born in the English village of Wickham Skeith, Suffolk, to James Matthew and Betsy Chandler. Edwin read missionary stories about David Livingstone, Hudson Taylor, Henry Townsend, Hope Waddell and Mary Slessor before the First World War. His thoughts were of Africa. Often when he spoke at a meeting, it would be about Ebed-Melech, the Ethiopian eunuch, Simon from Cyrene, or some other African-related Bible story. He had a strong interest in missionary work in West Africa. Edwin became a London pharmacist and, in 1896, married Elizabeth Jarvis in Wandsworth, London. In 1899, he and Elizabeth sadly lost a son, Samuel, at 9 months and followed later by their second son, David, at less than two years of age.

Henry Elson noted that, at the time of the separation of Churches of God from the wider Brethren Movement, Edwin wholeheartedly identified himself with the 'remnant who sought to give effect to the truth of the house of God.' He took a decisive stand at that time. By 1901, Edwin Matthew was an overseer in the Church of God in London, in the company that met in Battersea. His brethren remarked of an exceedingly gracious and lovable personality, a man of a gentle and humble presence, but nevertheless one who had a purpose of heart and a tenacity of purpose which led him to accomplish not a little. He was commended by the Conference of Overseers of Churches of God to full-time service in preaching and teaching God's Word in 1919.

Edwin's heart was deeply exercised for many years towards work overseas and he never lost an opportunity for pressing the claims of that work. His vision and persistent purpose for the inception of this work was instrumental in its commencement. However, much work had to be done in the British Isles before the Community was sufficiently consolidated so as to be properly free to launch out in Gospel work overseas. When the happy moment arrived, Edwin and Elizabeth Matthew along with Fanny, wife of JPA Taylor, and William Terrell (1896-1961) sailed to Nigeria on the HMS Zaria from Liverpool on 17 March 1920 and on 5 April 1920 they arrived in Lagos.

By October 1922, Edwin was compelled to return to the UK on account of illness due to the tropical climate. However, he improved sufficiently in the UK for him to be able to return to Nigeria in May 1923 to resume his work in the preaching of the Gospel and the making of disciples. The periods of comparative good health were interspersed with attacks of his blood pressure trouble, sometimes with great severity and often his indomitable spirit made him persevere when assuredly one less zealous than he would have given up. It was his joy to witness the baptism of three disciples in 1924 – the firstfruits of evangelical work in Ibadan. On the 5 June 1924, Edwin Matthew gave his last address. By the following Tuesday his condition had deteriorated and the doctor was called. On 14 June 1924 the

Lord called Edwin Matthew 'home', and he was buried there in Ibadan.

John Park Allan Taylor (1869-1965) was a missionary who was born in Galway, Ireland on 2 May 1869. His Scottish parents, Colin Taylor and Margaret Allan, had moved to Barrhead in Scotland when John was eighteen months old.

In Nigeria, he became known for his efforts to improve local living standards in the communities where he worked, helping to change the beliefs of many and to introduce western education. John Taylor was accepted for full-time ministry in 1919 by what was then known as the British Isles and Overseas Conference of Overseers in the churches of God; his going to West Africa was already in view. He was married to Annie Piggott in 1896 in Edinburgh, Scotland, but she died on 8 February 1906, aged 33. Then in 1908, he married Fanny Crowder in Greenock, Scotland, and he came to Nigeria with her. Sadly she died on 4 November 1922. In 1925, he married Rachel McFarlane at Old Mill Street, Lagos. She was 29 and he was 56. Both lived until old age.

In 1890, he had been received among the Open Brethren in Barrhead, but stood with the Churches of God at 'the separation' of 1892-94. In 1905, he had been recognised as a 'leading brother' in Scotland. He was one of the five pioneering missionaries who came to Nigeria on the HMS Zaria in March 1920. He was also privileged to visit the Church of God in Grand Cess, Liberia. JPA Taylor previously had an important post in the ceramic industry, but had greater interest in missionary work. Much prayer was offered to God by the fellowship of Churches of God at the time. It was with great joy and much blessing to us that the Assembly in Lagos was planted on 8 May 1921. JPA Taylor's last visit to Nigeria was in February 1949, when he was 80 years old. He died on 5 November 1965 in Middlesbrough, England.

The tropical climate brought unwanted warmth and oppressive heat day and night. When it rained, it bucketed; sometimes with lightning and thunder, yet JPA Taylor loved Akarakumo, a village near Badagry, in Lagos State which was a place of palm trees, lagoon, sandy beach by the Atlantic and forest behind the village. They were privileged to see those who had been once idol worshippers now singing praise to our God as they worshipped on Lord's Days.

Africa is very appreciative of all the sacrifice and the huge cost that these pioneers paid, together with all the strenuous work and hardship they endured for us to be in the Fellowship today, and celebrating – by God's grace – the centenary of Churches of God on Nigerian soil

Can you help me with this?

Tattoos and other body art

Geoff Hydon, Mount Forest, Canada

Body art seems to be increasingly popular. Whether it improves appearance or not is a very personal matter, but there are some aspects that deserve careful thought by any Christian. We may know someone who has a faith- based tattoo, like the crown of thorns, or a Bible word, and these displays may have led to witnessing opportunities. Are there any compelling reasons not to use body art? First we should note this is a very old, pre-Christian, activity. Historically, it is known to have been used in various cultural settings for beautification of the body, acting as a supposed protection against bad spirits, as an identifying mark to distinguish between tribes, or to show a particular status. It is still commonly used in a similar way by gangs and sometimes in prisons. But, while those examples do need to be borne in mind, our concern is principally with its use by everyday people, especially Christian disciples.

Recent surveys suggest more people are now choosing to have body art (tattoos and piercing) than in previous decades.[1] It is now considered a mainstream practice in the western world. It's interesting that in a 2015 survey of 450 Colorado students, the majority of those who had used tattoos made their decision without accurate information as to associated health risks, and sometimes without being able to state just why they did it.[2] In terms of religious practice, although common in some religions, Jews and Muslims usually are forbidden to use body art (because of its association with idolatry); the Roman Catholic church permits body art if it is not sacrilegious, blasphemous or obscene. More importantly, let's see if we can find clear Bible-based examples or principles to apply.

Bible expectations and observations
- Disciples' bodies are 'temple of the Holy Spirit';[3] they belong to God.
- We have a responsibility to imitate good, not evil.[4]
- Moses' Law prohibited tattoos/cuts that symbolized idol worship.[5]

- Paul said that the violence against him left him branded by the marks of Jesus[6] (but they were not self-inflicted).
- Christ Himself bears in His body the marks of Calvary;[7] the marks of injury suffered. Christ-likeness calls for readiness to suffer on His behalf, not to copy the marks of suffering.

So, I should ask myself:
- How does my heart and my conscience convict me? Do I have freedom in Christ and a clear conscience before the Lord regarding the decision?[8]
- Am I passing judgment on a brother or sister because I don't personally feel I have freedom in Christ to do this myself?[9]
- Will I still want this image on me years from now? Our views on many things change over time. It is very difficult when young to weigh up future risks and benefits.[10]
- Will it be honouring to my parents (in the Lord),[11] and/or will my future spouse want me to have this?[12] There are examples of men who had the name of a girlfriend tattooed, but eventually married another woman!
- A Christian needs to earn a living.[13] How will it affect me getting work?
- Will I cause another brother/sister to stumble if I display body art?[14]
- Is my decision based on faith and will the result be glorifying to God?[15]
- Am I just imitating majority thinking, or those who act selfishly?[16]
- Have I properly considered the health risks, e.g. allergy, disease?[17]

Although there are clearly significant cautions to be taken into account, in the final analysis for disciples in churches of God this matter is one to be determined by individual conscience. And whatever we may feel ready to do, or not to do, let's aim to have a testimony that attracts others to the Person we follow!

References: [1] E.g. 2015 data Harris Poll: https://www.prnewswire.com/news-releases/tattoo-takeover- three-in-ten-americans-have-tattoos-and-most-dont-stop-at-just-one-300217862.html and BMC Italian data: http://www.biomedcentral.com/1471-2458/10/73https://sociologylectures.weebly.com/uploads/8/8/7/3/8873683/tattoosreseachpaper.pdf [3] 1 Cor.6:19 [4] 3 Jn 11 [5] Lev.19:28; Deut.14:1 [6] Gal.6:17 [7] Jn 20:27 [8] Rom.14:1-10 [9] Rom.14:13,21-22 [10] Ps.119:59 [11] Eph.6:1-3 [12] 1 Cor.7:4 [13] 2 Thess.3:12 [14] Rom.14:21 [15] Rom.14:23; 1 Cor.10:31 [16] 3 Jn 11 [17] 1 Cor.6:19-20

Meeting triumph and disaster

An interview with
Peter Hickling, Cromer, England

'If you can meet with triumph and disaster And treat those two impostors just the same…' Many people can remember those two lines of Kipling's 'If', but may not have a reason for calling triumph and disaster 'imposters'. It is an example of Victorian 'stiff upper lip' stoicism which is not currently fashionable, but there is a response to them which arises from Christian faith. Christians believe that there is a God who controls everything, and ultimately designs that *"for those who love God all things work together for good, for those who are called according to his purpose."*[1] If we believe that, we must accept that sometimes God does things whose purpose is known only to Him, and we must accept them because we trust His omniscient goodness.

A human example of this sort of thing is "Do your children always agree that what you want is good for them?" You may think that what I am writing is rather abstract, and separate from actual experience, so I have been prevailed upon to answer some questions about my own life. I was very reluctant to do this, because I am no examplar, but it may help some who have gone the same way:

NT: Have you known 'triumph' – moments of success and accomplishment in life?
I went to Liverpool University, where I obtained a degree in Civil Engineering, and met my wife Dorothy, who was in the Liverpool church. Later I went to Salford University, and while in the North West of England visited many churches. We had three children, Jocelyn, Duncan and Martin. We had a comfortable existence.

NT: What about 'disaster' – times of failure or loss?
Several, regrettably. My father died in January 1988 while driving his car, and we set off to drive across the country from Southport to my mother in Cromer. At a crossroads a driver on the minor road drove straight across into the side of our car, giving me serious head injuries, from which Dorothy was told that I had less than 20% chance of surviving.

People prayed for me around the world, and I did live, but Dorothy, who was injured herself, had to look after me – I couldn't walk or speak or get dressed.

A further disaster was the death of Duncan in 2009. He had been very active in the Church of God in Cromer, running two youth groups, as well as going into other Districts, even to Canada. The Church of God in Cromer cannot now sustain a youth work, and we cannot understand why Duncan was taken away: we can only say, with Job, *"The LORD gave, and the LORD has taken away; blessed be the name of the LORD."*[2]

NT: Didn't you ask why?
What good would that do? There is no way of finding an answer; the only Christian response is to trust God, who knows the end from the beginning. It may be that he had other things for me to do; perhaps I was unduly self-reliant, perhaps he was teaching me to trust.

NT: Those were single events, that might teach you a lesson. Is there anything else?
The biggest trial of all, which we cannot see any end of, is that Dorothy has been diagnosed with Alzheimer's disease, cannot go out on her own or drive and has a very limited memory. We are told that there is no cure, only palliative measures.

NT: What can you do about that?
We can pray. Over the years there have been many killers which were thought incurable at the time which have been much reduced or eliminated; e.g. smallpox, which has killed 300 – 500 million people, but which now only exists in a few laboratories. Is a cure for Alzheimer's impossible? Perhaps it is unlikely in our lifetime (since we are in our eighties), but it is not wrong to ask.

NT: What about the coronavirus pandemic?
It is a worldwide scourge; over a million people have died and 50 million have been infected. Those of us who live in areas of low infection can be thankful; many who have been infected have only had mild effects, and can be thankful for that too – that was the apostle Paul's message; *give thanks in all circumstances.*[3] Of course, I can't give any help to people who refuse to believe that there is anyone to listen to them – all they can do is to relapse into a sterile stoicism.

References: [1]Rom.8:28 [2]Job 1:21 [3]1 Thess.5:18
Bible quotations from the ESV.

Seed sowing

Information supplied by

Topesa Issa, Malawi

"Unless a grain of wheat falls into the earth and dies ... "[1]
There was a very large crowd at Phalula that day, perhaps two to three hundred people. It was Mary Katimba's funeral on a hot day in the so-called 'warm heart of Africa' – Malawi. Brother Patson Katimba and his family members were very satisfied with the strength of the support and with the words of tribute and clear sounding of the believer's certain hope in Christ. The preacher's initial impression of Malawian funerals was that they are heavily influenced by the multitude of family and friends in attendance. According to custom, it was a long, drawn-out affair over two days with a lot of waiting around.

Then, at the graveside particularly, there were prolonged bouts of loud wailing, lamentations and throwing of oneself on the burial mound as family members, each in turn, gave full vent to their emotions. In the West, Christian funerals are closer to a celebration and in that way give a dignified witness to unbelievers of the Christian hope. Here, however, the preacher's scriptural note of triumph at a believer's homecall to glory, seems almost negated by this cultural performance. To cap it all, a sector of the womenfolk seated in front of the preacher audibly reacted against the thirty minutes length of translated preaching. Understandable perhaps, if you've already been there for 24 hours and it's been a long time since breakfast! It had not helped that there had been a delay of somewhere between one and two hours because a local 'headman' had not got himself organised. But events start when they start in rural Africa.

But if there was a sense of disappointment from the preacher's perspective, there was to be a brighter sequel. Eight months later, came the news that the message proclaimed that day had 'touched many'. At the funeral at Phalula some had 'received the word'. At this, two of the overseers from Lilongwe visited Phalula. It is situated partway between Lilongwe and Blantyre and is the home village of Patson who is the Chairman of the elders of the Malawian churches of God. The visiting elders from Lilongwe encountered a group of about twenty in number.

After their visit, the members of this group began calling Brother Topesa daily, begging him to visit them and share the Word. They were taught the '7 steps' of the New Testament pattern for Christian discipleship.[2]

During Bro. Topesa's visit, he also taught the three aspects of salvation (believers are saved from the penalty of all their sins; can be saved from the power of their ongoing sins; and, at the Lord's return, will be saved from the presence of sin). Instruction was also clearly given explaining the Christian believer's eternal security: that once saved, someone can never be lost.[3] There was great joy at hearing these things plainly outlined from Scripture. The request from them is now for interviews: they desire to give their testimonies. To hear of this was belated encouragement for the preacher, because the lasting impression at the funeral time had been the reaction of one group of women who objected to the length of the preaching. In a fallen world, a sense of opposition is often a good sign because Satan opposes only what God is powerfully doing. When Satan is busy, God is even busier – and He will prevail.

The sowing of a body in the ground led to productive sowing of the good seed of the Word of God.[4] If so, how true for those who received the Word that it is better to go to the house of mourning than to go to the house of feasting![5] It's at least possible that there may be the planting of a Church of God in this place at some point. Phalula is not far from the location of the Church of God at Ntcheu. Joining the dots further, Phalula is within Balaka district, and Topesa next received an invite to preach to a group of people in Balaka town. These people were aware of the Church of God at Mwanakhu.

References:
[1]Jn 12:24 [2]Acts 2:41-42 [3]Jn 10:28 [4]Mk.4:3-8 [5]Eccles. 7:2

From the Editors' desk

Issue 2 2021

One of the great assurances made by the Lord Jesus Christ was that He had come to this earth so that we may enjoy an abundant life.[1] We might wonder what such an abundance looks like. Surely it would meet Peter's inclusive term of *"all things that pertain to life and godliness."*[2] Peter declared the key to such a life was a perceptive awareness of Christ, and His purposes.

So this magazine attempts in each quarterly issue to help us in that pursuit, by presenting varied challenges from the Bible for us to live up to. We hope, as you read through the different topics covered in this edition, that objective will be met. Of course, reading by itself is insufficient and we also need a sense of urgency as we try to put into practice what we learn of God's will for our lives.

Pursuing that tack, we may ask ourselves, how would we live our lives differently today if we expected to die tomorrow? Most of us may want this question to be hypothetical, but for many people in the past twelve months it has become a real concern; we have been subjected to constant reminders that we are not invincible. Sadly, the physical and mental weakness as death approaches may rob us of any real ability to make changes, so we must ensure we don't procrastinate. Paul settled the question well, saying that: 'now as always Christ will be honored in my body, whether by life or by death.'[3] The context of Paul's remarks in Philippians 1 is laden with a sense of resolve to go on doing what God had prepared for him to do.

And in this issue of NT we remind ourselves that, with one eye on eternity, we must see ourselves now as not just saved from sin's penalty, but saved to serve. Into such service the Lord can bring an abundance of opportunity and blessing.

Read on, and choose well!

Geoff

References:
[1]John 10:10 [2]2 Pet. 1:3 [3]Phil.1:20 ESV

He gives, we gather

Gilbert Grierson, Armagh, N.Ireland

The writing of this article was prompted by a walk through the old orchard next to our house in Northern Ireland one cold wintry morning early in January. The farmhouse we live in has two fires on which we burn sticks, logs and coal, and occasionally turf that has been dug from the bogs of this land. Over the years, most of the sticks for lighting the fires have come from the old orchard and the nearby trees. It was some weeks since I had last taken a walk to gather firewood, and on this particular day, after some high winds, I was able to collect quite a pile of dead branches that had been dislodged by the wind and fallen to the ground. All I needed to do was gather them! "Yet again, God's provision," I thought to myself.

I was reminded of the manna which we read about in Exodus 16 that God provided on a daily basis to meet the needs of the Israelites on their wilderness wanderings for forty years. There it was, faithfully provided morning by morning (with a double portion on the sixth day so the people could rest on the seventh day, the Sabbath). But it had to be gathered! Families, perhaps working together, had to go out from the camp, stoop to pick it up, fill baskets and carry them back to their tents for it to be prepared for meals – just like my sticks needed to be gathered and carried and chopped made ready for use lighting fires. The work of the Lord involves just that, doesn't it? Work! God has given us so much and entrusted us with so much to do. But we then have to work to make it useful in our own lives through diligent study and application; and then work to make it available to others, fellow believers or to those who are still outside of Christ, still in the 'darkness' of sin and unbelief.

Time and effort are required in any church – in prayer, planning programmes, preparing messages for young and old, distributing God's word around homes, in hospitals, waiting rooms, on the bus, in the market place, sharing the gospel wherever people are to be found. Individuals spend time writing letters, sending cards, emails, texts, communicating gospel truth via the wise use of social media, visiting sick neighbours and ring-fencing time each day to bring needy folks before the Lord. These are not easy tasks; it takes work. God's church register doesn't recognize the word 'unemployed'! In one of the parables that the Lord told (in Lk.19:11-27) a nobleman, who was going away to a far country, gave quite a sum of money to ten of his servants, with instructions to engage in business and make a profit until he should return.

The older versions of the Bible say in verse 13, *"Occupy till I come"* –
wise words that we could take to heart in our own day! There came a
day when their lord returned and servants were called to give an account
of their use of the money given them. Two had made a profit and were
commended; one had hidden it and had not made wise use of it. He was
severely reprimanded and suffered loss. We, too, have been given
something that we should not hide! We have the light of the gospel that
people in darkness need, and time that we can redeem and use
beneficially.

Knowing God

Stand like the brave!

Michael Johnston, Kirkintilloch, Scotland

Resolute in the knowledge of God
"...the people who know their God shall stand firm." (Dan.11:32)

A nation's freedom

The land that God gave to His Old Testament people is one of vital geographic importance. The safest roads connecting Africa or Arabia with Turkey (therefore Europe) or Syria (therefore Asia) all pass through the lands God gave to the twelve tribes. This meant that all traders, travellers and troops passing between these places had to go through Israel. This was a blessing when in the hands of kings like David and Solomon who leveraged these trade routes carrying all the finest goods to purchase similar goods to furnish the house of God. But it gave ample room for error also: the otherwise commendable king Josiah saw opportunity for himself when Pharaoh Neco of Egypt asked for safe passage to attack an enemy to the north. Josiah tried to secretly add his troops to the forces of Neco's enemy, presumably to turn the tide of the battle and weaken the neighbouring power of Egypt, but instead he was killed in the battle himself.[1] Not seen during the time of David, political games like Josiah's became more alluring to the kings of Israel and Judah as their kingdoms became weaker.

During the Cold War, the US and the USSR never fought against each other with armies, but instead fought for the allegiance of other countries that might change their patron power. Often those 20th Century political games spilled over into violent regime change (as in Cuba), and sometimes also into long wars, including the extant Korean war. The leaders of countries in that day thought that the benefits of Soviet or American backing were worth the risks, and similar opportunism lived in the days of the Old Testament. The seeds were there early: Asa, king of Judah, bought the allegiance of the king of Syria against the king of Israel in a war between the two.[2] He took treasures out of God's house in order to make payment for this alliance – a short benefit at the cost of the honour of the God who would ever defend Jerusalem. Similar deals with foreign powers were repeated in the later reigns of Ahaz and Hezekiah,[3] and the northern kingdom made alliances of its own, though they would not have been paying out of the temple treasury.

Those commended in Daniel's prophecy are those who would stand firm in their faith in God to be their deliverer, in contrast to those who instead put their faith in earthly powers. Although Hezekiah lived before Daniel, his change in attitude illustrates this mindset well, as he came to know that God alone was to be the source of the security of the people – and God vindicated that faith.[4] Those who put their faith in men, rather than God, for the national security of the kingdom were referred to in Daniel as those who *"forsake the holy covenant."*[5] Standing firm was a commendation given to those who wouldn't succumb to the pragmatic political game for the defence of Israel, but instead would know that *"the LORD is a refuge to his people, a stronghold to the people of Israel."*[6]

Preserving another freedom
When Paul wrote to the Galatians, he evoked a similar language to Daniel's when he spoke of his own resoluteness: *"to them we did not yield in submission even for a moment, so that the truth of the gospel might be preserved for you."*[7] He was utterly convinced of the truth of the new holy covenant, as it had been revealed to him from Jesus Christ Himself,[8] and so he remained resolute in holding fast to the truth of it. The forces arrayed against the New Testament people of God were not the armies of foreign kings, but the insidious teaching of those who sought to break the testimony of the churches by bringing them into 'slavery' – forcing additional traditions onto the people of God so that they might fail in keeping to the commandments that they had been given. That slavery was akin to the state of slavery to sin that they had known before their salvation:

"Formerly, when you did not know God, you were enslaved to those that by nature are not gods. But now that you have come to know God, or rather to be known by God, how can you turn back again to the weak and worthless elementary principles of the world, whose slaves you want to be once more? ... For freedom Christ has set us free; stand firm therefore, and do not submit again to a yoke of slavery."[9]

Paul passes on here the charge to 'stand firm' in their knowledge of Christ, even as he had not yielded to these false teachings. This instruction requires our active attention: it's the language of the battle line. Many films have a depiction of warfare that is more about style than accurate representation, and so battle sequences frequently involve people fighting in a chaotic melee, relying on their wits and their skill with weapons to fight off a sequence of individual combatants. This looks excellent as a choreographed scene on a big screen, but it would be a terrible analogy for the act of standing firm as a soldier.

Most armies in the time that the Bible was written were largely made up of unskilled conscripts, with a nucleus of the few trained soldiers that made up the king's bodyguard. Nevertheless, by adding to the size of the formations, these conscripts still played an important part of the battle. Very few people died in combat in that era; the vast majority of casualties occurred when one side gave in to fear and tried to flee. This provoked a chase and the slaughter of those who were running away. Therefore the role of a common person in an army wasn't to kill hundreds of the opposition, but to stand firm and not give in to fear, to keep panic from spreading through the whole army and putting everyone in danger.

The Christian mentality needs to be that befitting of such soldiers, contributing to the success of the whole by not fearfully retreating. The success of the fighting is the responsibility of kings and princes – and our victory has been completely won by Christ – yet God prizes those who do their duty in holding fast in faith to what they know of him. More than just not giving in to fear, we further need to understand soldierly discipline: *"Wake up from your drunken stupor, as is right, and do not go on sinning. For some have no knowledge of God. I say this to your shame."*[10] Paul might have been advocating the freedom of the believer from the works of the Law as he wrote to the Galatians, but he never promoted disregard for our requirement to live righteously. What guides our behaviour when we are not bound by the strict and detailed laws of the Old Testament? It's our knowledge of God. When writing to the Ephesians with the encouragement to stand firm, 'the truth' is one of the vital pieces of equipment Paul names: the knowledge of God itself produces in us the will and the ability to stand firm. This is how he can state in 1 Corinthians that we prove this knowledge is within us when we resist sin in our lives.

Sharing the knowledge of God

"… the wise among the people shall make many understand …" (Dan.11:33). The 'wise' in this verse means 'those that understand', and so the second commendation in this statement is of the passing on of knowledge. God gives particular understanding to some – perhaps through a natural ability, or because of a distinctly studious character, or through the provision of already learned teachers – but that understanding is never to be hoarded by the one who has been given it.

The entire people are commendable when those who have been given understanding dedicate themselves to helping others to understand. In the Old Testament, this was one of the roles of the priests, and so they were particularly called out for judgement when they fell short in this regard: *"...with you is my contention, O priest. ... My people are destroyed for lack of knowledge; because you have rejected knowledge, I reject you from being a priest to me..."*[11]

Paul's defence against a life of sin was that those who know God will reject it, and therefore it is a vital requirement of the health of a church of God that the Word of God is being ministered to it, so that they may more fully know God. When he wrote to Timothy, he made two requests of him in this regard: *"follow the pattern of the sound words you have heard from me... guard the good deposit entrusted to you."*[12] Timothy was singled out for this particularly because of his position as an overseer and a teacher, but we all carry these responsibilities somewhat, since we have become a holy priesthood[13] and therefore all share in that requirement to preserve the teachings of the House of God that have been entrusted to us by passing them on to others.

References:
[1]2 Chron.35:20-24 [2]1 Kgs.15:17-20 [3]2 Kgs.16:8; 18:15 [4]2 Kgs.19:14-36
[5]Dan.11:30 [6]Joel 3:16 [7]Gal.2:5 [8]Gal.1:12 [9]Gal.4:8-9; 5:1 [10]1 Cor.15:34
[11]Hos.4:4,6 [12]2 Tim.1:13-14 [13]1 Pet.2:5
Bible quotations from the ESV.

Ecclesiastes

Time and eternity

Ira Williamson, Trinidad, USA

God revealed Himself to Daniel as the Ancient of Days;[1] a title that stretches into eternity past. As the Alpha,[2] there is no beginning. God is the Ancient of Days – He has always been. Isaiah speaks of God's unfailing power and limitless understanding when he describes God as *"the Creator of the ends of the earth* and *the everlasting God."*[3] As the Omega,[2] He has no end. The word 'everlasting' captures the idea of the vanishing point. Like the horizon; as far as we can see, yet God goes further; much further. *"The LORD is the everlasting God"*[3] – He will always be. Yet God's memorial name, revealed to Moses at the burning bush, is *"I AM WHO I AM."*[4] The ever-present God. The God who is! The everlasting God, known and experienced in the present.

It is this backdrop of the everlasting perspective making the present memorable that helps to bring greater meaning to the beautifully poetic words of Ecclesiastes 3. As mortals, tied to the present with no control over the march of time, knowing there is a season for everything can feel depressing. Everything is a cycle. Day after day, season after season, year after year, generation after generation, and so it continues. There is a time for every purpose under heaven. All are known by God, yet busily enacted by us in the present as we press on into the futile future of seasons.

The fourteen couplets that follow verse 1 begin with two appointed times that encapsulate all the others: *"a time to be born, and a time to die."* We had no involvement in the first, and the second cannot be extended.[5] Perhaps the passing of time is most poignant to us because of the truth of verse 11 (NASB): *"He has also set eternity in their heart".* Here we have humanity's dilemma: knowing the certainty of eternity, yet only having the uncertainty of now, we look ahead with concern and do our best to use 'now' to make tomorrow better, or to forget the past, or to enjoy our next few moments. German author and Godless philosopher, Thomas Mann, wrote: 'To man, time is given like a piece of land, as it were, entrusted to him for faithful tilling; a space in which to strive incessantly, achieve self- realization, move onward and upward.

Yes, with the aid of time, man becomes capable of wresting the immortal from the mortal.'[6] If time is, indeed, all we have and now is all we get, then this knowledge of the everlasting adds sorrow to the passing of time.

Thomas Mann confessed the knowledge of the everlasting – the immortal – in his heart, but felt that happiness could only be found by wresting this knowledge away. How sad!

God placed eternity in our hearts and His work is everlasting – we cannot add to it or take away from it.[7] We didn't put it there, and we can't take it out!But can we, who know the everlasting God, not also miss the lesson? The God who is and who always will be, who holds our time in His hand,[8] who knows all our days before any existed,[9] has placed the everlasting in our heart to make the present precious.

The Lord's prayer teaches us to ask for daily bread: today's provision.[10] The Lord's own words teach us not to worry about tomorrow.[11] He warns us about trusting provisions stored up for the future, but He exhorts us to store up for the everlasting[12] – the vanishing point, the future beyond time.

Abraham planted a tree and called upon the name of *"the LORD, the Everlasting God."*[13] Abraham, the deedless yet promised, owner of the land. He looked beyond – past the things that were promised and to the one who promised them – the Everlasting God. He looked to the vanishing point, to a heavenly country.[14] We have also been called to look ahead. Not to tomorrow, but to the everlasting. Because if we only look to the future, to tomorrow – we have plenty of opportunity to return to the things from which God called us.[14] Can God only be trusted for our Eternity, but not for tomorrow or even now?

References:
[1]Dan.7:9,13,22 [2]Rev.22:13 [3]Isa.40:28 [4]Ex. 3:14 [5]Matt.6:27 [6]J.Allison & D.Gediman (Eds), This I Believe: The Personal Philosophies of Remarkable Men and Women [7]Eccles.3:14 [8]Ps.31:15 [9]Ps.139:16 [10]Matt.6:11 [11]Matt.6:34 [12]Matt.6:19-20 [13]Gen.21:33 [14]Heb.11:14-16
Bible quotations from the ESV.

Image-bearing

No man-made images

Geralde Mag-usara, Davao, Philippines

Worshipping idols not only remains commonplace in parts of the world today, but was also a big concern in Bible times. These pagan practices existed from the time of the patriarchs[1] to that of the Apostles.[2] Forsaking such practice was involved in God's call to Abraham to leave his country.[3] The same can be said regarding His people when they were slaves in Egypt, which was full of idolatry. God instructed Moses to tell Pharaoh, *"Let My people go"*[4] And then, after they had been delivered, He commanded them: *"You shall not make for yourself an idol, or any likeness of what is in heaven above or on the earth beneath or in the water under the earth."*[5] *'You shall not make for yourselves idols, nor shall you set up for yourselves an image ... to bow down to it; for I am the LORD your God.'"*[6]

It is clear that God wanted to forbid any carved, or graven, images that were thought to represent Him (for they only reduce Him to human thoughts). In fact, when God gave this command to Moses at Mount Sinai, the people only heard the sound of the words, but they saw *no form.*[7] Consistent with this, of course, Jesus taught a Samaritan woman, who perhaps worshipped idols, that God is spirit.[8]

"To whom then will you liken God? Or what likeness will you compare with Him?'[9] *"I am the LORD, that is My name; I will not give My glory to another, nor My praise to graven images."*[10] God is so serious about this that it is listed among the character of those who will face eternal judgment: *"... and idolaters ... their part will be in the lake that burns with fire..."*[11] Obviously, idols are lifeless.[12] They could neither declare former events nor announce what is coming; they are no account and nothing, and an abomination; they are false, worthless, only being wind and emptiness, or confusion.[13]

An example of their uselessness is found in the account of Micah in the book of Judges. He thought he was blessed when he had a shrine, an ephod, household of idols, and above all a Levite as priest to minister.[14] He confidently said, *"Now I know that the LORD will prosper me, seeing I have a Levite as priest."*[15] But what happened next was in fact the opposite. He gained nothing when the sons of Dan stole them and they were not able to save him from his enemies.[16]

Unlike Daniel's three friends, by contrast, who were willing to lose everything, face the furnace of blazing fire unto death, just to stand for the truth of the one true and living God. They strongly refused to be forcibly made to worship the graven image of Nebuchadnezzar. They confidently said to the king that whether or not God would deliver them, *"we are not going to serve your gods or worship the golden image that you have set up."*[17]

As a consequence, they were cast into an extremely hot burning fire – so hot that even those men who carried them were slain by its flame. But God saved the three faithful friends. The king was then enlightened as a result and made a decree in favour of God. And they were blessed by the king who prospered them in the province of Babylon.[18] How blessed we are by our King when we don't compromise our devotion to Him! *"Those who honor Me I will honor".*[19] However, let us also note that worshipping idols is not only limited to carved/graven images. Someone might say, "Well, I'm not guilty of that since I do not possess any of them." That's true. But there's another form of idolatry revealed in the New Testament that we need to take heed of. Paul urged and warned the believers at Colossae to *"consider the members of your earthly body as dead to immorality, impurity, passion, evil desire, and greed, which amounts to idolatry."*[20] They cannot inherit the kingdom of Christ and God.[21] Therefore, we must worship Him alone[22] and so let us guard ourselves from idols.[23]

References:
[1]Gen.31:19 [2]Rom.1:21-23 [3]Josh.24:2; Gen.12:1 [4]Ex.5:1 [5]Ex.20:4
[6]Lev.26:1 [7]Deut.4:12 [8]Jn 4:24 [9]Isa.40:18 [10]Isa.42:8 [11]Rev.21:8 [12]Ps.115:4-7
[13]Isa.41:22-29 [14]Jdgs.17:5-7 [15]Jdgs.17:13 [16]Jdgs.18:17-27 [17]Dan.3:18
[18]Dan.3:19-30 [19]1 Sam.2:30 [20]Col.3:5 [21]Eph.5:3-5 [22]Matt.4:10 [23]1 Jn 5:21
Bible quotations from the NASB.

The Atonement

The temple shrine: propitiation

James Needham, Birmingham, England

Hiding at the back, his eyes fixed on the ground and fists beating his chest, the publican occupied the place of the repentant sinner. Others around him might proclaim their own self-worth, but he knew the peril of his eternal safety and sought the grace that only God can provide. In the sincerity of his few words we find the kernel of that prayer repeated through the ages by all who have realised the severity and hopelessness of sin, and heeded without fail by the one true God to whom belongs both the power and willingness to save: *"God, be merciful to me, a sinner!"*[1]

The meaning of propitiation

At the heart of the tax-collector's prayer is the thought of propitiation: the averting of anger by the offering of sacrifice that grace might freely be given. Although propitiation is hardly common language today, the concept was familiar to pagan worshippers in the ancient world. Since their deities were forged from their own imaginings, Greek gods were invested with human characteristics – selfish disinterest, even wrath towards their adherents, which could be appeased by offering gifts or feats of valour to earn their favour. That idea – that anyone could earn or buy the favour of the living God – is wholly foreign to the Bible, of course. God's unchanging attitude towards men is grounded in His nature as one *"ready to forgive, gracious and merciful, slow to anger and abounding in steadfast love."*[2] That love, the enduring delight of His servants,[3] originates in Him, and when His creatures demonstrate love to one another, we exhibit not only something that God does, but something that He is in essential nature.[4]

But the Scriptures attest that is not all God is. When the Lord confirmed His steadfast love towards a fickle and sinful people, He emphasised it was not a love that came at the expense of justice. At Sinai God made clear that He who forgives iniquity, transgression and sin *"will by no means clear the guilty."*[5] While grace is essential to God's nature, He is also implacably opposed to evil, and when evil in humanity gives rise to sin, God must meet it with wrath.

Reconciling wrath and grace

Many attempts have been made to demonstrate that divine wrath is incompatible with God's kindness. Yet the Scriptures find no inconsistency in displaying wrath as an inherent part of God's nature,[6] just as much as grace. This wrath is not the uncontrolled outburst we may experience, exploding and subsiding in response to personal offence; it is the constant and settled state of God's relentless opposition to sin.

So the *"ungodliness and unrighteousness of men,"*[7] which blights this fallen creation, has not aroused something new in the heart of God; it has revealed His wrath, literally 'uncovered' that which was always there as His uncompromising opposition to evil. For now, His wrath is restrained by grace to give room for repentance in mankind, but in a coming day it shall be displayed in furious judgment.[8] No-one in their natural state is immune, for all are declared to be *"children of wrath"*[9] because of sin, whether revealed by transgression of the Law[10] or in disobedience towards the essence of God embedded in creation.[11] So it is that, on the day when God judges the world in righteousness,[12] His settled wrath, uncovered by human sin, shall be laid bare in fury towards those who remain under it.[13]

The shadow and its reality
How reassuring, then, that propitiation has long been disclosed within God's purposes for humanity. The Greek word for 'propitiation' is used in Hebrews 9:5 (and throughout the Greek translation of the Old Testament) to describe the mercy seat which rested on the ark of the covenant in the Most Holy Place. The mercy seat is especially associated with the Day of Atonement (called in the Septuagint the 'day of propitiation'), the one occasion in every year when the high priest was permitted to pass through the veil to sprinkle there the blood of the atonement. There in God's own presence, stained with the blood of sacrifice[14] and under the gaze of the heavenly beings,[15] the mercy seat stood as the divine witness that justice was satisfied and the people spared by grace.[16] Here was the hope that God's necessary wrath could yet be reconciled with His essential grace, not by the ignoring of sin, but by the price of justice being met in blood. And just as the mercy seat rested on the ark and its contents which spoke of Christ, so the reality which answers to the shadow depends entirely on the person and work of His Son.

Coming to the New Testament, we find no room for pagan thinking. It is not sinful humans who interpose with gifts to appease a capricious god, as though a soul's ransom could ever be earned.[17] It is God who intervenes, compelled by eternal love to send His own Son into the world, that by the sacrificial work of the cross, love itself might be defined: *"in this is love, not that we have loved God but that he loved us and sent his Son to be the propitiation for our sins."*[18] At Calvary, laying down His life for sinners, the Lord Jesus suffered the torment of the wrath that men had exposed by sin. The burning justice of a holy God was poured out on the Lord Jesus so fully that divine wrath was completely satisfied and God's own righteousness extended to those who were once excluded from it. Though all have sinned and fallen short of God's glory, now we may be *"justified by his grace as a gift, through the redemption that is in Christ Jesus, whom God put forward as a propitiation by his blood, to be received by faith."*[19] At the cross, God's essential nature was vindicated, both in wrath and grace, as He proved Himself both *"just and the justifier of the one who has faith in Jesus."*[20]

A threefold propitiation

That propitiation achieved at the cross is not exhausted by discharging wrath due to the sinner, for its efficacy continues both to the children and to the people of God. We who have been saved still struggle with sin, and for us the propitiatory work of the cross endures, since the one who bore our sins to Calvary now stands in heaven to plead our cause. He does so on the basis of His perfect atonement, pleading the ongoing merit of the propitiation He has already achieved,[21] so that we who know justification by blood are assured of our salvation from wrath.[22] And to those who have been gathered together to form God's new covenant people, the effectiveness of the cross extends still further. For them, He also serves in heaven as *"a merciful and faithful high priest ... to make propitiation for the sins of the people,"*[23] able to *"save to the uttermost those who draw near to God through him."*[24] Though the mercy seat must be sprinkled year after year, the self-giving of the Son has achieved propitiation for sinner, saint and people alike, which need never be repeated.[25]

As proof of the satisfaction God has taken in the work of Calvary, the place of His propitiation is no longer hidden behind the veil. Romans tells us that the Lord Jesus Himself has been put forward as a propitiation, occupying the gaze of heaven and earth alike. The original word implies a public display, and describes His eternal purposes which God *"set forth in Christ"* to unite all things in Him.[26] So today the 'man of the cross' is God's own declaration, both to this world and to all in the heavenly realms – an open display of His triumph over hostile powers[27] and the unchangeable demonstration of satisfied wrath giving way to *"the immeasurable riches of his grace in kindness towards us in Christ Jesus."*[28]

References:

[1]Lk.18:13 [2]Neh.9:17 [3]Ps.136 [4]1 Jn 4:7-8 [5]Ex.34:6-7 [6]Deut.32:35-36; Rom.12:19 [7]Rom.1:18 [8]Rom.2:4-5,8 [9]Eph.2:3 [10]Rom.4:15 [11]Rom.1:19-20; Eph.5:6 [12]Rom.3:5-6 [13]Col.3:5-6; Jn 3:36 [14]Lev.16:15 [15]Ex.25:20 [16]Lev.16:30 [17]Ps.49:7-8 [18]1 Jn 4:10 [19]Rom.3:23-25 [20]Rom.3:26 [21]1 Jn 2:1-2 [22]Rom.5:9-10 [23]Heb.2:17 [24]Heb.7:25 [25]Heb.9:24-26 [26]Eph.1:7-9 [27]Col.2:15 [28]Eph.2:7 Bible quotations from the ESV.

Virtue signalling

David Pattison, Leigh, England

'Virtue signalling' is another of those nuisance new words (neologisms) that the secular media has seen fit to attack us with over the past twelve months. Part of the package which also comprises its stablemate 'woke',[1] and the coincidental phenomenon of the 'snowflake',[2] both of which have been eloquently dealt with in previous issues of NT, this is a slightly different kettle of fish with, arguably, different implications for us as Christians.

'Virtue signalling' may be loosely thought of as the practice of publicly expressing sentiments intended to 'signal' one's good character or the moral correctness of one's position on a particular issue. Though a precise definition remains elusive, it is something you are still expected to recognise when you see it – typically 2020s, in other words. Its practitioners are said to make a meal of their liberal woke values, notably inclusive inoffensive multiculturalism, at the risk of holding themselves up to ridicule. A recent news item, for instance, concerned the renaming of streets in Birmingham, UK by the local council to include Diversity Drive and Freedom Close; this followed protests against the long-standing practice of honouring those involved in historical slave trading with a street name.

No surprise, then, that virtue signalling is spoken of in a generally negative context, either to a predictable chorus of 'political correctness gone mad' from the political right in response to the Birmingham example, or by its intended recipients as an act of condescension from so-called 'white saviours' whose tut-tutting about poverty and discrimination is regarded as mere self-serving career moves.

As with many trends, virtue signalling needs the right fermentation conditions, and coronavirus saw to that. While it would be generous to regard five per cent of popular journalism as essential work, suddenly the profession found itself elevated to key worker status and, coupled with an audience with unexpected time on its hands, a new gesture politics emerged in the UK: rainbows in the window, 'Clap for Carers', taking the knee as part of television's Match of the Day highlights – virtue signals all, fit for inclusion alongside established genre classics like that of the politician posing while kissing a baby.

Not that this is anything new. Isn't it what Absalom was doing when he used to "*stand beside the way to the gate; and when any man had a suit*

*to come to the king for judgment, Absalom would call to him and say,
'... See, your claims are good and right, but no man listens to you on
the part of the king ... Oh that one would appoint me judge in the land,
then every man who has any suit or cause could come to me and I would
give him justice.' ... so Absalom stole away the hearts of the men of
Israel."[3]*

Where does this leave us as Christians then? On permanent Woke
Watch, fearful of thinking, saying or doing the inappropriate? Could we
be seen to be guilty of our own virtue signalling? We trust not, for it is
not at all to draw attention to ourselves that we are told to: *"Let your
light shine before others"*;[4] *"all people will know that you are my
disciples, if you have love for one another"*;[5] and *they may see your
good deeds and glorify God on the day of visitation.*[6]

The Christian life isn't about our own virtue – far from it. We are rather
to signal the virtue of our Saviour. That is what should occupy us, as
Peter put it: *"you are ... a people ... that you may proclaim the
excellencies of him who called you out of darkness into his marvelous
light."*[7] Some Bible translations have it as 'to proclaim the virtues' of
the Lord.[8] And as one of our hymns says concerning our approach
before God in worship: 'We plead not our own virtues, They cannot
here avail, But by the blood of Jesus we enter through the veil.'[9]
Moreover, in contrast to such worldly fads as 'virtue signalling', ours is
a faith of permanence, which we already know has outlived many other
fads and fancies of secular- humanist practice, and which we know just
as well will survive our own individual involvements with the
conventions of this world.

References:
[1]aware, especially of social problems such as racism and inequality [2]an
insulting way of referring to someone who is considered by some people to
be too easily upset and offended [3]2 Sam.15:2-6 [4]Matt.5:16 [5]Jn 13:35 [6]1
Pet.2:12 [7]1 Pet.2:9 [8]The Amplified Bible and the Berean Study Bible render
it as 'to proclaim the virtues' of Christ. (https://biblehub.com/1_peter/2-
9.htm) [9]C.Belton, PHSS 96
Bible quotations from the NASB.

Job

Job's reaction

Graham Schleyer, Liverpool, England

In this article we'll attempt to draw some lessons for when we are tempted like Job to question God's ways and find fault with Him.

For what purpose?

The middle section of the book of Job, chapters 3 through 31, is a long cycle of speeches between Job and his three friends Eliphaz, Bildad and Zophar who come to comfort him, as we discovered in the first article in this series. What we have is a pattern that begins with Job presenting his view of his miserable situation followed by a friend stating his take on it, and then Job responds, and then another friend responds, and so on. This goes on for three rounds of speeches and we might well say, "For what purpose do we have this long meandering dialogue that appears to go round in circles and doesn't answer the central question of why Job is suffering for no apparent reason?" We learn far more from Job's reaction to his suffering than we do from his friends' attempts to comfort him. As we're never given the answer fully to the 'why' question, we must conclude that God wants us to learn about 'how' we should react to suffering, and realise that suffering is meaningful for us now as Christians having to navigate our way through life's perplexities.

Superficial theological argument

Job's argument for his situation goes along these lines: I'm innocent of what you are accusing me, therefore my suffering is not part of divine judgement and consequently either God isn't just or He isn't operating the universe according to His just principles. I simply need the opportunity to tell him so! We then see how Job's friends' misguided theology provokes Job into challenging God and His ways. Their argument follows these lines: God is just, therefore since God must be operating the universe according to His just principles, Job is suffering because he's done something badly wrong and sinned against God.

Job therefore feels the need to justify himself before God, *"How many are my guilty deeds and sins? Make known to me my wrongdoing and my sin,"*[1] and even thinks that God is treating him like an enemy and not His friend, *"Why do You hide Your face and consider me Your enemy?"*[2]

We should remember that Job is on an emotional roller- coaster whereby his responses are influenced by his physical and mental state, and lead him to say some things that are seemingly out of character.

Job protests

Job then comes to an emotional place where we can find ourselves too, appealing to God to do something about our situation, *"Oh that I knew how to find Him, that I might come to His home! I would present my case before Him and fill my mouth with arguments,"*[3] and even doubting God's ways, *"Why are times* [of judgement for the wicked] *not stored up by the Almighty, And why do those who know Him not see His days* [of judgment for the wicked]*?"*[4]

This surely resonates with many of us when we reflect on the trials that we've been through and are presently experiencing; possibly questioning God. How could we doubt His Calvary love? Paul says, *"Therefore we do not lose heart, ... For our momentary, light affliction is producing for us an eternal weight of glory far beyond all comparison."*[5] That's not easy to accept when we're in pain and the burden God has given us seems heavy. Job's trust in God reaches a high point when he saw beyond his suffering, as Paul did, to a glorious future with God when he said, *"after my skin is destroyed, yet from my flesh I will see God."*[6]

Final submission

In the end Job submits to God's sovereignty and infinite wisdom, *"Therefore I have declared that which I did not understand, Things too wonderful for me, which I do not know,"*[7] having never comprehended the 'why' but left in absolutely no doubt of God's holy will and loving care for him to the end of his days.

References:
[1]Job 13:23 [2]Job 13:24 [3]Job 23:3-4 [4]Job 24:1 [5]2 Cor.4:16-17 [6]Job 19:26 [7]Job 42:3
Bible quotations from the NASB (2020).

100 years in Africa

Vacation Bible Course

Augustine Ahabue, Igbede, Nigeria

We give thanks to God for open doors for us into secondary schools to reach out to students and teachers with the Gospel. It all started long ago from a visit to a school to give a Gospel talk. Students, numbering about 800-1000 were available to listen to the speaker, and after the talk they asked lots of questions. The late George Prasher Jr then floated the idea to invite the students to the church hall, thus linking them with the church. To get the students to the hall, it had to be during the holidays and that was how the Vacation Bible Course (VBC) came to be. In 1967 the first VBC was held in the Church of God meeting-place, 75 Falolu Road, Surulere, Lagos. The program was – and still is – a one-week non- residential course and the most suitable holiday season has been found to be the long vacation time in July/August.

Preparation

From earliest days, we have prepared a programme for the week-long course with details of what the students need to bring, when it will start, subjects to be considered, etc. We draw up three subjects: Character study; Encounter with Christ; and Contemporary Study. We schedule a 20-minute break period after the first two subjects during which time we offer the students refreshments before taking the last subject.

Visit to schools to book appointment

We then had 'Uncle' Bernard French and John Black who, for a while, were in the forefront of this exercise, accompanied by local brothers. The brothers became adept at approaching these school principals to obtain their consent to be allowed to address the students. There were about 30 secondary schools and they had to be addressed during morning assembly at 7.45am. This was a very great task with limited personnel.

Progress to date

From early in the 1980s, Bernard French and John Black were not able to visit as regularly, and so the responsibility for the VBC now rests squarely with the local brothers. For many years, only Surulere assembly conducted the VBC with others from Ajegunle coming to assist. We recorded a turnout of 100 to 200 students and 65-80% will attend the course consistently through the week. In all, we would typically pass the Gospel to over 500 to 900 students during each running of the programme. Thankfully, the VBC is presently organised by most of the churches of God in Nigeria.

Prospects for the future
We reckon it must have made an impact in the life of the students due to the fact that the principals pleaded with us to visit their schools to conduct assembly on Christian Assembly days in public schools. Only one brother could accept the challenge and, by God's grace, has continued to date. May God raise workers to take up this task as the doors are still open.

The VBC also boosted our Boys and Girls Camp as we were recording 200 to 280 attendees at the VBC Camp, as we now call it. The VBC starts on the first week of vacation and on Thursday of the second week we take them to camp till Lord's Day so that they can see how we conduct the Remembrance of our Lord Jesus.

We had planned to experiment with a week-long VBC Camp this past year, but Covid-19 did not allow it to happen. We thank God for all the hearts that have been touched for the Lord through the VBC over these many years of its operation, and thank God for opportunity to serve the Lord in the exercise. Only eternity will reveal the souls who have been saved while attending the course. Maranatha!

The Jerusalem Conference

Is Acts 15 a pattern for today?

John Kerr, Ayr, Scotland

This article looks at the necessity of such a conference as a means of maintaining unity among churches in fellowship with each other and compares it with what the Churches of God do today.

The churches who publish this magazine regularly convene a conference of elders. Where possible, elders from all the churches throughout the world meet on the basis of Acts 15.[1] For many years, I personally have seen the value of elders in churches of God coming together for discussion on a local, national and international basis. While the world today is so different from the one in which the apostles lived, the principle is surely the same, i.e. there must be a means by which all churches maintain unity of practice and teaching. Paul and Barnabas were teaching that previous Mosaic ceremonies had ceased and that faith alone in Christ brought salvation, so inevitably a dispute arose.

In this incident, if the dispute had been unresolved, it would have done terrible damage to the developing churches. So, wisely, representatives from the churches affected were chosen, commissioned and sent to Jerusalem for a decision. Judaizing teachers were facing what (to them) were major changes and, considering how strongly each side held their views, much grace was going to be needed. When change is required, we all need an attitude of willing subjection to enable unity to continue. I have seen this attitude of subjecting to one another working, when all gathered need to have an attitude of humility. Having seen it in practice, I am convinced it has been a major factor in contributing to the success of such present-day conferences producing unity in a worldwide fellowship.

As in New Testament times, down through the centuries there always have been those who want to add to the basic simplicity of the gospel message. So even today we must be ready to uphold the truth of the gospel. When we face any challenge in the churches over serious disagreements these surely must be addressed promptly or else a split is a likely result. This cannot be what God wants and it is a bad testimony to unbelievers.

As we continue the story, on arrival at Jerusalem the group of church representatives were received by the Church in a friendly manner. A conference was convened for apostles and elders exclusively, the purpose being for these leaders to review the facts and confirm God's will. After much debate,[2] Peter was able to report the first clear case of Gentile conversion[3] – a powerful input to the conference discussion, which none could gainsay. Then came Barnabas and Paul who corroborated this by reporting their experience of Gentile conversions.

When a good chairman, guided by the Holy Spirit, accurately sums up the general tone of the conference, others recognise the mind of the Spirit and readily accept the decision. This is what happened in Acts 15 when James the chairman guided the conference. It must have been a lively affair, but after considerable discussion James summed up the matter with a quote from Old Testament scripture.[4] That was a very important part of the decision- making process, for the Scriptures must back practical decisions.

The agreed conclusion was then conveyed by letter as well as in person, which in Bible times would be important to confirm that the letter was genuine. The letter acknowledged the Judaizers' error and gave clear guidance with minimum requirements for Gentiles who had believed.[5] The initial controversy had been limited in geographical terms at the time, but the concluding decision was conveyed in writing to all churches of God in a wide area for a standard application throughout.[6] This is important and confirms that the churches were in a fellowship with one another, teaching and practising the same thing.

Other scriptures[7] confirm this intention. For this to apply today there must be something that corresponds to the Acts 15 conference. So, for the Churches of God now, it is therefore correct for the elders in our churches to meet and resolve issues and then communicate the result to all churches in the worldwide fellowship. For any churches further afield at the time of Acts 15, who did not receive the apostles' letter, the itinerating apostles would have communicated the content in their teaching as and when they travelled. Churches of God today are united and imitate the decision-making procedure of Acts 15, for it is scriptural and what would be the alternative?

References:
[1]see also Acts 21:15-25 [2]Acts 15:7 NASB [3]Acts 11:14-15 [4]Amos 9:11-12 [5]Acts 21:25 [6]see Acts 16:4 [7]e.g. 1 Cor.4:17; 7:1

Can you help me with this?

Why baptize?

Peter Hickling, Cromer, England

Most Christian churches baptize people, but there is a bewildering variety of views about the purpose of the ceremony. Can we find out what we ought to do, and why? To answer this question we need to set out our basic assumptions.

What are our premises?
We accept the Bible as the Word of God, normative for church teaching and practice. This means that we don't start by listing other people's practices and pointing out their errors.

John's baptism
John, a relative of Jesus, *"appeared, baptizing in the wilderness and proclaiming a baptism of repentance for the forgiveness of sins."*[1] This wasn't the same as Christian baptism, because it was before the death and resurrection of Christ. Repentance is still a prerequisite, of course, for forgiveness of sins, but it's not the whole story. Forgiveness comes through the acceptance of what Christ has done in His death and resurrection.[2] Many came to be baptized by John and accepted his teaching, but some of those never heard of Christian baptism. One example was Apollos, of whom the Bible records: *"Now a Jew named Apollos, a native of Alexandria, came to Ephesus. He was an eloquent man, competent in the Scriptures. He had been instructed in the way of the Lord. And being fervent in spirit, he spoke and taught accurately the things concerning Jesus, though he knew only the baptism of John. He began to speak boldly in the synagogue, but when Priscilla and Aquila heard him, they took him aside and explained to him the way of God more accurately."*[3] Everything that is said about Apollos commends him, but he didn't quite have the whole story.

Christian baptism: Who were baptized?
Peter preached to the Jews who had gathered together at Pentecost,[4] and accused them, *"Let all the house of Israel therefore know for certain that God has made him both Lord and Christ, this Jesus whom you crucified."*

Now when they heard this they were cut to the heart, and said to Peter and the rest of the apostles, "Brothers, what shall we do?"[5] Peter told them to repent and be baptized in the name of Jesus Christ, *"and those who received his word were baptized."*[6]

Note that their repentance and belief in Christ came before their baptism, not after it. It is a general principle that a physical action can never produce a spiritual change. Another example was the Ethiopian court official whom Philip was sent to meet. He was returning from Jerusalem, and on his journey he was reading a passage from Isaiah,[7] which he asked Philip to explain. From that, Philip told him the good news about Jesus. The sequel to that was that they came to some water, and the eunuch said, *"See, here is water! What prevents me from being baptized?" And he commanded the chariot to stop, and they both went down into the water, Philip and the eunuch, and he baptized him."*[8] The sequence was again that the eunuch heard the Word, believed it, and was baptized.

Is there more than one kind of baptism?

All the instances we have read about so far refer to baptism in water, where it was possible for the person being baptized to go down into the water, and not merely to have water poured over them. This has its symbolism: that of death and burial. Again, the act of baptism itself does not do anything to the person; it is a confession before the onlookers of what has already happened. God counts believers in Christ as having been crucified with Him; saying, *"you also must consider yourselves dead to sin and alive to God in Christ Jesus."*[9] There is another kind of baptism – baptism in the Holy Spirit. Every believer in Christ receives this, for *"anyone who does not have the Spirit of Christ does not belong to him."*[10] This spiritual baptism binds together all believers in Christ in a unity called the Body of Christ: Scripture says, *"in one Spirit we were all baptized into one body ... and all were made to drink of one Spirit."*[11]

Summary

People who are repentant of their sin against God admit that Jesus Christ, the Son of God, died for them. They submit to baptism, which is a confession that they have died with Christ and a declaration that they intend to be disciples of Him. Faith in Christ brings simultaneous baptism in the Holy Spirit, which makes believers members of the Body of Christ.

References:
[1]Mk.1:4 [2]see Rom.10:9 [3]Acts 18:24-26 [4]Acts 2:5 [5]Acts 2:36-37 [6]Acts 2:41 [7]Acts 8:30-31,34 [8]Acts 8:36-37 [9]Rom.6:11 [10]Rom.8:9 [11]1 Cor.12:13
Bible quotations from the ESV.

Keep close to God

An interview with

Daisy Celmar, Davao, Philippines

Can you tell us something of your background?
I am married to Fidel and we are blessed with 6 children. My parents are purely Catholic and I was devoted to it until 2006. We were not encouraged to read the Bible, and so it brought no changes in my life. The following year, I heard someone preaching in the busy market who invited me to their church called Victory Chapel. I became their member for six years. I liked it because we were encouraged to read the Bible. But this church always emphasized giving money so as to be more blessed by God. I obeyed in the hope of gaining material things and to avoid experiencing problems, but it did not happen in reality. And most concerning of all, I was still not sure of my salvation … until, on Christmas Eve in 2013, I invited my friend Teresita to join with our family to celebrate Christmas. She told me about the Church of God. Three months later, she brought Geralde to speak with me and I understood fully about my salvation through Ephesians 2:8-9.

Here, finally, was a church that not only encouraged me to read the Bible, but also to study and apply it. They emphasized living righteously in God's kingdom by keeping the will of God in our lives, and being content with God's provision for our needs, not our wants. My gambling vices stopped. By April 2014, I was numbered in the Church of God at Davao.

How was life when you began to serve in God's kingdom?
It was tough. We lost our home. We used to live rent-free at the house of my uncle in Matina (part of Davao). But my cousin John got angry when he learned I allowed someone from the Church of God to regularly conduct Bible study in his house. And I was offended because I wanted my whole family to hear the truth. We voluntarily moved to live at the house of my mother-in-law, who is a devoted Catholic. But after a year of living there, she also was against us. She wanted to support one of my daughters to study in Cebu at a Catholic school to become a nun, and I refused. I resisted because I now knew the truth. After that, she no longer allowed my fellows in the church to conduct cottage prayers in that house. And so we again packed all our things.

We decided to move to Surigao del Sur, my birthplace. We were about to put our things in the vehicle, ready to go, when Geralde suddenly came, not knowing our plan. When he said there's no Church of God there, I changed my mind. Instead of heading to the bus terminal, we brought our things instead to the church hall in Uraya, and temporarily lived there.

A few weeks later, through the help of the Churches of God, we found a piece of land in Ula. And in 2015, God blessed our little business and we were able to build our own house in Ula. God's Word is true that when we seek first His kingdom, He will provide for our needs.

That's inspiring. Apart from that, what else have you faced and how have you coped?
I was burdened for my husband. Following me, my six children were numbered in the church, and he was the only one not a Christian. It was a great struggle for me teaching ourchildren in the way of the Lord and yet they were watching their father who had vices like drinking wine to excess and smoking. I kept telling him the Gospel, but he wasn't responsive. I continued praying for him and included him in the church prayer and weekly cottage prayer list. God performed a miracle. Fidel accepted the Saviour, and was baptized and added to the church in January 2018. His vices had finally gone. That's the great victory in my life.

During the Covid-19 lockdown, your husband lost his job, and you moved in the mountain of Malabog to plant crops, but you gained no profit and life became harder still. Did you ask God why he allowed this?

I certainly did not. Because I've been in many difficulties in the past and God helped us. So I trusted He would do the same again. God's promise doesn't change. He's in control of everything. I'm even thankful that lockdown occurred because God had a purpose in it. We were able to witness to our neighbours here. And thirteen of them were baptized and added to the Church. In the Malabog company of the Davao church, I'm delighted to say that my husband has begun participating in praises and prayers regularly since last December 6. He says 'Amen' to all I'm sharing.

Do you have a message for our readers?
Whatever trials we may face, keep close to God. Let His things be central in our lives.

Wherever you sow

Geoff Hydon, Mount Forest, Canada

"How blessed will you be, you who sow beside all waters."[1]

Isaiah's words promised bountiful blessing from spreading seed, and it has often been applied to spiritual sowing, of course. But sowing the good seed of the Word of God has been problematic recently, because of the limitations on public preaching, or even face-to- face meetings. Many of those most 'Covid-vulnerable' choose to stay safely at home; they are 'shut-ins', but they still need to hear the word of God. How?

Technology may help. But how do you get people to see and click the link to your video recordings? We might first ask, what are people actually watching anyway? Answer: whatever is on the TV! Canadian official statistics reveal over-60s watch the most TV: the same group that these days is unable to attend church gatherings. They may indeed be missing them.

On local TV channels here, community content is aired free of charge. There is a shortage of local material, because virus prevention has severely curtailed usual events. Our community TV channel, which serves many thousands of homes in this region, is now very willing to include in its TV listings recordings of our regular church ministry meetings. We simultaneously record these talks, when they are shared live with those in the local church by video link. Of course, we have to do some editing to meet TV station specifications, but this is easily manageable. Broadcast quality videos can be produced using free software, supported by helpful online instructions. We are not trying to become TV celebrities or compete with Prime Time TV! All community TV is produced on shoestring budgets. It requires careful planning, not big money.

So we have been 'on TV' weekly since July 2020. Here are some of our learning experiences, in case you have local opportunity to do the same. We first had to think about who is likely to watch our TV broadcast, and familiarize ourselves with typical competing programmes. Then we tried to build content that will attract interest. We targeted mainly older, but active, 'shut-ins' who likely have some familiarity with the Bible, and may be missing 'going to church', as they would call it. As well as a talk, we think they will like hearing traditional hymns and we want to always include gospel content; we don't know whether unsaved people will be watching. Obviously our church elders need to be comfortable with what is broadcast.

After friendly contact with the TV production person, we knew exactly the length and format our video must be in and what their production timelines are, so we can always provide our video in good time. The TV producer praised the sample video we provided, and we always appreciate their review before they air it (a captive audience for us!).

Those who produce the regular videos for the churches of God are familiar with what presenters should avoid when making videos, and conversely the best ways to produce good ones. These tips apply equally to television.

It is wise to always smile, and develop a consistent, warm look to our TV programme, including using the same lead-in and concluding material and musical accompaniment each time. (You can sample this from one of our broadcasts at https://bit.ly/2TkW1A7.) We also avoid using jargon that average television viewers won't appreciate.

Where possible, we alternate speakers, since people have different preferences and a new face adds interest. However, using the same person to briefly introduce every speaker helps to satisfy audience expectations. Interest may be sustained by pre-advising what the next talk will address, God willing. We readily modify and re-use good material from other churches of God that will be new to our audience (our video library is available to you). Each broadcast is clear about how people can contact us. We point them to our local website (www.mountforestchurch.ca). Since we started airing the TV broadcasts, visits to our website have increased (exceptionally peaking at 150 different visitors on a single day!). We constantly try to increase local awareness of the broadcasts, so we encourage everyone to pass the word on and we think about how to advertise effectively.

This window of opportunity may be short-lived if things return to normal after the pandemic and TV slots disappear, but what we do now may bring eternal blessing and can help to enhance our local testimony.

Reference:
[1]Isa.32:20 NASB

From the Editors' desk

Issue 3 2021

I was struck recently by the fact that Paul rejoiced to see the discipline and stability of others.[1] The former will lead to the latter. Stability doesn't sound very flashy or exciting but it is something that God values, and that we should rejoice in when we see it in each other. Jeremiah talks about a healthy tree[2] that has roots extending deeply into the well-watered soil (a picture of resilience, in trusting in God, for those facing the drought of exile). But root systems develop over time for us, our roots should extend deeply into the soil of God's Word, and our lives will be saturated with the life of God. There is something organic about that natural development over time as a result of disciplined abiding, of living with God and His Word. It's not something we can readily fake. Roots are hidden from external appearances (and their development is, in a sense, secret work) but they have visible consequences in the green leaf, the fruit and the stability of the tree.

NT can't do the hidden work of root development for you — but this magazine can be an aid to the discipline of reading and study that leads to stability: so draw on the truths in the articles here. You'll find precious teaching on the Lord's atoning work at Calvary, on the Son as the image of the invisible God, on the wisdom of the Teacher in Ecclesiastes, on what the counter-cultural life with God looks like. Let's get on with the work of root development and rejoice in one another's stability.

Stephen

References:
[1]Col.2:5 [2]Jer.17:7,8

Ecclesiastes

Chance occurrences

Gareth Andrews, Belfast, N.Ireland

The chances of some things happening are very remote, but that doesn't mean they won't happen. For example, if you are a parent, the probability of having three children (who are not triplets) all sharing the same birthday is roughly 1 in 135,000. And yet, in the UK alone, there are around a million families who have three children, and so this coincidence actually does occur every few years! [1]

Recently, there has been some concern about the potential side effects of certain COVID-19 vaccines, with a risk of blood clots. While statistically really rare, millions of doses are being given and sorely needed, so these chance occurrences do unfortunately happen from time to time. In living our lives, we all have to identify and assess risk in different ways every day - calculations of benefits versus risks.

As Christians, though, can we expect that bad things won't happen to us? Can we, even unconsciously, expect that being faithful to God will somehow lower our exposure to risk? How would we react if, or indeed when, bad things happen to us? If, as we're told, on average one in two people will develop some form of cancer during their lifetime,[2] can we suppose that it simply won't happen to us or to any of our loved ones? Or to put it another way, can we earn 'health and wealth' as a reward from God in return for us being good?

The teacher in Ecclesiastes notes that: *"I again saw under the sun that the race is not to the swift and the battle is not to the warriors, and neither is bread to the wise nor wealth to the discerning, nor favor to the skillful; for time and chance overtake them all."*[3] The teacher is realistic in assessing that life is uncertain, and although talent and hard work may shift the balance of risks in our favour somewhat, in the end, time and chance occurrences will overtake us all. The notion that our own rewards or prosperity are earned or guaranteed in this life, is surely punctured and burst by the teacher in chapter 8: 14: *"There is something else meaningless that occurs on earth: the righteous who get what the wicked deserve, and the wicked who get what the righteous deserve. This too, I say, is meaningless."*[4]

Toiling to earn rewards only in this life on earth is meaningless - this short-sighted desire for immediacy is the fallacy of falling for a deceptive substitute while ignoring all the inherent risks.

This vanity has been described by several commentators as going after candy floss (or cotton candy) - it may seem attractive to us, but will prove to be ephemeral, unsatisfying and, ultimately, not very good for us.

In contrast to this risky view 'under the sun', raising our gaze up to a heavenly perspective is a longer term view that will allow us to lay up our treasures in heaven - safe, secure, substantial and ultimately satisfying. Jesus said: *"Do not lay up for yourselves treasures on earth, where moth and rust destroy and where thieves break in and steal ... For where your treasure is, there your heart will be also."*[5] That's not to say that we shouldn't value anything or anybody in this life because some chance occurrence may happen to us or to them. Rather, it's a question of following and prioritising the everlasting God (with whom there is ultimate certainty), the commandments and characteristics of the unchanging one[6] who loves and values us so much that He gave His life for us.

Tim Keller has put it succinctly like this: 'Christians don't face adversity by stoically decreasing our love for the people and things of this world so much as by increasing our love and joy in God.'[7] With this eternal perspective and living hope, we are then able to commend joy, no matter what might occur in this life: *"Instruct those who are rich in this present world not to be conceited or to set their hope on the uncertainty of riches, but on God, who richly supplies us with all things to enjoy."*[8]

References:
[1]https://www.bbc.com/future/article/20120426-what-a-coincidence
[2]https://www.nhs.uk/conditions/cancer/ [3]Eccles.9:11 NASB (2020) [4]Eccles. 8:14 NIV [5]Matt.6:19-21 ESV [6]Heb.13:8 [7]Timothy J. Keller, Walking with God through Pain and Suffering [8]1 Tim.6:17 NASB (2020)

Knowing God

A counter-cultural lifestyle

Sam Jones, Aberkenfig, Wales

The Lord Jesus' teaching often runs contrary to the ideas of our society. His teaching about our lifestyle is no different. Society's attitudes to the way it expects us to live are often expressed as 'you only get one life, hang on to it for as long as you can'; 'pursue your dreams and make yourself happy'; or 'do things your own way'. The Lord, however, teaches the opposite, saying: *"If anyone would come after me, let him deny himself and take up his cross daily and follow me. For whoever would save his life will lose it, but whoever loses his life for my sake will save it."*[1]

Taking the Lord Jesus' counter-cultural approach to making the most of our lives means, figuratively speaking, to 'lose' them. That involves giving up on doing things our own way, surrendering the pursuit of our wants and desires and, instead, committing ourselves to following Him with a goal of knowing Him better and becoming more like Him. In practice, this is extremely difficult. We are put under constant pressure to align ourselves with the lives of our peers by pursuing values, goals or material things which would, in their eyes, give our lives more worth. Maintaining our pursuit of Christ, and preventing ourselves from being distracted by other things in these circumstances, is a challenge. Perhaps we can get some help from Paul's experiences as someone who was once deeply engrained in the Jewish society of his day.

It is Paul's experiences that we will focus on for the remainder of this article. Ultimately, we will see that it was a desire to increase his knowledge of God, in the person of the Lord Jesus Christ, that moved him away from pursuing a social standing and kept his life in step with the Lord's example.

Paul's pursuit of social standing

Prior to his conversion, Paul's adherence to Jewish culture and customs was extremely important to him. In his letter to the Philippians he writes: *"If anyone else thinks he has reason for confidence in the flesh, I have more: circumcised on the eighth day, of the people of Israel, of the tribe of Benjamin, a Hebrew of Hebrews; as to the law, a Pharisee; as to zeal, a persecutor of the church; as to righteousness under the law, blameless."*[2]

Here, he outlines several characteristics that he held up as trophies - values and achievements in which he proudly put his confidence before coming to Christ. First, his list refers to his heritage - he is a Hebrew of Hebrews; a true ethnic Jew who spoke the ancient Hebrew language and could trace his ancestry back to Jacob through Benjamin, the tribe which produced his namesake, the first king of Israel.

Second, he refers to his ambitions; as the son of a Pharisee[3] he aspired to live as a Pharisee - the strictest sect of the Jewish religion.[4] More so, he was recognised to be advancing in it beyond his peers.[5] Third, he refers to his passion; citing his persecution of the church of God in Jerusalem[6,7] as evidence for his sincere, unquestionable devotion to Judaism. Finally, he notes his success in achieving his goals: in terms of the legal righteousness so prized by Jews he was blameless - nobody could bring a charge against him.

These characteristics describe the pedigree of Paul's Jewish lifestyle and the achievements he worked hard to attain. They gave him a reputation, status and authority that would have seen him held in high regard among his peers (in fact, his reasoning for listing them here is to lend weight to the authority of his Christian teaching in the eyes of a Jewish audience).

Paul's pursuit of Christ

Yet, despite the significant value these things had to him, Paul goes on to write: *"But whatever gain I had, I counted as loss for the sake of Christ. Indeed, I count everything as loss because of the surpassing worth of knowing Christ Jesus my Lord. For his sake I have suffered the loss of all things and count them as rubbish, in order that I may gain Christ and be found in him, not having a righteousness of my own that comes from the law, but that which comes through faith in Christ, the righteousness from God that depends on faith."*[8]

After responding to the call of Christ on the road to Damascus, Paul's appreciation of the value of a personal relationship with the Lord Jesus eclipses his desire for anything else. He no longer aspires to maintain his Jewish pedigree - doing so just would take up valuable time that could be dedicated to knowing Christ. He no longer values the self- given righteousness he obtained through law-keeping - it was worthless compared to the God- given righteousness that came through faith in Christ. Instead, he counts these previous aspirations and successes as nothing more than rubbish - along with all other things that distract his focus from his life's new pursuit: increasing his knowledge of Christ.

As those who have responded to a similar call, we are challenged to make a similar decision. We are to identify anything in our lives that hinders our pursuit of a knowledge of Christ, casting them off as 'rubbish'. Paul suffered loss as a result of giving up on things valued by his culture, and the same may be true for us.

Paul's new lifestyle

There is little doubt that Paul's new pursuit involved the study of Scripture, but he also desired to increase his knowledge of Christ through his lifestyle. He writes that he now lives: *"... that I may know him and the power of his resurrection, and may share his sufferings, becoming like him in his death, that by any means possible I may attain the resurrection from the dead."[9]*

The word 'know' here refers to knowledge that comes through lived experience. Paul's desire to know Christ meant that he was willing tobring something of Christ's death and sufferings into his daily experience, and this appears to be the means by which Paul looked to attain a fuller experience of the resurrection.

Eternal life is centred on, and defined by, knowing Him.[10] Like Paul, by taking up our Master's yoke and walking alongside Him we have a daily opportunity to learn more about Him,[11] experiencing this resurrected life in a fuller sense in the process.

Paul presses towards his goal

Ultimately, human weakness and the presence of sin means that the fullest experience of this cannot be obtained now and we must wait until a future day when we shall know Him more fully.[12] However, this did not deter Paul in his pursuit of it and he goes on to write: *"Not that I have already obtained this or am already perfect, but I press on to make it my own, because Christ Jesus has made me his own. Brothers, I do not consider that I have made it my own. But one thing I do: forgetting what lies behind and straining forward to what lies ahead, I press on toward the goal for the prize of the upward call of God in Christ Jesus."[13]*

Not content to leave the prize of a fuller knowledge of the Lord Jesus to a future day, Paul makes it his goal to press forward to make it his own, as best possible, today and every day. It was this desire that moved him away from pursuing social standing and kept his life in step with the Lord's example. Salvation is just the start of a new life in relationship with the Lord Jesus. However, perhaps the assurance that accompanies our salvation means we are at risk of becoming complacent - being content to leave a relationship with Him to a future day while we pursue other things now. Doing so may gain us accomplishments, status or material things that look good to those around us, but we miss out on the ultimate purpose of our lives.

Paul goes on to encourage us to follow his example so that we do not miss out.[14] By living counter- culturally, taking up our cross daily and dying to our own aspirations we may miss out on short term gains, but we develop a greater experience with Christ that lasts for eternity. As we pursue Him we will find that all other things lose their appeal. As the songwriter wrote:

> Turn your eyes upon Jesus,
> Look full in His wonderful face
> And the things of earth will grow strangely dim
> In the light of His glory and grace.[15]

References:
[1]Lk.9:23-24 [2]Phil.3:4-6 [3]Acts 23:6 [4]Acts 26:5 [5]Gal.1:14 [6]Acts 9:1-2 [7]Gal.1:13-14 [8]Phil.3:7-9 [9]Phil.3:10-11 [10]Jn 17:3 [11]Matt.11:29 [12]1 Cor.13:12 [13]Phil.3:12-14 [14]Phil.3:15-17 [15]Helen H Lemmel, Gospel Songs 126, cf. Heb.12:1-2
Bible quotations from the ESV.

A world in crisis and conflict

Don Williamson, Littleton, USA

The Lord asked His disciples an interesting question: *"Do you not see all these things?"*[1] It may have been that the disciples were much like some ofus, so caught up with getting by each day that we miss the big picture. What a struggle this year has been! We were all happy to see 2020 end and had hoped for a return to normal living, but the struggle continues and our impatient nature is once again brought to light. The world is on edge. COVID still represents a major battle, but many of the countries in the West are making rapid progress with their vaccination campaigns.

Sadly, many families have lost loved ones and deaths are numbered in the millions. Our hearts are going out to those in Eastern countries, particularly for those in India. A recent article in the *Los Angeles Times* declared that the COVID-19 crisis in India was a 'nightmare'. The numbers are stunning: at the time of writing, there are 400,000 new cases a day. Hospitals are overwhelmed, the supply of oxygen is running short, and new variants seem to be complicating the fight. We are thankful for the relative safety of our brothers and sisters in the Indian churches, but we must pray on that our merciful God will intervene and bring relief from this humanitarian crisis.

But the battle is not only against the virus, it is going on between countries. *"For nation will rise against nation, and kingdom against kingdom, and there will be famines and earthquakes in various places."*[2] Take a moment to reflect on the political sphere of this world. The complex issues of Brexit reveal the struggle that nations face in the growing influence of world markets and regional pressure for financial control and the huge battle for economic power between the western world, primarily the United States, and the growing power of China. Many countries in the world rely on the power of the American dollar, yet there is a constant effort by countries like China and Russia to undermine and devalue the currency. It is not just money, but the ever-growing threat of war. China and Taiwan are at a boiling point with the potential for many nations to get involved if a direct attack by China takes place. The Middle East remains a problem with no solution and Israel has again shown herself ready to aggressively defend her sovereignty. Saudi Arabia is in a current conflict with rebels in Yemen, funded by the global terrorist nation of Iran.

All around are the signs of *"wars and rumors of wars"*.[3] The moral and ethical fabric of our countries is collapsing. " *... because lawlessness is increased, most people's love will become cold.*"[4]

There is a serious breakdown of the family structure in many of the Western nations and it is spreading to Eastern countries as well. With the prophetic words pointing us to the last days, we will see an increase in such structural fractures in society, as the Lord has warned us.

It is interesting to see how the world looks at the present chaos and lays blame on racism, poverty and unfair lack of opportunity. But the real reason for the situation is the destruction caused by sin. We live in a fallen world and the evil one is set to destroy what God values in His creation, such as family. Marriage is on a serious decline in our present society; 40% of births in the United States will occur prior to any marriage. In generations past, having a baby out of wedlock was a shame; today it calls for a celebration. Yet the statistics suggest that children brought up with only one parent have a greater chance of failure in life than a child brought up in a two- parent married family.

Some are worried about global warming, but this has the potential of destroying the very fabric of society. We need to wake up and look around us for our Redeemer is drawing near. Borrowed from a later time-point, the words of the Lord Jesus could be applied to you and me, *"Therefore be on the alert, for you do not know which day your Lord is coming."*[5] We do not know the day or the hour of His return for His church, but God does. Look up!

References:
[1]Matt.24:2 [2]Matt.24:7 [3]Matt.24:6 [4]Matt.24:12 [5]Matt.24:42
Bible quotations from the NASB (2020).

Image-bearing

The image of the invisible God

Andrew Dorricott, Hamilton, Canada

Icons - they're everywhere. They used to only be seen on products themselves on some hidden or subtle label. Then they became more widely seen in print and on television ads. Now icons are on page after page of our smartphones, on the uniform of our favourite sports team and loudly presented on the clothing some of us wear.

The modem icon, as an extension of a brand, tells us something about what we can expect. Henry Ford once said, "You can't build a reputation on what you are going to do." It's all about what has happened, and that sets the expectation for what will happen. A brand, including its logo (or icon), is a representation of a past experience with that company's product or services, and it can be either positive or negative. Each experience influences our overall view of that brand. When we see the Amazon logo, for example, we expect a certain experience based on what has happened before. And it's the same for an app on our phone, a food brand or a type of car. That logo serves as an expression of the promise the company is trying to make to its users. When we see the icon, we know what we're going to get.

Colossians 1:15 says of God's much loved Son: *"He is the image of the invisible God, the firstborn over all creation."* The word 'image' is the Greek word *'eikon'*, from which we get the word 'icon'. The sense from the original text is that the Son of God as Jesus is a representation of the invisible God. He is not just any representation, but a full and exact representation as Hebrews 1:3 tells us: *"the brightness of (God's) glory and the express image (Gk: charaktir) of His person."* Jesus is the expression of God, and of all His promises[1] and qualities to us.

To put it another way, to know Jesus is to know God,[2] and how we respond to Jesus is how we respond to God the Father[3] - they are not dealt with separately. The Son of God coming to this world as a man, Jesus, made the invisible God visible – *"all the fullness of the Godhead bodily."*[4] He made God to be seen and heard and touched by people. We are now able to approach the unapproachable God, and we are allowed great insight into the heart of God through Jesus.

Thankfully, we have the Word of God, the Bible, to read about Jesus and some of the things He did, said and felt. We see intimate moments between Him and God the Father as recorded in John 17. We see tender moments with broken people seeking the help only He could give.[5] We learn so much more about God through these experiences of Christ.

Christ is the perfect expression of God the Father, but in another way, members of the Body of Christ are to be an expression of Christ to the world. By the grace of God, through faith in Jesus Christ and what He has done, we are unified as believers with the intention that this should become visible in churches of God.[6] Not only that, we are gifted in specific ways, each of us equipped and empowered by the Holy Spirit to express to the world the character, the teaching, the love and the power of Jesus Christ. What an amazing thought! As the world encounters a follower of Jesus, what is it they expect? What do they experience? As believers we have been given both a great commission to make disciples,[7] and a great commandment to love God as well as one another.[8] Is that evident when non-believers meet with me? Are they drawn towards Jesus?

As Colossians tells us, Jesus has made the invisible God visible, as He is the *eikon* of the invisible God. We also learn in the New Testament that we are called to make Jesus visible to non-believers, through the power and working of the Holy Spirit. A modern design icon tells us about what we can expect based on an experience. As believers, is this what we are to those around us?

References:
[1]2 Cor.1:20 [2]Jn 14:9 [3]Matt.7:21-23 [4]Col.2:9 [5]Mk.5:25-34 [6]1 Cor.12:12-14,27; Jn 17:21 [7]Matt.28:19-20 [8]Matt.22:37-39; 1 Jn 4:21
Bible quotations from the NKJV.

The Atonement

The law courts: justification

Stephen Hickling, Birmingham, England

In this series, we are considering some of the word pictures used in the Scriptures to help us to understand the atonement. If 'redemption' took us to the marketplace and 'propitiation' led us to the temple shrine, then 'justification' is surely the language of the law court. The imagery conjured by the word 'justification' causes us to consider our own appearance in the dock to face the judgment of the cosmic Judge, before whose eyes everything we have thought, said and done is uncovered and laid bare.

Justification, then, is a legal pronouncement, the verdict of the Judge. It is the opposite of condemnation' since, when justification takes place, God bangs the gavel and declares a person to be not guilty, but just in His sight. I have sometimes heard justification explained by the phrase 'just as if I'd never sinned,' but I suggest that this definition is somewhat deficient and might lead someone to the assumption that God is complicit in a legal fiction - simply ignoring a person's sin. That phrase also fails to convey the wonder of the great exchange that had to take place for us to have a righteous standing before God.

Martin Luther's famous phrase - *simul justus et peccator* (a Latin phrase meaning, 'at the same time just and sinner') - might sound like a contradiction in terms, but it more accurately expresses this gospel truth. Justification is God's provision for sinners so that, while they are still sinners, they may be reconciled to Him and declared righteous by Him.

The big question that justification raises is how a holy God can declare an unjust person to be just? Let's explore the answer to this as we look at three phrases the apostle Paul used to explain our justification. We shall see that this is no legal fiction!

Its origination - by grace

The first phrase, *"justified freely by his grace,"*[2] points us to the source, the origin, of our justification. It is the prerogative of the Judge to condemn or to justify. Grace, in this context, refers principally to the disposition of the Judge. He is gracious, that is, He is minded to find a way to acquit us. The fact that justification is by grace reminds us that it is not our entitlement.

Indeed, Paul spends the opening two- and-a-half chapters of his epistle to the Romans firmly closing the door to any attempt by humans to reach God's required standard by their own efforts before his summary statement in Romans 3:23-24 – *"for all have sinned and fall short of the glory of God, and all are justified freely by his grace through the redemption that came by Christ Jesus."*

The point is that we have no leverage over the Judge; neither can His pardon be obtained by deception or bribery. There is nothing that we can offer Him to tip the scales in our favour. We are fully reliant on His grace. So, justification is wholly a result of the gracious disposition of the Judge toward the ungodly. Unless God had wanted to be the justifier of those who have faith, there would be no justification.

Its basis - by blood
But how can God be so graciously disposed towards people who have spurned His laws and scoffed at His love? To simply declare the unrighteous righteous would be contrary to God's self-revealed standards of justice.[3] As Judge, God must Himself act righteously in giving His verdict on the unrighteous. Yet Paul's staggering claim is that God does indeed justify the wicked.[4]

Without the atoning sacrifice of Christ, Paul's claim would be preposterous. But the atonement is the basis of God's gracious justice; the blood of Christ's cross enables God to be the justifier of those who have faith in Jesus, whilst all the time remaining supremely just.[5] This leads us to our second phrase, *"justified by his blood"*,[6] which reveals God's righteous way of providing for our justification - its basis and its cost. Indeed, a good definition of justification is God's 'righteous way of 'righteousing' the unrighteous'.[7]

There are two elements to the problem: on the one hand God is absolutely holy and just; and, on the other, men and women are universally unjust, all falling short of His glory. To a two-fold problem, God has presented a two- fold solution, involving a double imputation: *"God made him who had no sin to be sin for us, so that in him we might become the righteousness of God."*[8]

First, our sins have been imputed to Christ, that is they have been transferred to His account in order that the full penalty accruing to them might be justly paid. That is what it means when we read that *"He himself bore our sins in his body on the cross."*[9] God held Jesus to account for our sins and punished Him for them at Calvary. And, second, the Lord's righteousness has been credited to our account.

In pronouncing us to be just, God is not saying that we have righteous character; He is declaring that we have righteous standing because when He looks at our account, He sees the record of Christ's performance on the ledger.

If the phrase 'just as if I'd never sinned' implies a miscarriage of justice, we must be clear that the Judge has neither acted unjustly nor suffered amnesia in cancelling our debt at the expense of His Son. But that is only half the story: we remain sinners and, indeed, we continue to sin; yet we are now cloaked in the righteousness of Christ's perfectly obedient life. You might say it's 'just as if I'd always obeyed!'

The consequence of our legal standing in Christ is that we now have peace with God, meaning that we can appear before Him with confidence.[10]

That confidence and the assurance of our justification is rooted in the resurrection of God's Son,[11] since the resurrection is the evidence of Christ's righteousness - the necessary vindication of a life that could not be bound by death and the confirmation of the good standing possessed by all who trust in His name.

Its appropriation - by faith

The last of the three phrases is *"justified by faith."*[12] This phrase calls attention to the means by which justification is received or appropriated. A person is justified by faith and by faith alone. Righteousness is and always has been the pre-requisite for justification. But God, recognising that humans are incapable of reaching the required standard through human endeavour or effort, credits righteousness to the account of those who have faith. So it was in the case of Abraham, whose simple yet profound faith in God's promises was credited as righteousness.[13]

This doesn't mean that Abraham was justified for mustering such a righteous faith. It would be a complete misunderstanding of the work of justification to think that a person is righteous because he has faith. That would turn faith itself into a work - the work of believing. Yet the faith that God accepts, crediting it as righteous, is faith that acknowledges our complete dependence upon God and that rests fully in the perfect life, the atoning death and the triumphant resurrection of His Son. Indeed, boasting is excluded precisely because no room is left for any human co-operation or contribution in the matter of our justification.[14] Faith, then, does not merit the Judge's verdict; it simply receives what the Judge freely dispenses, in His grace and on the basis of the cross. And even our faith is a gift![15]

How should we respond to this wonderful picture of the atonement? Let us praise God for His glorious grace, so freely given to us in the Son He loves. Although human boasting is excluded, there is a joyful boast associated with our justification, as we eagerly anticipate a day in which we will no longer fall short of His glory, but share in it[16] - our character matching our standing. And that final link in the golden chain (of Romans 8:30) is as certain as our justification, since *"those he justified, he also glorified."*[17]

References:
[1]Rom.5:18 [2]Rom.3:24; see also Tit.3:7 [3]Ex.23:7 [4]Rom.4:5 [5]Rom.3:26 [6]Rom.5:9 [7]Stott, J. R.W. (2006). The Cross of Christ (p.187). Downers Grove, IL: IVP Books. [8]2 Cor.5:21 [9]1 Pet.2:24 [10]Rom.5:1-2 [11]Rom.4:25 [12]Rom.3:28; 5:1 [13]Rom.4 [14]Rom.3:27-28 [15]Phil.1:29; Eph.2:8 [16]Rom.5:2 [17]Rom.8:30
Bible quotations from the NIV (2011).

100 years in Africa

Missionary profiles

Eric Sampou, Port Harcourt, Nigeria

The open door

The so-called 'London meeting' was to become a prominent milestone in Fellowship history, as well as an outstanding forward step in the progress of taking the Gospel overseas. Leading Brethren of the Churches of God met in Clayton Hall, Peckham in September 1918, concerned about work in 'Regions Beyond'. Africa was ready to receive the Gospel and our pioneering missionaries dared to undertake this venture. Our brothers had received the call of God. They had no doubt God wanted them to preach Jesus Christ in the African continent. That sense of direction was from the Holy Spirit and the word of God.

The long boat trip

Whenever ships transporting missionaries entered the harbour, Tom Wallace would be on the quay in Apapa, Lagos, to welcome them. On 17 March 1920, William Terrell waved goodbye to family and friends and boarded RMS Zaria for the 18-day trip from Liverpool, UK, to Lagos, Nigeria.

The goal and motivation

Paul said: "*I make it my ambition to preach the gospel, not where Christ has already been named, ... but as it is written, "... those who have never heard will understand.*"[1] They were prepared to risk their lives for people in unreached regions. Their interest was to preach Christ as the Son of God; His death on the cross; and that He rose again, was exalted and glorified. "*How ... are they to hear without someone preaching? And how are they to preach unless they are sent? As it is written, "How beautiful are the feet of those who preach the good news!"*"[2] They were aware of both the righteous wrath and the eternal love of God. They were constrained by the love of Christ. Their lives were sanctified to Christ as Lord and they desired the glory of God. Some of them were:

William Charles Taylor Terrell (1896- 1961)

Born in Paisley, Scotland, WCT Terrell was commended to full-time service at age 22 by the Conference of Overseers in 1919. Brothers in Paisley described him: "He is a true-hearted disciple of the Lord Jesus Christ, his life bearing evidence that his one desire is to serve Him loyally and well."

He married Jean Davidson in Lagos, and John Terrell, who was chairman of the Conference of Overseers (1976-1991), is one of his sons.

George Egbert Stockwell (1888-1991)
He was born in Middlesbrough, England and later married Muriel Doble in Cardiff in 1925. George did vital work in translating hymn books and leaflets into the Yoruba, Isoko and Ibo languages

William Holmes Stewart (1909-1989)
Willie was born in Glasgow, Scotland and later married Susan Travers. In 1945, he was commended by the Conference of Overseers to full time service at the same time as Rice Horne, Guy Jarvie and George Prasher Jnr. His ambition was to go to West Africa: missionary work had fascinated him from early days. Dr Terrell referred to Willie's homecall in 1989: "The loss to the Fellowship of men 'out to the work' is always keenly felt, none more so than the 'sounding of the trumpets on the other side' (to quote Bunyan) for beloved Willie Stewart ... a man greatly beloved. The fragrance of his life and witness remains and we thank God for it."

George Prasher Jnr. (1916-2008)
Born in Bridgend, Wales, George, like his father, became a Lord's servant (in 1945) and a leading brother in the churches of God (1965). In 1946, George married Margaret Crabtree. George and Margaret served over eleven years in Nigeria in four instalments: Feb. '56 to May '57, accompanied by Jessie Galbraith of New Zealand; Aug. '58 to May '59; April '63 to July '64; Nov. '65 to April '67. He was an outstanding teacher and helped in the Vacation Bible Course.

Our missionary brothers experienced the shock of life in Nigeria, but met its challenges and opened the way. Some died 'in service' there and were buried in Ibadan. They will never be forgotten. We have happy memories of them. What message did they bring to Africa? One of hope, redemption, peace and forgiveness through the Cross of Christ, but also that we too can sacrifice our lives for others. In addition to Liberia and Ghana, the missionary work has expanded through Search for Truth Radio to the east and south east of Africa including Kenya, Malawi, Mozambique and Zimbabwe.

References:
[1]Rom.15:20-21 [2]Rom.10:14-15 ESV

Job

Elihu - the wisdom of youth

Karl Smith, Kirkintilloch, Scotland

Elihu was the original angry young man. He was angry at Job's friends because they heartlessly declared Job to be wrong, but hadn't found an answer as to where the wrong lay. His anger with Job was because he went to the other extreme of justifying himself, not God, (like the Pharisee at the temple in Luke 18) with a long list of his own virtues. By contrast, Elihu would *"ascribe righteousness to my Maker."*[1] To call himself perfect and God unfair would not help Job's suffering. Nevertheless, unlike the three friends, Elihu said, *"I would take pleasure in justifying you."*[2] He was on Job's side.

Job demanded a fair trial from God, as we are inclined to do if we can't see a reason for our hard circumstances. Elihu replies that God doesn't need to investigate Job. He knows all about him already, *"For He does not need to consider a person farther, that he should go before God in judgment."*[3] God's omniscience, however, is comforting because we know He hears *"the cry of the afflicted."*[4]

God's silence in the face of his suffering disturbed Job, but, according to Elihu, God speaks in two ways: first, **through dreams**, [5] which seem to have been a prominent feature of God's revelation before Scripture was completed, and second, **through suffering.** [6] Elihu says this can be a rebuke[7] to correct the person's course. The person in his example is driven to prayer and realises that a ransom has been found. [8] The price has been paid and he is rescued.

The experience draws him to deeper worship of God. Maybe Elihu had deliverance from physical suffering in mind, but we all know that this does not always come, just as it didn't always come to the righteous, even in Bible times. When Job had spoken of redemption,[9] he had the perspective of a triumphant hope beyond death: *"I know that my Redeemer lives, and at the last, He will take His stand on the earth. Even after my skin is destroyed, Yet from my flesh I will see God .."*[10]

Therefore we can apply the joyful song of Elihu's hypothetical man, saved in the midst of his suffering, to our own sense of eternal and not just temporary salvation: *"He has redeemed my soul from going to the pit, And my life will see the light."*[11] At times Elihu can sound as harsh as Job's three older friends, but his perspective is markedly different. God doesn't commend him at the end, nor does He condemn him.

He does, however, come the closest to God's perspective. The descriptions of God's power seen in nature in chapter 37 fittingly introduce the poetic voice of God as He reminds Job of His creative and sustaining power in the following chapters.

Elihu focuses on the image of the clouds, which God sends for three reasons, which we may apply also to the suffering under discussion: *"Whether for correction, or for His earth, or for goodness, He causes it to happen."*[12]

The correction we have thought of, but sometimes the heavy rain serves a purpose for the benefit of the land. In God's inscrutable purposes we sometimes see a benefit in our growth from the dark clouds around us - and in some cases we will only realise what was being achieved from the perspective of glory. We can say that 'for love' stands behind the other reasons. Elihu encourages Job - and us - to go on trusting that whatever God permits is an expression of His love, bringing out the true quality of our faith. My cousin Andrew found the book of Job, with its avoidance of glib answers, an immense help during his experience of Leukemia, from which he eventually died. He wrote: 'the suffering of the righteous...is a token of God's love and a refinement of their righteousness'.[13] He could say this with an authority I do not have, not having experienced such depths, or perhaps such intensity of relationship with God.

In the meantime, Elihu advises us not to be tempted to give in and choose sin rather than suffering,[14] but to extol God's work. [15] He concludes by introducing the appearance of God: *"From the north comes golden splendor; Around God is awesome majesty."*[16] Perhaps this sense of longing for God's presence and His righteousness, not our own resources, is the unique perspective that Elihu brought to Job in his suffering.

References:
[1]Job 36:3 [2]Job 33:32 [3]Job 34:23 [4]Job 34:28 [5]Job 33:15-18 [6]Job 33:19-22 [7]Job 33:19 [8]Job 33 :24 [9]Job 19:25-27 [10]Job 19:25-26 [11]Job 33:28 [12]Job 37:13 [13]Drain, A. Code Red (London: CMF, 2020), p.84 [14]Job 36:21 [15]Job 36:24 [16]Job 37:22
Bible quotations from the NASB (2020).

The race

Tony Smith, Kirkintilloch, Scotland

The apostle Paul describes Christian life as a race. It starts with salvation and ends in glory. Of course, salvation itself is not a reward; it is a gift. However, there are rewards and a prize to be awarded for runners who strive for the crown on completion of the race. Paul wrote: *"Now there is in store for me the crown of righteousness, which the Lord, the righteous Judge, will award to me on that day - and not only to me, but also to all who have longed for his appearing."*[1]

The main thing is to finish the race well and hear the "Well done!" The apostle sums it up this way: *"I consider my life worth nothing to me, if only I may finish the race and complete the task the Lord has given me - the task of testifying to the gospel of God's grace."*[2] When Paul was stopped in his tracks on the road to Damascus, he was appointed as a servant and a witness to testify to the gospel of God's grace. Later he could say, *I was not disobedient to the vision from heaven.*[3] Centuries earlier the prophet Habakkuk was told by God: *"Write the vision; make it plain on tablets, so he may run who reads it."*[4] So, Paul ran with it. At the end of his life he could write, *"I have fought the good fight, I have finished the race, I have kept the faith."*[5]

The word 'fight' in the original Greek is *'agon'*, from which we get our English word 'agony'. Doubtless, Paul would have agreed with this modem derivative - that his had been a hard-fought race, demanding stamina and endurance. We would not expect the Olympic Committee to knock on our door to ask us to run a marathon in the next Olympic Games, especially if the only running we had done was from the sofa to the fridge! The remarkable thing is, that the Lord Jesus has picked us to run in His team and complete the task of testifying to the gospel of God's grace. An average Olympian trains for four hours a day and for three hundred days a year. For the Christian, there is a lifetime of training. Paul says, *"Do you not know that in a race all the runners run, but only one gets the prize? Run in such a way as to get the prize. Everyone who competes in the games goes into strict training. They do it to get a crown ..."*[6]

Believers are expected to compete in a good sense. The English word 'compete' comes from the Latin, *'cam'*, which means together and *'petere'*, which means to strive; literally, to strive together. Today's athletes do it to win a medal and in ancient times a crown was the prize. As the apostle Paul goes on to say, *They do it to get a crown that will not last; but we do it to get a crown that will last for ever. Therefore I do not run like a man running aimlessly; I do not fight like a man beating the air.*[7]

A verse from Dr. J.S.B. Monsell's well-known hymn says:

'Run the straight race, through God's good grace;
Lift up thine eyes, and seek His face.
Life with its path before thee lies,
Christ is the way and Christ the prize.'[8]

Simon Kindleyside, a 34-year-old paralysed man, took part in the 2018 London Marathon. Wearing robotic leg attachments, it took him 37 hours to cover the 26.2 miles of the marathon. He came in last, but he finished the race. He kept going, enduring pain, encouraged by public supporters and raised £8 million for paralytic treatments.

The race we are involved in as Christians is not a dash; it, too, is a distance event. Not a sprint, but a marathon demanding stamina and endurance. The writer to the Hebrews says, *"Therefore let us also, seeing we are compassed about with so great a cloud of witnesses, lay aside every weight, and the sin which doth so easily beset us, and let us run with patience the race that is set before us."*[9]

The question is, are we still on course to run the race marked out for us? There are two critical times in a marathon race. First, starting too fast, expending our reserves of energy at this early stage. Second, giving up at the halfway point, when the strain begins to tell on our tired limbs, in what runners call 'hitting the wall'. Athletes need to push through the halfway barrier and not be discouraged by others who may be gaining on them. Paul highlighted the dangers of this when he wrote, *"You were running a good race. Who cut in on you and kept you from obeying the truth?"*[10] Has anyone cut in on you or caused you to stumble? Are you tempted to give up? There is a poem attributed to D.H. Groberg about a boy who ran a race, falling many times, yet finishing the course: And to his dad he sadly said, "I didn't do too well." "To me, you won," his father said. "You rose each time you fell."[11]

Three words could sum up Hebrews 12 verse 1 to motivate us in our Christian race:

Encouragement
In addition to those heroes of faith described in chapter eleven of Hebrews we, too, are to run the race before us as they had done. This is not the imagery of stadium spectators viewing our progress and cheering us

on. It is the picture of men and women of faith, whose witness in their day serves as an example and encouragement for us today. They were not always successful, failing at times, but God kept them running in such a way as to inspire us to keep going until we reach the finishing tape.

We think of those who, in our lives, have encouraged us as followers of Christ: youth leaders, Bible class teachers, spiritual mentors, and those elderly Christians who regularly prayed for us. They knew the law of the track and exhorted us not to look back, not to be discouraged although others appear to be overtaking us, not to grow weary or lose heart but to finish the course.

Encumbrances

Athletes who compete in a race must be fit and wear the necessary lightweight running kit. So too, the Christian runner must travel lightly and lay aside every weight that would hinder their progress. The Hebrews scripture differentiates between 'weight' and 'the sin'. The word weight means something superfluous holding us back - an encumbrance.These 'weights' may be harmless in themselves, but are handicaps preventing us from achieving our best performance. Forfeiting time spent on entertainments, pleasures and certain luxuries frees us up to achieve a crown that fully recompenses our loss of these things. The besetting sin which can so easily get in the way of the runner could be thought to be unbelief, which has the effect of hemming us in on all sides and is possibly at the root of all sin and failure. Let us feel the exhilaration of running unencumbered, with nothing to hold us back in our service for the Lord.

Endurance

The scripture says, *"Let us run with patience the race that is set before us."*[9] The word 'patience' used here can be understood as endurance or perseverance. We need 'staying power' if we are to finish strongly. To mix our metaphors, life throws its curve balls at us and at times knocks us off our feet. It is then that we need to get up again and carry on with the race.

Eric Liddell, whose life was featured in the film 'Chariots of Fire', ran in several races, such as the 100-, 200- and 400-meters. In one 440-yard race, he tumbled on the track and one of the officials shouted, "Get up and run!" He jumped to his feet and took off. Right at the finishing tape, Liddell stuck out his chest and won the race. *The Scotsman* newspaper later wrote, 'This must have been the greatest track performance ever seen.'

There is something noble and honourable about not quitting. Of course, it is not about coming first in the Christian race, but, instead, finishing well should be our goal. So, will we 'get up off the sofa' and run the race? In a distance race, a bell is sounded when runners begin the last lap and athletes make a supreme bid for success. Exerting every limb to the utmost with eyes fixed on the finishing tape. The eye outstrips and draws forward the hand and the hand in tum draws the foot and looking straight ahead they run to attain the goal and win the prize.

Let us follow the single-minded example of the apostle Paul who wrote, *"But one thing I do: Forgetting what is behind and straining towards what is ahead, I press on towards the goal to win the prize for which God has called me heavenwards in Christ Jesus."*[12]

References:
[1]2 Tim.4:8 [2]Acts 20:24 [3]Acts 26:19 [4]Hab.2:2 ESV [5]2 Tim.4:7 [6]1 Cor.9:24-25 [7]1 Cor.9:25-26 [8]John SB Monsell, PHSS 369 [9]Heb.12:1 RV [10]Gal.5:7 [11]DH Groberg, The Race [12]Phil.3:13-14
Bible quotations from the NIV (1984) unless stated otherwise.

Can you help me with this?

God's healing through prayer

Mario Magallanes, Tagum, Philippines

At the time of writing, Mario was recovering after being seriously ill with an aggravated bout of hepatitis. Prayer was made throughout the Philippine churches for him. A godly man, he found it salutary and reflects on it...

In the Bible book of 2 Chronicles it says, *"if my people who are called by my name will humble themselves, and pray and seek my face, and turn from their wicked ways, then I will hear from heaven, and will forgive their sins and heal their land."*[1] Let us try to examine ourselves, deep within us. Is there real humility in our hearts before God? Are we truly turning away from our sins? Jeremiah declares firmly: *"The heart is deceitful above all things, and desperately sick; who can understand it?"*[2] Only God looks at the heart. He knows our desire, even our thoughts afar off. He alone knows if we are truly forsaking, and dealing with, our sins and humbling ourselves. The Lord our God in heaven is ready to hear our prayers, forgive our sins and heal us.[3] *"But your iniquities have made a separation between you and your God; and your sins have hidden his face from you, so that he does not hear.[4] Nothing will be impossible with God."*[5]

Why then are there some prayers still unanswered? Now we are God's children, we know that all our sins have been forgiven for His name's sake.[6] We have been *"washed ... sanctified ... justified in the name of the Lord Jesus Christ and by the Spirit of our God."*[7] We are forever justified, not based on what we can do, but based on what the Lord Jesus Christ has done for us. But, in daily Christian living, we need to take care of our sins by confession, because this is the only way to maintain our intimate, close fellowship with God. Confess your sins before God, for *"he is faithful and just to forgive us our sins and to cleanse us from all unrighteousness."*[8]

Now about diseases, is it true that God can heal us today? Absolutely, He can! *"And this is the confidence that we have toward him, that if we ask anything according to his will he hears us."*[9] However, we need to learn how to wait for Him patiently. Sometimes, we have prayer for our well-being but there is no quick response. Is the problem within us?

Having done our part (confessing in prayer), we just need to wait for whatever is God's response. Of course, not all the sickness and disease we experience is due to God's disciplining of us. What are some reasons why we may get sick?

Because of the works of the Devil

Remember the case of Job: He was a righteous man, but God proved him, saying to Satan: *"You persuaded me to let you attack him for no reason at all, but Job is still as faithful as ever." Satan replied, "A person will give up everything in order to stay alive, now suppose you hurt his body he will curse you to your face." So the Lord said to Satan, "All right, he is in your power, but you are not to kill him." Then Satan left the Lord's presence and made sores break out all over Job's body."*[10] Job suffered at the hands of Satan. As Christian disciples, we may suffer persecution today at the hands of wicked people who are motivated by Satan.[11]

Because of our unwise actions or unhealthy environment

If we should eat anything that is not wholesome (either unhealthy or contaminated food), that can cause us to be ill. We need to be wise in our habits. However, we are powerfully reminded at this time of pandemic, that despite our best efforts, we live in a fallen world in which we can at any time be innocently exposed to germs, viruses and other dangers.

Because of God's discipline

This is only one category. *"For the Lord disciplines the one he loves."*[12] *"My son, do not despise the LORD's discipline or be weary of his reproof."*[13]

Because of God's glory

This is more positive: so that the works of God might be displayed.[14]

References:
[1]2 Chron.7:14 [2]Jer.17:9 [3]Jas.5:14-18 [4]Isa.59:2 [5]Lk.1:37 [6]1 Jn 2:12 [7]1 Cor.6:11[8]1 Jn 1:9 [9]1 Jn 5:14 [10]Job 2:3-7 GNB [11]2 Tim.3:12; 1 Jn 5:19 [12]Heb.12:6 [13]Prov.3:11 [14]Jn 9:3
Bible quotations from the ESV unless stated otherwise.

Saved to serve

An interview with Gospel Worker

Topesa Issa, Milepa, Malawi

Tell us about your parents and your childhood?
My parents were originally from different countries: my father from Malawi and my mother from Zimbabwe. They were Christians. I was born in Zimbabwe on 17 November, 1963.

That's interesting: that you should be born in Zimbabwe, living in Malawi, and now also busy evangelizing by visiting Mozambique! Tell us, how did you personally hear the Gospel and become sure of your salvation?
My parents either attended, or belonged to, several different denominations. I distinctly remember the Church of Christ asbeing one of them. For a time, too, they were with the sect known asChristadelphians. My father died in 1981. At that time when I was only a church-goer, it was easy to me to drop it and start living a pagan life: drinking, stealing and looking for the help of witchdoctors to become rich. We were seven in our family and I was the youngest. I plainly recall that it was in 1984 when I was saved.

This happened when I was in attendance for a service by the Full Gospel Church. The message preached that day was based on Mathew 11:28. I knew I was weary and burdened and wanted spiritual rest, so I simply responded to the invitation and came believing toChrist as my personal Saviour. After responding to the message, I wanted to follow my own spiritual journey, not the example of my parents.

What family do you have?
In 1985, I married a believer, Rode. Because we were both believers, we were careful to have our wedding ceremony before we started our own family. We thank God for giving us seven children: four daughters and three boys. I've been a farmer ever since I left primary school and on my own since my parents died.

What motivated you to begin a life of preaching the Gospel?
After my conversion, I was sure that God had called me to serve him as an evangelist. God graciously added His blessing when I shared the message of salvation in Christ, and many came to be saved through my witness.

What brought you to the Churches of God?
This happened when I heard about 'the seven steps' that are followed in the Churches of God, taken from Acts 2:41-42. Although I was a preacher, I discovered it was incorrect doctrine that I'd been following. I thank God who brought me to His house, the churches of God. [1]

This wonderful event took place in 2002 when two men, Peter Jonga and Luck Nazombe, visited me at my home. They had brought with them a copy of this magazine, Needed Truth! These men also invited me to their outreach, and it was there I learned the seven steps as preached then by Churches of God Nigerian evangelist, Mark Imoukhuede. Afterwards, I went home and prayed with fasting that I should discern if this was the right way for me to go. I thank God that He revealed to me that I should leave my past denomination, and serve Him at the place of His own choice (as in Old Testament times[2]). When I came to the Church of God, my mum left the Church of Christ through my testimony to her and was herself associated with the Churches of God from 2004. She was called home to be with the Lord in 2016.

When are you most happy?
Using whatever God-given ability I have in evangelism, I am full of joy that now more people are being brought to the Lord than before - and also now to serve Him in His house! I thank God that while the Holy Spirit motivates me to preach, I do not have much free time for selfish desires, as many outreaches are being made. Indeed, I am most happy when people are receiving the Lord Jesus and being baptized and added to the Churches of God.

What are your ambitions?
My ambition is to see all areas of Malawi covered by churches of God united in God's house, as it is the pillar of the truth.[3] I can think of how I was given the support of the motorcycle I am using. For many years I served on foot, occasionally bicycling, but now I'm able 'to catch people with the Gospel' faster! To God be the Glory!

Who are your closest helpers in the Lord's work?
My wife, being a farmer and using her produce, is my close supporter in the Lord's work, as are well-wishers in the churches.

Bible references:
[1]Heb.3:6; 1 Pet.2:4-5 [2]Deut.12:5 [3]1 Tim.3:15

The Best Time

Samuel Moses Gummadi

Greetings. I am doctor Samuel Moses Gummadi, 61 years old, with a PhD in chemistry, and have served as a professor and principal of Government degree colleges in Andhra Pradesh, India for 35 years. But what's more important. I am happy to state that along with my wife, Dr Kamala, and four members of my family I have been numbered with the Church of God in Rajahmundry and involved in serving the Lord for the last 21 years. Brother Brian Tugwell has been our excellent Bible teacher during that time. Previously we were also blessed through exposure to the teachings of brothers Andy McIlree, Alan Toms and Phil Brennan and in more recent times Craig Jones.

I am writing now at this time to seek say a big "thank you" for sending the weekly video sermons from our excellent experienced speakers in the churches of God during this time of pandemic and uncertainty. I feel immensely blessed that God gave me the opportunity to translate around 20 different international speakers belonging to our churches in the first six months of the pandemic. This is truly a unique opportunity for all of us in the churches of God in India, and we give all the glory and honour to our great God. Exposure to the teachings of these 20 experienced brothers of churches abroad is really a great blessing to us from our Lord at this time. We thank the Lord for the great opportunity.

In fact, I must say that in all my 21 years of service in the Church of God in Rajahmundry, although now under pandemic conditions, this seems like the sweetest and best time in my life to do God's service by translating into Telugu and forwarding to our Telugu-speaking churches in India God's wisdom and the Lord's knowledge from our dear brothers. Most of those in the Church of God at Rajahmundry together with our leaders and a few of the saints in the other 13 Telugu-speaking assemblers in Andhra and Goa, plus a few saints in Chennai (like brother Venkat) have all greatly benefited from the translation of these recorded video messages through the Internet. You may be already aware that all these sermons are uploaded in a YouTube channel for the benefit of present and future generations and indeed are receiving a good number of 'likes' from a considerable number of people.

As it says in Hebrews 10:25 we are not to forsake the assembling of ourselves together, as is the manner of some, but exhorting one another, and so much the more as you see the day is approaching.

There have been many months during the pandemic when it has not proved possible to gather physically, but those in our church (around 40) who have Internet and smartphone facility as well as other leaders of other assemblies are all inquiring often whether the weekly message for the Lord's day has come or not? I am really happy you have never disappointed us.

I thank you all from the bottom of my heart for your priceless service and we give all glory and honour to the Lord.

At the time of writing (some time before publication) we are all in a confused state regarding the opening of church halls here in Andhra Pradesh. The virus is still rampaging through our towns and villages. There remains therefore a real risk of infection with this dreadful disease. Consequently, most of our halls have not yet opened on Sundays (or any other days). Pray for us and continue to send the valuable sermons from our dear brothers abroad.

Once again, with heartfelt appreciation from India to all the speakers who gave sermons and shared God's wisdom with us in this way.

From the Editors' desk

Issue 4 2021

On her 21st birthday in 1947 Princess Elizabeth, now the Queen of the United Kingdom and fifteen other commonwealth realms, dedicated her life to the service of her people with the broadcast words "I declare before you all that my whole life whether it be long or short shall be devoted to your service and the service of our great imperial family to which we all belong." That dedication was evident in everything that she did; she returned to royal duties only four days after the loss of her husband of 73 years during 2021. The Queen is a Christian believer, although she must be disappointed with some of the things that have happened within her family.

None of our readers will be called to the monarchy, although all of us will be called to something. It probably won't be anything particularly outstanding: scripture says *"consider your calling, brothers: not many of you were wise according to worldly standards, not many were powerful, not many were of noble birth."*[1] It is salutary to consider that we follow one who is wisdom personified, who has all authority in heaven and on earth, and who is King of Kings.

So, the Bible says, *"Have this mind among yourselves, which is yours in Christ Jesus, who, though he was in the form of God, did not count equality with God a* thing *to be grasped, but emptied himself by taking the* form *of a servant, being born in the likeness of men. And being found in human form, he humbled himself by* becoming *obedient to the point of death, even death on a* cross. *Therefore God has highly exalted him and bestowed on him the name that is above every name, so that at the name of Jesus every knee should bow, in heaven and on earth and under the earth, and every tongue confess that Jesus Christ is Lord, to the glory of God the Father."*[2] He took the form of a servant, and we must ask ourselves, "What can I do to serve?" Scripture makes it very clear that if we seek to exalt ourselves, we will be abased.

Peter

References:
[1] 1 Cor.1:26 [2] Phil.2:5-11
Bible quotations from the ESV.

Fishing

Tony Smith, Kirkintilloch, Scotland

Mark 1:16-20 tells how Jesus called His first disciples, Simon, Andrew, James and John. These hardy fishermen responded to Jesus' call to *"Follow Me, and I will have you become fishers of people."*[1] The call of these disciples is also recorded in Matthew 4:18-22 and Luke 5: 1-11. In John's Gospel it is revealed that Andrew and another disciple (thought to be John) attended the preaching of John the Baptist when he proclaimed Jesus to be *"the Lamb of God, who takes away the sin of the world!"*[2] Andrew found his brother Simon and told him, *"We have found the Messiah."*[3] However, it appears that these men had returned to their fishing business after their first encounter with Jesus.

In Luke's account of the call, Jesus was preaching by the seashore. It is estimated that Jesus spent around 90% of His ministry in Northern Palestine, with many Bible references to being on or around the Sea of Galilee. Luke gives us more detail of how Jesus got into Simon's boat and sat down to teach the crowds of people.[4]

Following this, a great miracle takes place as Simon is told to launch out into the deep and let down the nets for a catch. There were so many fish that the nets were breaking and even with the help of their partners both boats were beginning to sink. A similar miracle takes place again after the Lord's resurrection when Christ on the beach in Galilee directs His disciples to throw the net on the right side of the boat for a catch. [5] This time the net was full of large fish but did not break and it took the strength of rugged Peter to haul the net to the shore.

These fishermen felt the call of the sea, but a greater call was given by the Messiah, *"Follow Me, and I will have you become fishers of people."*[1] Thirteen times in the Gospels Jesus said, *"Follow me"*. It is a personal call that demands a response. Jesus did not say, "Follow My rules; follow My morality; follow My ways," though of course these are important for disciples of the Lord. But above all, "Follow me!" That involves knowing Christ, worshipping Christ, obeying Christ, serving Christ and loving Christ. Can you hear His call again today? Peter heard it on two occasions: on the seashore of Galilee[1] and then again in John 21:22. Perhaps we, too, need to be reminded of the call of the Master.

The call of Jesus has two parts: not only an invitation to life under a new master, but also the adventure of embarking on a new mission. Who is master of my life? Does Christ have mastery over me? These are questions that challenge us today. Jesus said, "If *anyone would come after me, he must deny himself and take up his cross daily and follow me.*"[6]

Perhaps we would gladly say, "I will follow Jesus", but let's keep the two parts together; that is, not only to be followers, but also to be fishers. Disciples making disciples.[7] When Jesus calls you to Himself, He never calls you to keep Him to yourself.

Fishing for people is not just for those who like that sort of thing - the keen ones, the 'door- knockers' or the open- air preachers, but for all followers of Jesus. So, the question is, "Is Jesus my master and am I willing to make Him known?" Evangelism was of great importance to the Saviour. He began His ministry and ended His ministry with a call to make disciples. That is, to use disciples to make disciples.

Fishing needs patience and perseverance to cope with the failure and success involved in the task. Fishing for people is as much a team effort as an individual one. Remember how the fishermen called their partners on that later occasion to help with the physical catch of fish on the Sea of Galilee. Fish do not just jump into a boat; fishermen need to go to find them. This involves launching into deep waters or trying another side of a boat to catch more and even bigger fish.

Finally, we must draw in the net and gather in precious souls for Christ. Alan Toms wrote in Needed Truth in 1978, 'We know there is no occupation more worthwhile in life than to win others for Christ.'

JC Ryle in his commentary[8] on Mark 1:17-18 wrote, 'The meaning of these verses is clear and unmistakable. The disciples were to become fishers for souls. They were to labour to draw people out of darkness into light and from the power of Satan to God. They were to strive to bring people into the net of Christ's church, so that they may be saved and not perish everlastingly.' When Jesus says to us, *"Follow Me, and I will have you become fishers of people",* this is not a suggestion for our consideration, but a calling for action. How will we respond to the Master and to the mission to which He has called us?

References:
[1]Mk.1:17 NASB 2020 [2]Jn 1:29 [3]Jn 1:41 [4]Lk.5:3 [5]Jn 21:1-14 [6]Lk.9:23 [7]Matt. 28:19 [8]JC Ryle, Expository Thoughts on the Gospels
Bible quotations from the NIV (1984) unless stated otherwise.

Knowing God

Walking in the light

Ben Jones, Hamilton, Canada

John's first epistle takes the reader on a fascinating and challenging exploration of biblical truths: the ability we have to pass from darkness into light, the appreciation of God's boundless love for us, and our need to consistently display love to those around us. The impression we walk away with is the solemn and yet joyous responsibility we have to know God by becoming more like Him as His disciples, and the importance of the consistency of our walk and testimony.

The apostle begins his epistle by reminding his readers about the message they had previously received – *"the word of life."*[1] He introduces a theme that we see repeated throughout his epistle by outlining that the fellowship between disciples, and the fellowship that those disciples have with God, are inseparable.[2] This thought is repeated in verse 7, where the foundation for the fellowship that disciples have with one another, and with God, is revealed as *"walk[ing] in the light, as he is in the light."*[3] This light is metaphorical here for the divine glory and the revealed nature of God. It would be no surprise if John had in mind what he observed on the mountain when the Lord Jesus was transfigured before him, showing His divine glory and majesty, which was manifested as His face *"shone like the sun, and his clothes became white as light."*[4]

The evidence of knowing God, who is light

John continues by contrasting the light of God with the darkness of the world. *"God is light"* - a direct contrast to the darkness of the world.[5] While outlining this contrast, John also reveals to us the amazing truth that we have the opportunity to pass from darkness into that light, if we acknowledge and confess the sin that keeps us in darkness. This must be our starting point for any fellowship with God, any experience of knowing Him - that the sin that keeps us in darkness be removed. At this point we should also take note of the audience and tenses that John uses in describing this transition from darkness to light; he is writing to believers, as evidenced in the first few verses of the epistle, and he writes in the present tense. Walking in the light[3] is a continual act, something that John's audience were to continually devote themselves to - and by extension, the need for continual confession and continual forgiveness.

The fact that John is speaking of a continual walking in the light is further emphasized in the following chapter. Verse 8 of chapter 2 speaks of a transition period, with the darkness [of the present evil age] passing away and the true light [of the age to come] - light that is from God and descriptive of His nature - shining (and, by implication, growing) in the world.

As disciples further their walk with God and deepen their fellowship with one another, the light of God shines more and more. John must be referring here to an increase in God's light evident in the world. The evidence of this light comes from the actions and the fellowship of the disciples - from walking in the same way that the Lord Jesus walked.[6]

The command that John is giving to his readers here is made clear in chapter 2 verses 9-11 - as brothers and sisters in the Lord, we are to love one another. We are not to love the world, [7] but instead our love (which must be evidenced by action, as James 2:14-18 makes clear) should be focused on those who are also striving to live in the light. The two are antithetical - love of the world is inconsistent with the disciples' testimony since the light of God's nature must drive out the darkness of the world.

But how does this fellowship cause the light of God to increase in the world? John's next chapter points us towards the end goal of the transformation he has spoken about - that the transition we are making from darkness to light, is about making us more like the light. That is, we are becoming more like God Himself. Verse 2 of chapter 3 contains the remarkable revelation that *"when he appears we shall be like him, because we will see him as he is."* When we piece this together, the picture we get is of transformation. When unbelievers, we started out in darkness. God in His infinite grace provided us with a means to be reconciled to Him, and to pass from the darkness of sin into His light.

John, in this letter, now shows that for Christians there follows a lifetime of continual striving, showing more and more of the light of God in the world through our actions, until finally, the Lord Jesus Himself appears and our transformation into beings of righteousness and light is complete. This is not to say that our life on earth and our eventual future is to become gods ourselves. On the contrary, our transformation is not about our own grandeur or glorification but is about the glory of God being displayed through us. When we become like Him, it is still His splendour and His righteousness that we display. As John makes clear at the start of his epistle, none of us is without sin, and so all of our transformation is solely attributable to God's saving grace.[8]

Actively knowing God
In Chapter 4, John further expands on why fellowship with, and love for, our brothers and sisters is such a key part of this transformation that we are undergoing.

It is because of that wonderful truth that God is love.[9] As we become like God, and show out His qualities and nature, love should be clearly displayed in what we do. That love is directed to those around us and, in loving our brothers and sisters, we are actively knowing God. To love someone truly, is to know what love is and, in so doing, we know God, because God is love. John also reinforces for us the importance of love being not just in word, but displayed in action. Verses 20 and 21 of chapter 4 make it clear that true love for God must be evidenced in visible love for the brethren. This visible, demonstrable love is the outworking and evidence of the transformation that John has referred to previously. As we transition from the darkness of sin to the light of God, we more fully reflect the nature of God. Since God is love, that love finds its beneficiaries in our fellow disciples - those who are also undergoing the same transformation from darkness to light.

The evidence of knowing God, who is love
If we are to know God, we must know that God is love. In amongst all of His divine attributes, it is His love that perhaps mostly fully describes His nature and being. In saying that God is love, John reminds us that all that God does comes, ultimately, from love. His creating power, His revelation of the law, His guiding of His people, the salvation He gives us, even the coming judgement for sinners, all comes from His heart of love. Since this is true, to know God is to express and live out love to those around us.

This is not to say that God loves everything. We know that there are things that He hates - things that are abhorrent to Him. [10] God's love is very often unmerited - here the wonder of God's love is that He takes hateful, sinful people, and transforms them through His love into people that are counted worthy of His love. If we are being transformed to be like God, then we too must be showing out His love to our brothers and sisters, seeking to encourage them in their righteousness and as they strive to follow God's commandments and depart from sin.[11]

References:
[1]1 Jn 1:1 [2]1 Jn 1:3 [3]1 Jn 1:7 [4]Matt.17:2 [5]1 Jn 1:5 [6]1 Jn 2:6 [7]1 Jn 2:15 [8]1 Jn 1:10 [9]1 Jn 4:7-8 [10]Deut.12:31; 16:22; Prov.6:16-19; Amos 6:8 [11]1 Jn 5:16-18
   Bible quotations from the ESV.

Ecclesiastes

Growing older

Philip Allen, Cardiff, Wales

Recently, I was looking through some old photographs and I came across one of my mother, who passed into the Lord's presence some 36 years ago. I was reminded that when I was a young boy, she would often quote to me verses from the Bible. One in particular I remember reads, *"Remember your Creator in the days of your youth, before the days of trouble come and the years approach when you will say, "I find no pleasure in them".*[1]

I suppose that, at the time, I understood little of its real meaning, nor did I grasp the importance of using the vigour and enthusiasm of youth in the pursuit of spiritual things. For many younger people, life seems to stretch out before them, full of limitless opportunities and possibilities and there may be little thought given to life's transient nature or to the creator who brought all things into being. Perhaps this is an experience that is familiar to many of us. Maybe it is only later in life that we realise how important it is, from earliest days, for a person to think about their Creator and to consider who made them and what they were made for. Maybe it takes many years for us to recognise that a person is not created for self- gratification of their passions, but rather to use their energies and capabilities in accordance with God's will and purpose.[2]

Such attitudes to life are dealt with by the writer of Ecclesiastes, the preacher who makes the sobering point that all things under the sun are futile and that ultimately we will all be accountable to God for the way we have lived our lives.[3] It is interesting to note that in the New Testament the equivalent phrase for 'under the sun', would be 'in the world' (Gk. *kosmos),* e.g., John 16:33.

The preacher expresses very graphically the process that takes place in each one of us as we move from being young into the state of old age. Physically we weaken, our energy levels drop, our senses are no longer acute, our appearance alters, we become fearful and everything becomes a burden. Eventually, the change and decay inherent in the human condition overtakes us and we become increasingly aware of our mortality. In due course, our body returns to dust, and our spirit returns to God who gave it.[4]

In his final analysis of life under the sun, the preacher concludes that life is meaningless.[5] However, the preacher doesn't leave it there. God had given him great wisdom and he had gained a great deal of knowledge and experience as to the vanity of the world, often at great cost to himself. After all his deliberations, he seeks to use what he has learned to explain to the people his conclusions on how they should live.[6]

When the preacher says that 'all is vanity', this is not his verdict upon life in general, but only upon the misguided human nature that treats the created world as an end in itself and has no eternal perspective. The preacher concludes his advice with the words *"Fear God and keep his commandments, for this is whole duty of man. For God will bring every deed into judgment, including every hidden thing, whether it is good or evil."*[7] For the believer, our perspective takes us far beyond the things under the sun, the things of this world, for *"we fix our eyes not on what is seen, but on what is unseen, since what is seen is temporary, but what is unseen is eternal."*[8]

It is vital for us as believers on the Lord Jesus Christ, to recognise the ultimate futility of things under the sun, but not with an attitude of despair. In the gospel of John we read that *"whoever hears my word and believes him who sent me has eternal life and will not be judged, but has crossed from death to life".*[9] Consequently, we should live our lives in the fear of the Lord, being joyful and motivated to serve Him as we *"wait for the blessed hope - the appearing of the glory of our great God and Saviour, Jesus Christ."*[10]

References:
[1]Eccles.12:1 [2]Rom.12:1-2 [3]Eccles.11:9 [4]Eccles.12:2-7 [5]Eccles.12:8
[6]Eccles.12:9-12 [7]Eccles.12:13-14 [8]2 Cor.4:18 [9]Jn 5:24 [10]Tit.2:13
Bible quotations from the NIV (1984).

Image-bearing

Renewed in God's image

Richard Hutchinson, Vancouver, Canada

Through this series on image- bearing, we've had it clearly laid out for us how we were made in the image of God, to shine out His glory and beauty by exhibiting His character in our lives. It is a lofty calling, and one sadly inhibited by our other image-bearing burden, that of *the man of dust,* as Paul refers to Adam in 1 Corinthians 15:48-49. Despite our being made by God with His image imprinted into our being, we must acknowledge how His image is shrouded by our earthliness, the weakness that our pride and self-interest breeds within us. The weakness of Adam is seemingly the much more prevalent image in humanity, but for those of us who have been born again by the will and word of God, and thereby qualified to be called children of God, we will *"bear the image of the man of heaven"*, our life-giving Lord Jesus.

Remarkably, that was always the plan. We were predestined to be conformed to the image of God's Son[1] as part of God's eternal deliberations. This was the great purpose of salvation, to redeem a people who fulfil the true purpose of humanity and who will worship God in spirit and in truth.

In 1 Corinthians 15, Paul has in mind our transformation at the rapture with the resurrection of the dead: *"the perishable puts on the imperishable"* (v.54), but we know from 2 Corinthians 3:18 that there is a process happening currently: *"And we all, with unveiled face, beholding the glory of the Lord, are being transformed into the same image from one degree of glory to another. For this comes from the Lord who is the Spirit."*

Two things to note here are that the one being transformed is *"beholding the glory of the Lord"*. In the context of the passage that means seeing the fullness of God's grace and loving- kindness in *"the ministry of righteousness."* [2] The second is that the transforming is a work of the Lord, the Spirit. We are not transforming ourselves, but the Spirit is at work within us, as is God's Word, [3] which is doubtless integral to the process also.

The ongoing process is also seen in Colossians 3. The first four verses tie in with the thoughts of 1 Corinthians 15 above: we have died to the world and have been raised in Christ, and the pending change of 1 Corinthians

15 is what we will experience when *"Christ, who is your life appears."* [4] The verses that follow take that great hope as the basis for reordering our lives here and now – *"put to death therefore what is earthly in you ... put on the new self, which is being renewed in knowledge after the image of its creator."* [5]

'Knowledge' here is the Greek *epi-gnosis,* which the NASB translates as 'true knowledge'. It's knowledge by experience, knowledge that impacts you and our new self is being renewed based on how we develop in our experience of God, allowing that knowledge to shape us, through the work of the Spirit and the Word within us, into an ever-closer resemblance of the one who made us in His image.

In verses 12-17 of Colossians 3, Paul shows how knowledge drives renewal. We are to clothe ourselves in spiritual qualities of compassion, kindness, humility, meekness, patience and, above all, love - qualities we have learned from knowing our Saviour; beholding His glory, not only on the page of Scripture, but in how He has worked in our own lives to bring peace and joy to us through that same compassion, kindness, humility, meekness, patience and, above all, love.

Why, then, would we be conformed to this world, to the image of *the man of dust,* when we can be transformed by the renewal of our minds?[6] Let us instead allow the Lord the Spirit to recalibrate our perceptions and motivations through a deepening understanding of God's inexhaustible love, so that we may have that most precious characteristic, the most desirable trait for a heart tuned to the heavenly: Christlikeness.

References:
[1]Rom.8:29 [2]2 Cor.3:9 [3]1 Thess.2:13 [4]Col.3:4 [5]Col.3:5,10 [6]Rom.12:2
Bible quotations from the ESV.

The Atonement

The family: reconciliation

David Woods, Manchester, England

It's a scandalous story of truly shocking behaviour: the dignified landowner running to meet his returning rebel son. In the culture of the day, a man of such reputation would not run anywhere. Ever. But he sees his 'lost' son returning, and in overflowing compassion runs to meet him.[1]

The son had previously demanded his inheritance early and had left home to live life his own way. After wasting everything on a lifestyle that lost more than it gained, he finally came to his senses. As he reflected on his self- inflicted poverty, he remembered how well his father looked after the servants in his household. Their living conditions, under the father's care, were far superior to those the son had created for himself. So, he headed back to his father, repentant for his actions: *"Father, I have sinned against heaven and against you. I am no longer worthy to be called your son; make me like one of your hired servants."*[2] He was hoping he might be received back into the household as a servant, since he'd forfeited any right to be considered a son and heir (he'd already spent the inheritance, after all). Instead he was greeted by the father's exuberant love. The father ecstatically welcomed him as his son and invited everyone to share in his joy: *"Let's have a feast and celebrate. For this son of mine was dead and is alive again."*[3] The returning rebel is immediately given the place of honour reserved for sons; the lost relationship is restored.

It's a well-known Bible story that helps us to understand something about reconciliation. Jesus used the story to expose the bigoted views of the religious leaders of His day who despised and disregarded irreligious people who, they thought, were beyond saving. The good news of God is that those who have disqualified themselves from God's kingdom can be reconciled to God! Rebel sinners can become children of God who share in the inheritance that belongs to His eternal Son Jesus Christ. The gospel is a scandalous story of undeserved reconciliation.

When we think of the word reconciliation, we usually have in mind the restoration or reestablishment of a previously good relationship that has been broken or damaged in some way. In our natural state as sinners, there has never been a good relationship with God. We naturally harbour hatred towards God - we are *"God- haters"*[4] and this, in turn, results in God's holy opposition toward us as arrogant sinners.

We can't escape the language of the Bible - God's wrath remains on those who reject him and hate him[5] and *"The LORD detests all the proud of heart. Be sure of this: They will not go unpunished."*[6]

We don't often hear people talk about God in this way today. Much is made of 'God is love' and for good reason - He is love! But when we stop to think about how true love really operates, according to the Word of God, we understand that God must act against anything that threatens the free expression of His love to all that He loves. As the creator of all things, and the provider of life to all creatures, God is deserving of each creature's honour and worship. For humans to not honour God, and to not give God what is His due, is an offence of infinite degree. We have all been guilty; the truth about God as creator and provider is plain to us, yet the natural choice of human beings is to suppress the truth and embrace a worldview that removes God from the equation and elevates us to be the centre of everything.[7]

This natural choice expresses itself in rebellion, when human beings fail to give thanks to God for all that He has provided and have the arrogance to believe that God has no part in their existence. The consequence of this is alienation from God through active rejection of Him. As Paul says repeatedly in Romans 1, God *gives them over*[8] to these God-rejecting thinking and behaviours, granting them the alienation from God that is the natural desire of sinful humans. It's frightening.

When Paul wrote to some first century Christians, he reminded them: *"Once you were alienated from God and were enemies in your minds because of your evil behaviour. But now he has reconciled you by Christ's physical body through death to present you holy in his sight."*[9] He said it plainly - those in the church of God in Colossae were once God's enemies. Yet, because of God's reconciling work, their 'enemy status' had been overturned. How did this happen?

Look at what Paul says about God's reconciliation in 2 Corinthians 5:16-21. He wrote that *"God was reconciling the world to himself in Christ, not counting people's sins against them"*[10] and *"God made him who had no sin to be sin for us, so that in him we might become the righteousness of God."*[11] Here is the heart of the gospel: that Jesus Christ was treated by God as guilty of believers' sin when He was innocent of any sin; He experienced the wrath of God due to them. For those who believe that Jesus is the sin-atoning sacrifice, His perfect life of sinless innocence is then imputed by God to them, and all fear of God's wrath against them as sinners is removed. God's fearful hostility against His enemies is turned away; God has *"made peace through the blood of [Christ's] cross.* "[12]

God then teaches us that not only are believers in the Lord Jesus Christ no longer considered enemies, but they have, in fact, become children of God! This is an amazing change of status: "*to all who did receive him, to those who believed in his name, he gave the right to become children of God.* "[13]

When Paul writes about believers becoming children of God, he uses adoption language. Look at Ephesians 1:5-6: "*[God] predestined us for adoption to sonship through Jesus Christ, in accordance with his pleasure and will- to the praise of his glorious grace, which he has freely given us in the One he loves.*" The NIV translation notes helpfully inform us: 'adoption to sonship is a legal term referring to the full legal standing of an adopted male heir in Roman culture.' This deepens our understanding even further - believers become God's adopted heirs!

Read these related statements from Paul and Peter and praise God for the eternal blessings of His work of reconciliation in Jesus Christ: "*The Spirit himself testifies with our spirit that we are God's children. Now if we are children, then we are heirs - heirs of God and co-heirs with Christ, if indeed we share in his sufferings in order that we may also share in his glory.* " [14] "*In his great mercy he has given us new birth into a living hope through the resurrection of Jesus Christ from the dead, and into an inheritance that can never perish, spoil or fade. This inheritance is kept in heaven for you, who through faith are shielded by God's power until the coming of the salvation that is ready to be revealed in the last time.* " [15]

Just as the rebel son was welcomed by the loving father, so the repentant sinner, trusting in the Lord Jesus Christ as saviour, is welcomed by God the Father. The rebel son was reinstated as the father's son; the rebel sinner becomes a son and an heir of God and is given the responsibility of speaking of their change of status to others. Look again at 2 Corinthians 5:16-21 - Paul wrote about the message of reconciliation having been committed to those who've experienced God's reconciliation for themselves, and that such people are ambassadors of Christ. Paul had been the "*worst of sinners*"[16] and now recognised the honour and responsibility that accompanied his new status as an heir of God. He's an example of how no one is beyond the astounding mercy and grace of the God of love who reconciles sinners to Himself in Christ Jesus.

References:
[1]Lk.15:11-32 [2]Lk.15:18-19 [3]Lk.15:23-24 [4]Rom.1:30 [5]Jn 3:36 [6]Prov.16:5 [7]see Rom.1:18-23 [8]Rom.1:24,26,28 [9]Col.1:21-22 [10]2 Cor.5:19 [11]2 Cor.5:21 [12]Col.1:20 *NKJV* [13]Jn 1:12 [14]Rom.8:16-17 [15]1 Pet.1:3-5 [16]1 Tim.1:16
Bible quotations from the NIV (2011).

100 years in Africa

Missionary profiles
Eric Sampou & Fred Ntido, Nigeria

Looking back with nostalgia over 100 years of the testimony in Africa, we can affirm like Samuel: *"Thus far the LORD has helped us"*[1] by guiding and guarding the pioneering men and those who have built on their noble foundation. However, it will be an act of injustice on our part in summing up our debt of gratitude, to not mention the women who were a source of strength and encouragement in the African work.

Lucy Griffin
Lucy was received into the Church of God in Derby in 1920. By then she was a qualified nurse and had met Mrs Sivier who taught her *"the way of God more accurately."* [2] In March 1928, Lucy left Liverpool on the Accra bound for West Africa, where she served the Lord until 1956.

Mary McClymont
On 29 December 1953, having passed the required exams, Mary was enrolled as a midwife and set out from the Port of London on board the SS Calabar bound for West Africa. She had interests around community nursing, and in Nigeria she set up a health visiting course in the 1960s. Mary had received an honorary Doctorate of Science from the University of Hertfordshire in 1996 and had been due to be awarded the MBE by the Queen in the New Year's Honours list of 2000, but sadly died shortly before the list was announced. These ladies followed in the steps of Mary Slessor who advocated for rescuing children from infanticide in Nigeria. They were busy people, yet passionately engaged in the worship meetings on Lord's Day morning; also healthcare services and then open air gospel meetings, prayer and Bible study meetings in the evenings almost every day.

Gladys Dorricott
On 9 June 1926, Gladys left Liverpool, bound for Lagos, on board the Accra. Its record shows Gladys as a missionary to Southern Nigeria.

The African work is privileged to still have brethren alive who are a link to the early days of the testimony. These men are fondly remembered for their remarkable labour of love.

Bernard French

Bernard was born in Crowborough, England in 1932 and later married Eunice Swift. He was accepted to full-time service in 1969 and travelled on the MV Aureol to arrive in Lagos, Nigeria, on 1st January 1970. Bernard and Eunice worked together in West Africa for 30 years, mainly in Nigeria but also in Ghana and Malawi. Bernard is a missionary, preacher and teacher, a pastor, a mentor and our friend.

John Black

John was born in Kilmacolm, Scotland in 1940. He arrived in Nigeria in 1965 to join Willie Stewart and George Prasher Jnr. and he later married Eppie Sands (Eppie was 'called home' in May 2020). John's visits have been to Nigeria, Liberia and Ghana over the past 55 years.

John and Bernard loved the African people, reaching out to them in open air meetings, in schools through the Vacation Bible Courses, teaching the saints and building potential leaders. They consolidated the work in Africa. The fellowship of churches of God invested godly men and women in Africa: Rae Taylor, Margaret Prasher, Susan Stewart, Eppie Black, Lorraine Strachan, Elsie Stockwell, Jane Bennison, Eunice French, Elizabeth Taylor and others. In all 15 Ministering brothers and 76 brothers and sisters.

We place on record our debt of love to the local men who have laboured, and are labouring, in the field: Zachariah Travi, Eric Sampou, Mark Imoukhuede, Anthony Nemi, Lawrence Onyokoko and Gbenga Fagbenle.

It is our fervent prayer that as the awakened continent of Africa responds to the preaching of the whole counsel of God, that others of the ilk of these pioneers will arise to continue this great work: from Nigeria, Ghana, Liberia, Kenya, Malawi, Mozambique, Zimbabwe to the uttermost parts of Africa.

All who came to Nigeria endured the strenuous work at personal cost but there were rewarding times. Some believed God's message through their voice, then followed expansion to other countries: Liberia, Ghana, Malawi, Kenya, Mozambique and Zimbabwe. The Radio work, championed by Brian Johnston, is forwarding the work into Zambia, Rwanda, Uganda, South Africa, Tanzania ...

Finally, we convey the collective appreciation of the African continent for this commemoration of the Lord's work in our midst. We are all only unprofitable servants, and this is the Lord's doing and it is marvellous in our sight.

References:
[1]1 Sam.7:12 [2]Acts 18:26 NKJV

Job

God - the last word

Phil Brennan, Buxton, England

Job chapter 38 opens with, *"Then the LORD answered Job."* After the initial scene-setting of chapters 1 and 2, there are 35 chapters containing the words of five men - Job and four others. Now, finally, the Lord speaks. The voices of men have been silenced by, *"Who is this that darkens counsel by words without knowledge?"*[1] Beyond the controversy of God with Satan; and the controversy between Job and his friends; the voice of God sounds with perfect equity and judgement. It is the final word. It always is. The Lord appears here, not as plaintiff, but as judge, asking the questions and directing the proceedings.

The paradox of man

First, Job comes to a realisation of his nothingness. From the depths of Sheol to the stars above, Job is confronted with the greatness of God's power as manifest in the universe and its creatures, and he confesses "I *am insignificant*".[2] This is the bar by which the popular notion of self-worth must be measured. Job speaks here of his lacking weight; his sheer smallness in relation to matters that were simply too wonderful for him. David would express the same sense of wonderment.[3] Consciousness of the greatness of God, as revealed in creation, produced consciousness of the insignificance of man. But then, the Lord's invitation to Job, to *"gird up your loins like a man"*[4] reveals the glory of man. Kepler, the 16th century mathematician, said, 'Geometry is one and eternal shining in the mind of God. That share in it accorded to men is one of the reasons that Man is the image of God.'[5] As well as revealing the insignificance of man, the fact that man is able to comprehend anything of the greatness of God, reveals the dignity of man in his ability to conceive of it.

The power of God

There is a further conclusion that Job must realise: if he found himself unequal to the task of managing the universe, how could he be equal or perfect in his understanding of God, or bring an accusation against Him? It is remarkable that the Lord makes no reference to Job's suffering and gives no explanation. God brought Job face to face with the universe and asked if he were able to govern it. In the resultant realisation by Job lay the cause of having confidence in the God who does. The two untamable beasts, behemoth and leviathan, are given as examples of things Job cannot control. He has no means of capturing and domesticating them.

In the face of his impotence, he is called to acknowledge God's omnipotence. There are matters that are being allowed to be played out, but be under no misunderstanding, above the mystery of his suffering there is One who reigns with sovereign power.

The purpose of God

Finally, we see the paradox of man and the power of God wonderfully blended in the purpose of God. In his retraction[6] Job repudiates the position he had reasoned before his friends. Here is the laying down of all that unregenerate man counts as wisdom; [7] here is the realisation of the words of Eliphaz;[8] here is the blessing found by Paul in renouncing self and accepting grace;[9] here is the meaning of the beatitudes breathed by the Lord Jesus.[10]

Job had never been abandoned by God. Looking at his suffering we sometimes say that Job had lost everything. He hadn't. He still had God, and to have God is to have everything. God had *"work[ed] all things after the counsel of His will,"*[11] and those divine purposes perfectly vindicated what the Lord had said about Job in the beginning.[12] It is not only Job's fortunes and family that were restored: We find him at the close of the book in the same intercessory role as in the beginning.[13] Thus God brought His servant through the severe lesson of suffering to a deeper knowledge of himself and of God, to worship and into divine partnership in service.

References:
[1]Job 38:2 [2]Job 40:4 [3]Ps.8:4 [4]Job 40:7 [5]Johannes Kepler in an open letter to Galileo Galilei, Dissertatio cum Nuncio Sidereo (1610) [6]Job 42:6 [7]1 Cor.1:19 [8]Job 22:21 [9]Phil.3:7 [10]Matt.5:3-4 [11]Eph.1:11 [12]Job 1:8 [13]Job 42:10; cf. Job 1:5 Bible quotations from the NASB 1995.

Some essentials for preaching

Martin Archibald, Glasgow, Scotland

The essence of preaching

The Biblical preacher aims to convey at some point a message that God Himself intends for the listener. How will this vital element be recognised? It may become evident in how the Scriptures are unfolded with relevance to the listener's own life, past or present. It helps if the speaker plainly loves the Bible, not as a demanding book to be 'mastered', but as a supreme guide to living: the Word must have first spoken to him and won his loyalty if he's to sound convincing to others. So the message should be a lot more than explanation and analysis of the chosen passages. There has to be clear purpose to move both mind and heart to a richer, higher life for God.

A message for living

When the Lord Himself met His audiences, He aimed to win a hearing, raise hopes, focus energies and impart the life of the written text - for the rest of the day and all their future. So He'd begin, *"Blessed* (or happy) *are the poor in spirit..."* How could that ever be? The reason, *"...for theirs is the kingdom of heaven"*,[1] made the people listen the more because they wanted to know what it meant. It was a puzzle, but first they had been called 'happy', and then some were told they personally owned something important. Soon they were assured that even mourners were happy too. They realized that, yes, if they'd been bereaved, and were people of faith, they had found fresh life when they trusted God, as Isaiah 46 had said they should - happy memories, new friends and new interests, with a sense of God's abiding care. Jesus spoke truth about their own lives.

Then the people of Galilee heard their local builder speak about the day's business in field or market, and life around the home. He sounded as though He cared about the person who ground the meal; and as though His building would last. If He gave wise advice about family relationships, He spoke as one who knew it would actually work and could be tried out in the coming week. He showed that the sacred Scriptures were about life in this world - joys, trials and disappointments - as well as about the promise of the heavenly.

In the same way, the Apostle Paul began in Athens with having seen an altar in the city devoted *TO THE UNKNOWN GOD.*[2] Or to the Jews, he explained the direction and purpose in their national history.

In expounding doctrine to the church, he mentioned people they knew, who were achieving (or failing in) what he commended for daily life.

Speaking - not writing

Paul was so much a preacher that he came to write in spoken style - especially in practical appeal. The preacher must speak as often as possible in clear, direct language that is familiar to his audience. The gist of a spoken sentence has to be understood without having to wait through many clauses for the main point. Key thoughts are best repeated in fresh terms so that they can be readily grasped and remembered. Brief notes fix each point more usefully.

They'll lead to brevity in speech; and lodge more easily in memory. Making sure of a few main points has some chance of being heeded. This doesn't mean that we can be content with shallow sound-bites. John Wesley was able to say, "I offered Christ to the people for three hours" - but in such potency that they went back for more.

Delivery also wins a hearing

In this task we need the Spirit's counsel in the King's message. We search the Scriptures for their power to challenge and guide. We consider the audience and their need. Lastly, all this must have a spokesman - the preacher, who longs to give of his best. But consider the demands of opportunity. The Lord may not grant another one. So the *"Preacher sought to find acceptable words ... words of truth ... like goads."*[3] Refining the message to highly charged sayings, choosing apt illustrations and drawing the audience in by asking for their view, takes practice, stripping out the lesser things that dilute. Then we may persuade others in the fear of the Lord,[4] as He sees fit.

References:
[1]Matt.5:3 [2]Acts 17:23 [3]Eccles.12:10-11 [4]2 Cor.5:11 ESV
Bible quotations from the NKJV unless stated otherwise.

Volatile values

Martin Jones, Hamilton, Canada

How much is a three-inch piece of card worth? You might be surprised! One of the more counter-intuitive impacts of COVID-19 in the West has been on 'values.' While social values have arguably declined, 'market' values seem to have gone through the roof. Speaking of which, house prices in many Canadian cities are at all-time highs, and even sleepy suburbs have seen year-on-year price rises of 40- 50% as people looked for more space in lockdown. At least property has some intrinsic value given 'they ain't making more land'!

But what about vintage sports cards? My neighbour recently found one of Bart Starr of the Green Bay Packers American football team[1] from the 1950s in a shoebox. I sold it for her for Cdn$1,000.[2] A similar card, in better condition, sold on eBay for US$11,000! If that blows your mind, incredible sums are now being paid for NFTs (non-fungible tokens) which include non-physical media. Twitter founder Jack Dorsey's first tweet recently sold for US$2.9m, and a YouTube video of a young boy biting his brother's finger garnered US$761,000 - crazy! Then we have the manic and volatile speculation of 'meme stocks' and cryptocurrency.

What's behind all this? At an economic level, it's partly driven by governments effectively rescuing their citizens with 'free' cash via COVID handouts and cheap debt via close-to- zero interest rates. At an emotional level, perhaps it's the FOMO effect - the Fear of Missing Out - and the desire to have something that no-one else has. We can only hope that this doesn't ultimately lead some to catastrophic financial loss.

You know, the price tag of any of these items pales into insignificance when we think about the price God paid for us. [3] Peter reminds us: "it *was not with perishable things such as silver or gold that you were redeemed ... but with the precious blood of Christ." [4]* Were we rescued by cheap grace? By no means! Today, precious metals are seen as a hedge against inflation when other assets lose their worth - a very current problem. But how much more precious is the blood of Christ, which can never lose its value.

Did you know that most trading of gold and silver today is for 'IOUs' and not the actual assets? Not so with God's salvation transaction – *"the Son of God ... loved me and gave himself for me".[5]* There are a lot of crazy asking prices on eBay, but you only know the true value of an item by what someone actually paid for it! Jesus did pay with His own blood, as He perhaps depicted in the parable of the treasure hunter.[6] The man sold all he had to buy the field it was buried in.

He wasn't remotely interested in the acres of dirt he had to pay for, but buried in them was something for which he was prepared to go 'all in.'

But let's flip this around for a second. What value do we place on the Lord's things? And how can we even measure that? One way, perhaps, is the relative value we place on other things - Paul said he counted all his credentials and achievements as garbage compared to knowing Christ. [7] It's good to check who or what we are investing in to make sure it's not leading us into serious spiritual loss. The hymn says, '...love so amazing, so divine, demands my heart, my life, my all.'[8]

Yes, it does, but sadly we have to admit that sometimes we fall short. That's probably equally true when we think about how we value our brothers and sisters in Christ - yes, as the term indicates, we're very much 'blood-related' because every one of them is someone for whom Christ died.[9] It's a reason why we should be *kind to one another, tenderhearted*. [10] The Greek word for 'tenderhearted' carries the thought of a 'gut reaction' that causes you to say, "My heart went out to them." It's the scriptural vaccination against the virus of selfish inward-looking thoughts and actions that considers ourselves of more value than others.[11]

Notes & references:
[1]equivalent to sports interest in Manchester United or David Beckham [2]approx. US$800 or £600 [3]1 Cor.6:20 [4]1 Pet.1:18-19 [5]Gal.2:20 [6]Matt.13:44 [7]Phil.3:3-11 [8]Isaac Watts, PHSS 13 [9]1 Cor.8:11 [10]Eph.4:32 ESV [11]Phil.2:3
Bible quotations from the NIV unless stated otherwise.

Can you help me with this?

Churches

Peter Hickling, Cromer, England

The word 'church' appears 74 times in the English Standard Version of the New Testament. That's quite to be expected, given the nature of the text. However, the words don't always mean the same. That, too, is to be expected, because we use the word in ordinary speech with different meanings. For example, when I am coming home, the first thing I see in Cromer is the tower of the church, the highest in Norfolk; but that is not one of the scriptural meanings. 'Church' never refers in Scripture to a physical building. In contrast, a few yards down Church Street, the Baptist building has a brick relief title saying 'Meeting House of the Baptist Church' - a more precise description.

What does the Bible word 'church' mean, anyway? In his Expository Dictionary of New Testament Words, W.E.Vine explains that the Greek word *ekklesia* derives from *ek,* out of, and *klesis,* a calling; thus it was used of a body of citizens called together to discuss affairs of state. That gathering was not specifically religious; in Acts 19:32,41 the word is used of a riotous mob called together by Demetrius the silversmith to defend the profits of his trade, which were endangered by Christian preaching.

In relation to Christians, *ekklesia* has two principal applications: (a) to the whole company of believers in this present era. Those are people whom the Lord Jesus has called to Himself, and by that call He is building what He called *"my church."*[1] This church is further described as *"his body, that is, the church."*[2] This metaphor is appropriate because of the organic relationship between the individual believer and Christ Himself - Scripture uses the expression *"in Christ."*[3] The great scheme of redemption lay at the root of all this - the creator of all things took human form so that He might take our place. Scripture sums this up:

"For it was fitting that he, for whom and by whom all things exist, in bringing many sons to glory, should make the founder of their salvation perfect through suffering. For he who sanctifies and those who are sanctified all have one source. That is why he is not ashamed to call them brothers, saying, 'I will tell of your name to my brothers; in the midst of the congregation I will sing your praise.' And again, 'I will put my trust in him.'

And again, 'Behold, I and the children God has given me.' Since therefore the children share in flesh and blood, he himself likewise partook of the same things, that through death he might destroy the one who has the power of death, that is, the devil, and deliver all those who through fear of death were subject to lifelong slavery."[4]

The second major application, (b), is to people who have been called together into a local church. There are a number of examples of this in the New Testament, particularly in the letters that Paul wrote to individual churches. We should note at the beginning that there is a difference in the status of people under (a) and (b). The Lord Jesus described those whom He had called to Himself as *"my sheep"*[5] and said,

"My sheep hear my voice, and I know them, and they follow me. I give them eternal life, and they will never perish, and no one will snatch them out of my hand. My Father, who has given them to me, is greater than all, and no one is able to snatch them out of the Father's hand. I and the Father are one."[6]

Thus the link between Christ and the believer is indissoluble, even through human frailty. But it is far different in the case of (b). People can leave churches of God if they lose interest in them, or if they fall out with others, or even, regrettably, if they have to be expelled. Paul wrote to the church in Corinth, *"It is actually reported that there is sexual immorality among you, and of a kind that is not tolerated even among pagans, for a man has his father's wife. And you are arrogant! Ought you not rather to mourn? Let him who has done this be removed from among you."*[7] But that is a disruptive occurrence in a church of God. It ought to be a gathering of like- minded people who share together and express the love of God to Him and to each other.

References:
[1]Matt.16:18 [2]Col.1:24 [3]Rom.8:1 [4]Heb.2:10-15 [5]Jn 10:27 [6]Jn 10:27-30 [7]1 Cor.5:1-2
Bible quotations from the ESV.

Serving a living saviour

An interview with

Talent Lungu, Chegutu, Zimbabwe

NT: Can you tell us how trusting in the Lord became very real to you?
In 1998, my father left Zimbabwe to go to Zambia. For a long time we heard nothing and became concerned. One day something strange happened. A letter was delivered to our neighbour. The name and address were somewhat confused, but we did recognise it as having been written in my father's handwriting.

NT: How strange, and what did the letter say?
It was an appeal to come and help him. He had fallen ill there. We were now most anxious, but no information as to any address had been supplied. However, I had an aunt who lived in Zambia, and so we assumed he might have been with her, or at least she would possibly have some information as to his whereabouts. And so I travelled to Zambia. On the bus journey, I explained my situation to some other passengers who promised to assist me when we got to Zambia, but then we got separated when changing buses. I was now by myself, not knowing what to do next or where to go. That is when it happened.

NT: What was that?
I was guided by a whispered voice to a place where I boarded a local bus to Kanyama township. But after riding the bus for a while, I again heard a whisper to "alight at the first stop." I did so but became more confused as what I saw was not what I expected. I felt completely lost. As I stood there, I noticed a girl vendor by the roadside and I approached her for help. She couldn't understand English and neither could I speak her language. Then, once again the whisper came, "Look to your right." As I looked to my right, I saw a young man.

I approached him and told him I was looking for my aunt. He asked me, "Is your aunt a believer?" I said, "Yes". He said, "Then I'll take you to one of the believers I know. I am sure you will get help there." He took me to a Catholic lady. When we got there, I explained my story. The lady took my bags and said, "Follow me, I am taking you to a lady who has no relatives here in Zambia. I assume she is the one."

NT: And was she?

Yes, when we got there, a woman whom I'd never met before stood before me. She looked like my uncle, my mother's brother. As I introduced myself to her, she did not wait for me to finish but interrupted me with a prayer in which she gave thanks to God for directing me to her place. She led me to the back of her house where my father was seated. He was in deep depression to the extent that he could neither recognize me nor my voice. I moved close to him and shook him by his knees. He acted as if he was awakening from a deep sleep. When he finally recognized me, it was a very emotional time for us both.

NT: How did this experience influence your thinking?

If I had any doubts previously, my faith in Jesus as a powerful, living saviour became very real to me at the time of that experience. I was very shortly after that baptized with an evangelical group known as Victory Life Ministries (VLM). From then I began to have the courage to tell others of Jesus as the saviour who died for our sins according to the Bible (Isa.53:5), and that they, too, through believing the word could receive Christ and be saved from the punishment their sins truly deserved.

NT: How did you come into contact with The Churches o/God?

I was not satisfied that VLM was fully biblical in its teachings. I would describe myself then as searching for the truth. I work in the office of Brother Thomas Ngwenya, and one day an acquaintance, Ephraim Chinga, visited us and shared the biblical teachings of the Church of God in Chegutu. I knew then that I had found what I was looking for!

NT: Is there anything you want to add?

I have known the power of prayer among Churches of God. In July 2021, my granddaughter was abducted in Capetown, South Africa. We received taunting messages demanding money with menaces. They were threatening to mutilate and kill her. Some in the UK churches joined with us in prayer, and the police tracked her phone that the kidnappers were using to make threats and demand money. Thank God, she was found alive. Please continue to pray for her settled rehabilitation to Zimbabwe and full recovery from the emotional scars of the serious assault she suffered. [Fuller details supplied have been redacted - Eds]

A reason to smile

Contributions from

Patson Katimba, Lumbadzi & Oscar Soko, Bangwe, Malawi

We are delighted to hear of the good hand of God continuing to be upon the Churches in Malawi, as a result of which a further Church was planted on Lord's Day, 27 June, 2021. On behalf of the acting District of South, East & Central Africa (SECA), they were welcomed as they found their place among the Churches of God in the Fellowship of His Son, our Lord Jesus Christ. In addition to brother Patson Katimba, also present were the other local Lumbadzi overseers: Luke Beka and Sam Phiri, who had laboured long and hard among them in a work that began many years ago. God be praised for the fulfilment finally seen in this planting! Some 38 of them had already been numbered for some time with the Church of God in Lumbadzi. At the planting, they were transferred to form part of the new Church of God at Chuzu. Others had been recently baptized by our brothers Luke Beka and Sam Phiri and were received into the fellowship at Chuzu. This church of God has been planted in the Chuzu Dowa district of Malawi. It is the result of outreach started by a brother who was in Lumbadzi assembly in 2008. The brothers named above all went to support this outreach.

In 2008 when we were meeting at Lumbadzi, one brother was coming from Chuzu. His name is Disimus Phiri. He was baptised, and in 2009 he decided to start a small group in the Chuzu area because of its distance from Lumbadzi. One other brother, Alfred Longwe, continues until now and was recognised as a deacon in 2010.

Western friends Bob Hawthorne, Kevin Jones and David McCarty all supported when an Open-Air Gospel Campaign was held at Chuzu. From this time, many people started to know about the Church of God. Then, in September 2019, 30 were baptized and added to Lumbadzi assembly. And on 25 July 2021, thirteen more were baptized by our brother Kevin Beal of Canada.

Brother Patson writes: "By the grace of God, the church was planted on 27 June 2021. This memorable occasion was graced by our brother Kevin Beal. Please pray for us that the Gospel should penetrate into other districts of the central region of Malawi."

Nkhotakota (Ndalama village)

We also thank God for another memorable occasion in having another church planted at Ndalama village (Nkhotakota) in what, from the point of view of our churches, we regard as the 'far north.' There are 36 people breaking bread. Brother Patson writes: "Our brother Kevin Beal again graced the occasion. We all have a reason to smile. Zikomo (Thanks - to God)!"

This second delightful event took place on Lord's Day, 4 July. It was then that they, too, on behalf of the acting District of South, East and Central Africa (SECA), were welcomed to find their place among the Churches of God in the Fellowship of His Son, our Lord Jesus Christ. SECA consists of Malawi, Zimbabwe and Mozambique, and on that inaugural morning, SECA leadership was represented by Kevin Beal; and Malawian elders were represented by local Lumbadzi overseers: Luke Beka & Sam Phiri, who had laboured long and hard among them.

The work of the Lord at Nkhotakota began some years ago when our brother Oscar Soko (now of Bangwe assembly) was living there. At that time, to support his own witnessing, he invited Luke Beka's help. Now we praise God for the fulfilment finally seen in this planting. At the time of the planting, some had already been numbered for some time with the Church of God in Lumbadzi and were transferred to form part of the new Church of God at Ndalama village in Nkhotakota district. Others had recently been baptized by our brothers Luke Beka and Sam Phiri and Kevin Beal and were received into the Fellowship here at Ndalama village. May they continue to know God's blessing in their service for Him.

From the Editors' desk

Issue 1 2022

The chronicler, traditionally presumed to be Ezra, writes in 1 Chronicles 9 of those belonging to the Old Testament people of God who were making a new start upon their return from enforced exile after the Babylonian captivity. As we launch out into 2022, we also may anticipate a more definite restart of conventional ways of serving the Lord after some measure of 'enforced exile' imposed by the Covid-19 pandemic.Back then, we're told that the first to repossess their cities were the priests, Levites and temple servants. Their keenness to re-engage energetically with their duties is noted inspirationally for us in the divine record. By the time we reach verse 17, the spotlight falls on Shallum (perhaps a family name, see v.19, 31) as notable among those who were gatekeepers for the house of God. There were, besides him, chief men among these Temple gatekeepers who were recognised as being in an office of trust. To all of them was assigned the task of not allowing anything improper to enter upon the sanctuary service of God's people at His chosen location. They had charge of all that was deposited in the treasuries of God's House.

In one of our new main series, charting God's desire to dwell among us, Andy already hints at where the series is headed: towards identifying the spiritual house of God in the New Testament. As we resume more normal service in it, may we as God's people be as zealous to guard the treasure of the good deposit that God has given in trust to us.[1] Tony reminds us that we do so as stewards looking for our Master's soon return. May God help us to be overcomers like Mark through becoming more Christlike. Both Jhonrou and Steve emphasize, of course, that this is all based on God's amazing grace. And there's so much more to profitably enjoy. Happy reading in the New Year!

Brian

Reference: [1] 2 Tim.1:13-15

Editors would like to place on record their warm and grateful acknowledgement of the many years of highly efficient service by Robert Fisher who has now retired from his role of commissioning editor of the magazine.

Living under grace

Jhonrou Sarsale, Nabunturan, Philippines

As a Christian believer it's very important that we should know and understand God's amazing grace that provides for us so that our lives in this world align with the way God wants us to live. The core of this article will focus on Romans 6:14, which says, *"For sin shall not be master over you, for you are not under the Law but under grace."* The 'law' here refers to the law in general found in the books of Moses and containing moral, ceremonial and judicial laws. We have to understand that the Law was given to Israel, God's chosen people: they were the people obligated to follow the Law accurately as God chose them to keep the Law and live within it, as a testimony to the nations around them. The Law was given to show humanity's inability to keep away from sin. It was not given to justify us, for through the Law comes the knowledge of sin but not the forgiveness of our sin *"because by the works of the Law none of mankind will be justified."*[1] However, God demonstrates His amazing grace through His Son, Jesus Christ. Paul says in Romans 8:3- 4:

"For what the Law could not do, weak as it was through the flesh, God did: sending His own Son in the likeness of sinful flesh and as an offering for sin, He condemned sin in the flesh, so that the requirement of the Law might be fulfilled in us who do not walk according to the flesh but according to the Spirit."

Here is the perfect presentation of the unmerited grace of God revealed in the life of our Lord Jesus Christ alone. He condemned sin by the holy way He was able to live here as a man, fulfilling the Law perfectly. Through Him we have eternal life at the moment we receive Him as our Saviour by faith. He – God's own Son – died for the sake of our salvation. It's amazing, isn't it? Since we are saved by the grace of God, we are no longer under the Law but under grace. This grace enables us also to fulfil the principle of the Law, as Jesus did in His earthly life. This, Paul tells us, is by the help of the Holy Spirit. So the fact that we're under grace doesn't mean the Law is abolished, but that we are not condemned by the Law, since we died to sin with Christ so that we might live to God in Christ.

Jesus said in Matthew 5:17, *"I did not come to abolish [the Law] but to fulfil [it]."* We cannot deny the fact that the Law Jesus talks about contains the principle of holy living. Jesus Himself, as we said, lived in the principle of the Law itself, showing this to surpass the righteousness of the scribes and Pharisees. We can see this fully as we read the Gospels: Christ subjected Himself to the Law.

Moreover, even if we are no longer under the Law, we too have to live according to the principle of the Law for it still remains today. God expects us to live in holiness as Christ did. Furthermore, the grace of God instructs us to live in a way that would please our Father in heaven. Of course, that concerns our day-by- day Christian living. As Christian believers, saved by grace, our first ambition is to please God by doing the things that He wants us to do and to avoid sin.

All in all, living under grace describes a kind of life that aims to keep us far away from committing sin. It's living in holiness, as Paul writes: *"What then? Are we to sin because we are not under the Law but under grace? Far from it!"*[2] In other words, there should be no room for sin in our lives; as saved people it is our responsibility to be holy[3] for this is one reason why God saved us.

References:
[1]Rom.3:20 [2]Rom.6:15 [3]1 Pet.1:15

Bible quotations from the NASB (2020).

Justice

Justice and righteousness

David Viles, Hayes, England

Glancing up at the Old Bailey courthouse in London or at the top of many other judicial buildings in the western world, we may well see a statue representing justice. She is personified as a young, blindfolded woman holding a sword and scales. The image is derived from Egyptian, Greek and Roman concepts of justice, but they must in turn be founded upon the biblical revelation of God because He is the "*only … lawgiver and judge.*"[1] Since humanity is created in the image of God, all our passionate strivings after justice and (to a lesser extent) righteousness originate in Him. As God's righteousness and justice are described as 'high' or 'exalted'[2] it is fitting that lady justice should be physically positioned right where she is.

The firm foundation

She is usually shown standing on a book, representing the constitution of the particular country in which the courthouse is located. For Britain, the USA and many other nations, the constitutional foundation goes back to Magna Carta – 'To no one will we sell, to no one will we deny or delay right or justice'[3] – but what do these terms actually mean? In both Hebrew and Greek the words 'justice' and 'righteousness' when applied to the character of God are often used together and sometimes translated interchangeably; their meanings, unlike in English, are closely connected. God's nature and being are presented as always being righteous; therefore, all He does must be right and just. "*Righteousness and justice are the foundation of Your throne*;"[4a] and *righteous and upright is He.*"[4b] In such verses, God's righteousness and justice are often linked to other qualities of His indivisible character, such as mercy and truth – we will return to these later.

Teasing the Hebrew expressions apart, the word used for the righteousness of God is often closely associated with the word 'upright'[5] or straight. So God's righteousness is clearly an expression of His absolute holiness and moral rectitude; He acts consistently in accordance with His own holy character, always keeping His promises.[6] While it's arguable whether any country's constitution is entirely morally righteous, God sets the absolute standard of what righteousness is; furthermore, in everything that God does He acts righteously.[7] So while righteous is what God is, justice is at the basis of what He does.

Unlike many human judges, He always acts equitably, showing no partiality or corruption, caring for the solitary and needy.[8] God's concern to demonstrate to Abraham that He exercised justice fairly and equitably in the cases of Sodom and Gomorrah, and Lot and his family[9] is an object lesson in the way He acts in a just and righteous way.

Whereas modern society tends to exalt justice as a public good and all too often deprecates righteousness as a purely personal matter, in God's holy character the two are perfectly united and balanced with all His other divine attributes. *"I am the Lord, exercising lovingkindness, judgment, and righteousness in the earth. For in these I delight."*[10] So while human attitudes to what is right may diverge from God's unchanging standards and humanity's urgent cries for justice seem increasingly to go unanswered in this world, those who delight in the Lord have a sure and firm foundation upon which to base their own standards and understanding of God's character.

A passion for righteousness, justice and mercy

Lady justice's blindfold and her set of scales emphasize impartiality and the careful weighing of evidence as key factors in administering human justice. These are indeed high and worthy principles that should underlie all our judicial systems; God is clear about His hatred of injustice and judicial oppression, corruption and bias – *"for the judgment is God's."*[11] *"Hate evil, love good; establish justice in the gate"*, He states through the prophet Amos at a particularly dire time in Israel's history. *"Let justice run down like water, and righteousness like a mighty stream."*[12] While good human jurisprudence emphasizes judges conducting themselves objectively and dispassionately, God reveals Himself quite otherwise. He is absolutely passionate about righteousness, justice and equity[13] because these qualities are central to His own holy nature. The psalms portray God as a just judge who is angry with the wicked every day. Sin personally affronts Him and He manifests a deeply-felt indignation about injustice.[14]

Furthermore, God needs no probing of the evidence to get at the truth, for *"all things are naked and open to the eyes of Him to whom we must give account."*[15] Sobering words indeed, as everyone is weighed in the scales of God's judgement and the verdict is clear – *"there is none righteous, no not one ... all have sinned and fall short of the glory of God."*[16] How can God come to this conclusion – that, despite our best endeavours, the scales of divine justice are so weighted against us? The apostle Paul in the first three chapters of the letter to the Romans elaborates on the answer to this vital question. We frail humans prefer to deal in relative terms, measuring our worth and achievements against others.

But in the light of God's righteous character and absolute holiness everyone falls short of His standards which, like His character, are absolute. He Himself is the ultimate standard of what is right, and in Him there is no unrighteousness.[5]

Against this dark background comes the blinding light of the Gospel – *"in it the righteousness of God is revealed."*[17] Romans 3 verses 21 to 26 transport us to a dramatic courtroom scene where the only lawgiver and judge reveals His righteousness in a cosmic act of both judgment and salvation. The God who is passionate about justice is also plenteous in mercy and grace – *"the LORD will wait, that He may be gracious to you…that He may have mercy on you. For the Lord is a God of justice."*[18] So without in any way compromising His righteousness – in fact, to demonstrate it – God poured out the full measure of His righteous anger on His beloved Son.

Justice was fully satisfied, and through that sacrifice God's grace and mercy as the Justifier of repentant sinners was revealed in all its majesty – justified freely by the grace of a just God and made righteous in His Son.[19]

The sword of justice

Lady justice's sword represents punishment; this is an important aspect too of God'srevelation of Himself as the righteous judge. In most modern systems of justice, the principle of punishment or retribution has become tempered with more liberal concepts of reform or rehabilitation of the guilty party. This was not so in ancient times. The Roman Emperor Justinian (482-565) said: "Justice is the constant and perpetual wish to give everyone his due." If this were even partially true of a Roman Emperor's concept of justice, it is completely true in relation to God's attitude towards sinners. For those who wilfully reject Him there is nothing to look forward to other than God's retribution – *"the day of wrath and revelation of the righteous judgment of God."*[20] The basis upon which judgment will be dispensed is to give everyone his or her due – *"the Son of Man will come in the glory of His Father…and…He will reward each according to his works."*[21] This is a terrible prospect given God's verdict that all have sinned, and should energize our efforts to proclaim the forbearing love of God to a sinful world.

We may prefer to think of God as a God of love which He certainly is, so how can we square this with His judgment of sinners as something which is good and righteous?[22] The fact is that the Bible has a great deal to say about judgment and punishment. The Lord Jesus, *"ordained by*

God to be Judge of the living and the dead,"[23] spoke frequently about present and future judgment during His earthly ministry because it is such an important aspect of God's revealed character.

Could any reasonable person really believe that the great criminals of history – the Stalins or the Pol Pots – will escape accountability to God for their crimes? But God, as we have seen, is holy and righteous and His wrath must therefore be revealed against *"all ungodliness and unrighteousness of men"[24]* without exception. A God who made no distinction between right and wrong would not be righteous by His own definition, and failure to judge the world would indicate moral indifference. God cannot be other than true to His own revealed character. Abraham long ago asked *"shall not the Judge of all the earth do right?"[25]* God demonstrated to him then that He would not act unjustly by destroying the righteous along with the wicked. History is moving inexorably towards the day when that question will be authoritatively answered on a global scale, leaving no grounds for appeal. *"For He is coming, for He is coming to judge the earth He shall judge the world with righteousness, and the peoples with His truth."[26]*

References:
[1] Jas.4:12 RV [2]e.g. Ps.36:6; Isa.5:16 [3]Magna Carta 1215, clause 40; [4a]Ps.89:14; [4b]Deut.32:4 [5]e.g., Ps.92:15 [6]Neh.9:7-8 [7]Ps.145:17 [8]Deut.10:17-19 [9]Gen.18:16-33; 19:15-29 [10]Jer.9:24 [11]Deut.1:17; see also Zech.7:8-10; Lev.19:35 [12]Amos 5:15,24 [13]See Ps.11:4-7; Isa.61:8; Heb.1:9 [14]Ps.7:11; 82:1-4 [15]Heb.4:13 [16]Rom.3:10,23 [17]Rom.1:17 [18]Isa.30:18 [19]2 Cor.5:21 [20]Rom.2:5 [21]Matt.16:27 [22]Addressing the Athenians, Paul spoke of the day when God *will judge the world in righteousness by the Man whom He has ordained* (Acts 17:31) [23]Acts 10:42 [24]Rom.1:18 [25]Gen.18:25 [26]Ps.96:13
All quotations from the NKJV, unless stated otherwise.

Preparing for the Lord's return

Transformation

Tony Jones, Aberkenfig, Wales

One heart-stirring eternal purpose of God is to make us like His Son[1] so bringing into existence a family relationship[2] in which the Lord Jesus is pre-eminent. That object, which will be fully realized when the Lord Jesus comes back for us,[3] has an application now: making that relationship evident,[4] thus bringing God delight in our 'Christ-likeness'.[5]

It's surely a vital goal of each day.[6] John writes, *"continue in him, so that when he appears we may be confident and unashamed before him at his coming."*[7] John was present on that eventful final evening before Calvary, when the Lord used that precious time to draw attention to the need of disciples to keep closely connected to Him.Now, repeating the word he uses in John 15 (about branches 'remaining' in the vine), John surely wants us to consider that night's teaching as he writes again of continuing, or staying, in a given relationship.[8]

His inspiration is to give us a well-founded confidence so that we will not feel we have let the Lord down when we meet Him, having shown faithfulness in carrying out another of God's purposes in our salvation – fruit- bearing.[9]

A tourist visited a famous villa in a beauty spot of the Italian Alps, with its exquisite gardens of many rare, beautiful specimens. While conversing with the head gardener, the tourist learned he had held that post for 25 years, though the owner of the estate had only visited four times in that period, the most recent of which was ten years previously. No instructions were ever forthcoming; no check-ups took place. The gardener was left to his own devices. The tourist remarked, "You keep the garden in such a wonderful condition. It's as if you were expecting the owner tomorrow." "Today, sir. Today," the gardener replied.

This anecdote covers not only that avoidance of feeling shame, but also Paul's focus on the character of our lives as we anticipate the return of our Lord: *"For the grace of God ... teaches us ... to live self-controlled, upright and godly lives in this present age, while we wait for the blessed hope – the glorious appearing of our great God and Saviour, Jesus Christ.*"[10]

An increasing understanding of the grace of God in our lives will be a catalyst for the proper ordering of them. A continuous, thoughtful, thankful grasp of what God's grace accomplishes will contribute significantly to the manner in which we respond to that grace.[11] The impact? Lives that are *self-controlled* (moderate as to opinion, 'enabling the believer to be conformed to the mind of Christ' 12), *upright* (righteous NASB), *and godly* ('… characterised by a Godward attitude, does that which is well-pleasing to Him'[12]).

Paul adds that the Lord Jesus *"gave himself for us … to purify for himself a people that are his very own."*[13] This is the character of the people together, though each person has that well-known continuing struggle with sin during this life. This spoils our personal relationship with Him. John follows up on his practical advice about restoring that relationship14 by adding a further incentive. He writes about how we will be like the Lord Jesus when we meet Him; a perfect prospect in more than one way. John's motivation for us is that *"everyone who has this hope in him purifies himself, just as he is pure."*[15] Here is an example of the grace of God to us when we compare our way of purification with the Sinai Covenant sacrifices. If there were any upside to that temporary way, it may be that the very experience and cost would have encouraged purity. In our own struggle with sin, we need to focus on the incalculable cost to the Man of Calvary, remaining aware of the grace given to us.[16]

This God-honouring transformation is desirable for each believer,[17] as we await our Lord's return.

References:
[1]Rom.8:29 [2]Heb.2:11 [3]1 Jn 3:2 [4]Eph.3:10 [5]2 Cor.2:15 [6]1 Cor.11:1 [7]1 Jn 2:28 [8]Strong's Exhaustive Concordance [9]Jn 15:16 [10]Tit.2:11-13 [11]such as in Rom.5:17 [12]Vine's Expository Dictionary of New Testament Words [13]Tit.2:14 [14]1 Jn 1:9 [15]1 Jn 3:3 [16]Heb.12:14-15a [17]2 Cor.3:18

Bible quotations from the NIV (1984).

Paul's travel companions

Mark: the overcomer

Philip Allen, Cardiff, Wales

Mark's name first appears in the Bible when Peter escapes from prison and goes to the house of Mark's mother, Mary. Here, Mark is referred to as John Mark.[1] In the first century, John was the most common Hebrew name and Mark the most common Roman name. It wasn't unusual for someone to go by both a Hebrew and Roman name, as we see with Saul, also called Paul.[2]

Traditionally, John Mark is considered to be the author of the Gospel of Mark. It seems likely that the meeting with Peter at his mother's house was the start of a relationship between them that led to Mark's conversion[3] and which would eventually lead him to record Peter's account of Jesus' life and ministry.

The next time we hear of Mark in the Bible is as a travelling companion of Paul and Barnabas on their first missionary journey,[4] which had started at Antioch. It is interesting to note that Mark was a cousin of Barnabas.[5] Mark doesn't seem to have had a major role in any of the events on this missionary journey, but he is referred to as their 'helper' or 'assistant'.[6]

As their journey progressed, the missionary work appears to have been going well with little opposition. By contrast, when they reached Paphos in Cyprus, Sergius Paulus, the proconsul, asked to see them and wanted to hear the word of God.[7] It was here that Mark would have witnessed the first real challenge to the work. A sorcerer, Bar-Jesus, did all he could to prevent Sergius Paulus from hearing the word and Mark would have witnessed Paul dealing with him severely by declaring that he would be blind for a season.[8] Maybe this experience strengthened Mark's faith, or it may have had the opposite effect and made him afraid.

In due course, Paul and Barnabas left Cyprus and reached Perga in Pamphylia, an ancient city in modern-day Turkey. At this point John Mark leaves them and returns to Jerusalem.[9]

His departure seems to have been a sudden event and the Bible doesn't record his reasons for doing so. Commentators have put forward various possibilities to explain his leaving which include, among others, that he became ill, he was homesick, he was afraid of the physical dangers associated with the onward journey, or that he took offence at Paul's rising prominence[9] at the expense of his cousin Barnabas.

It is not certain if any of these reasons are correct and while there must remain some speculation as to the actual reason for his leaving, a plausible suggestion is that he was overcome by sudden fear,[10] triggered perhaps by the events he had witnessed at Paphos.

We may suspect the hand of the Adversary behind such an attack of fear[11] as well as then exploiting Mark's conduct to create a division between Paul and Barnabas, who had been advocating Mark's inclusion in their second missionary journey. As a result of this disagreement, Barnabas took Mark and went to Cyprus, while Paul returned to Asia Minor with Silas.[12]

Including John Mark was a problem for Paul because of Mark's previous conduct. However, Barnabas encouraged Mark and gave him a second chance. God would overrule for good, however, and the friction between Paul and Barnabas, as well as that between Paul and Mark, did not last. In God's good time, Mark and Paul were reconciled[13] and Paul referred to him as one of his fellow-labourers, and also as being profitable to him for the ministry.[14]

Despite his initial failings (which may be inferred) and with the support of Barnabas, God used Mark mightily. In addition to writing his Gospel, according to tradition he might well have been the first person to bring Christianity to Africa, at Alexandria.[15]

The Lord Jesus prayed, *"Holy Father, keep through your name those whom You have given Me, that they may be one, as We are."*[16] That prayer was fulfilled in Paul and Mark. For Jesus' sake, may we, too, seek its fulfilment amongst our fellow Christians today.

References:
[1]Acts 12:12 [2]Acts 13:9 [3]1 Pet.5:13 'my son Mark' [4]Acts 12:25 [5]Col. 4:10, though the word can also mean 'near relative' [6]Acts 13:5 [7]Acts 13:7 [8]Acts 13:11 [9]Acts 13:13, as compared with the order of names in e.g. Acts 13:2 [10]Prov.3:25 [11]2 Cor.2:11 [12]Acts 15:36-41 [13]Philn.1:24 [14]2 Tim.4:11 [15]In Church History, Eusebius records: "And they say that this Mark was the first that was sent to Egypt, and that he proclaimed the Gospel which he had written ..." [16]Jn 17:11 NKJV

The Holy Spirit

Learning from Paul

Geralde Mag-usara, Uraya (Davao), Philippines

It seems that God the Father and God the Son are frequently in the forefront in our Bible with regards to their work. God the Holy Spirit is perhaps not so obviously in view. Yet right from the beginning of creation, He was there,[1] and at the beginning of Jesus' ministry as well.[2] There's no surprise in that because He is a full member of the Trinity. Scriptures testify that He is omnipresent,[3] omniscient,[4] and omnipotent.[5] But what exactly is His work? Peter, John, Paul and, most of all, Jesus, have a lot to say about Him. But this article focuses on what we can learn about the Holy Spirit from Paul's inspired writings.

Baptized in the Spirit

We live in a world full of discrimination. It seems as though some people regard themselves as sitting in 'first class'; while they view everyone else in 'economy'. The Church of God in Corinth in part seems to have behaved like that. In 1 Corinthians 1:12 (NKJV), it's recorded that some said, *"I am of Paul,"* who bore witness before kings. Others said, *"I am of Apollos,"* as of someone mighty in the Scriptures. Some others said, *"I am of Cephas,"* the one to whom were given the keys of the kingdom of heaven; while still others said, *"I am of Christ,"* the greatest of all.

Something not altogether dissimilar exists in different Christian denominations today. Some appear to claim they are above others, by claiming they are the only ones who can get to heaven. But God used Paul to teach us that we are all equal 'in Christ'. Only the Lord Jesus is above us all. This became a reality when He baptized us in the Spirit.[6] Paul says, *"For in one Spirit we were all baptized into one body – Jews or Greeks, slaves or free – and all were made to drink of one Spirit."*[7] This precious truth was unknown to all generations before this. Previously, Jewish people discriminated against Gentiles, but Paul says, *"it has **now** been revealed ... that the Gentiles are fellow heirs and fellow members of the body, and fellow partakers of the promise in Christ Jesus through the gospel."*[8] And so, *"There is neither Jew nor Greek, there is neither slave nor free, there is neither male nor female; for you are all one in Christ Jesus."*[9] So, all Christian believers are baptized at conversion by Christ in the Spirit into the church, known biblically as His Body.[10]

Sealed with the Spirit

Sadly, some people in The Philippines refused Covid vaccines for what they considered to be a religious reason. They were influenced by misinformation coming from social media that claimed the vaccines contained material that would be used to eventually form 'the mark of the beast' or '666'. Unfortunately, some professing Christians are caught up in this. But the Bible gives the true information that the '666' era belongs to a time after the Lord has taken all true believers to be with Himself.[11] It will never affect any true Christian. One way to be assured of that is to realize that we are already marked eternally in a way that signifies we belong to Christ. And by this we refer to the fact that each Christian believer is sealed with the Holy Spirit.

At the time of conversion, God sealed us with the Holy Spirit as His mark of ownership that we belong to God: "...*when you believed in Christ, he identified you as his own by giving you the Holy Spirit.*"[12] This happened when we believed and – as we've seen – the Spirit united us in Christ's body, His church. More fully, we read: "*In Him, you also, after listening to the message of truth, the gospel of your salvation – having also believed, you were sealed in Him with the Holy Spirit of promise…And He put all things in subjection under His feet and gave Him head over all things to the church, which is His body, the fullness of Him who fills all in all.*"[13]

The Spirit also acts as "*a pledge* (or 'earnest') *of our inheritance.*"[14] Covid-19 vaccines, although they give us protection, give no assurance that we can no longer get the virus. Nothing can change the fact that our bodies are also 'groaning' and so vulnerable. But when Paul speaks about the Holy Spirit being the "*earnest of our inheritance*", he is emphasising the future transformation of our mortal bodies into glorious bodies like that of our risen Lord. Paul said, "*For indeed, we who are in this tent groan, being burdened, because we do not want to be unclothed but to be clothed, so that what is mortal will be swallowed up by life. Now He who prepared us for this very purpose is God, who gave us the Spirit as a pledge.*"[16] The 'earnest' (Gk. *arrabon*) of the Holy Spirit serves as a down payment (deposit) or is like an engagement ring[17] to give us assurance.[18]

The habitation of God in His Spirit

The baptism and sealing of the Spirit are both linked to our eternal salvation. No individual believer is discriminated against in any way, and every single believer is protected and secure. But the 'habitation of

God in His Spirit'[19] is linked to our service in God's house. Praise God, it is possible to plant churches of God anywhere today! In Old Testament times, God chose a unique, physical place and His people could only worship there. They were forbidden to build an altar elsewhere.[20]

But when Jesus introduced the true way of worship, *"in spirit and truth"*,[21] it implied worship is no longer associated with one physical place on earth, but God's people now worship Him spiritually in heaven itself by faith. We can plant churches of God in any place where He leads. And His Spirit unites all these churches of God in every place into one spiritual house of God in which He dwells.[22]

Let's clarify that being God's habitation in the Spirit is distinct from believers being individually indwelt by the Spirit. That's also true, but it refers to our own bodies.[23] That's not what's meant at the end of Ephesians chapter two where we read of becoming the *"dwelling of God in His Spirit."*

The unity, filling and gifting of the Spirit

As this habitation of God in His Spirit, we need to be diligent to preserve *"the unity of the Spirit."*[24] That begins with us being collectively founded upon the Apostles' teaching which came originally from the Lord.[25] In God's habitation, there are God's own guidelines for *"the saints ... including the overseers and deacons"*[26] as they engage with church activities. Each individual should be filled with the Spirit by way of submitting to one another.[27] In Romans 12 and Ephesians 4, we see God the Father and God the Son giving certain gifts to individual believers. God the Holy Spirit is seen to do this as well.[28] Gifts such as working miracles, different kinds of tongues, interpretation of tongues, and gifts of healing are no longer expected to be seen today. They served their purpose as the foundation was laid, while the apostles were then still active.[29] But the remainder of the gifts continue for our common good,[30] and we ought to use them in our service within His habitation.[31]

Walking by (while born of) the Spirit

We want to keep our homes tidy, don't we? Even more so in God's house surely, where He dwells in His Spirit. Each disciple should walk according to the Spirit. The world we live in is fascinated with material things. Unregenerate persons are consumed by this. But we, being born of the Spirit,[32] ought to walk *according to the Spirit*.[33] Our appetite must be on the things of God and not on the things of the flesh.[34] Our habit should be to desire and know the mind of Christ. We are born to be naturally 'curious' about the things around us. Having now received the Spirit of God, our curiosity should be directed to 'knowing the mind of Christ'.[35] This would help us stay away from having our minds fixed on worldly trends. Let's not be intimidated by what the world may say against us, especially not listening to those for whom believing God is foolishness. They do not have the Spirit of God and simply cannot understand the things of the Spirit.[36] But through His Spirit, *"we have the mind of Christ."*[37]

What a marvellous work God has done for us through His Spirit! Thank you, Paul, for sharing so much.

References:
[1]Gen.1:2 [2]Matt.3:16 [3]Ps.139:7 [4]1 Cor.2:10-11 [5]Zech.4:6; Lk.1:35 [6]Matt.3:11 [7]1 Cor.12:13 ESV [8]Eph.3:5-6 [9]Gal.3:28 [10]Eph.1:22-23 [11]1 Thess.4:13-18; see also Rev.13 [12]Eph.1:13 NLT [13]Eph.1:13, 22-23 ESV [14]Eph.1:14 NASB (1995) [15]Rom.8:23 [16]2 Cor.5:4-5 [17]George Prasher, The Holy Spirit and the Believer, p.8, Hayes Press [18]2 Cor.1:23 [19]Eph.2:22 RV [20]Deut.12:5,12-14 [21]Jn 4:24 [22]Eph.2:19-22 [23]1 Cor.6:19 [24]Eph.4:3 [25]Acts 2:42, sometimes known as 'the faith', Jude 1:3 [26]Phil.1:1 [27]Eph.5:18,21 [28]see 1 Cor.12:8-10 [29]Heb.2:3-4 [30]1 Cor.12:7 [31]1 Pet.4:10 [32]Jn 3:5 [33]Rom.8:4 [34]Rom.8:3; 1 Jn 2:16 [35]1 Cor.2:9-16 [36]1 Cor.2:14 [37]1 Cor. 2:16
Bible quotations from NASB (2020) unless stated otherwise.

Jesus Christ

A model for acceptance

Craig Jones, Toronto, Canada

It's increasingly unmistakable that we live in a world that places a high value and priority on 'self'. Bookstore shelves creak under the weight of the sheer number of 'self- help' volumes written to supposedly empower people to take control of various aspects of their own lives in order to fulfil their desires, their pleasures, their ambitions and thereby realize their full potential for this life. Some of it comes across as explicitly self-centred, focused on how to get the best out of life for yourself, even at the expense of others. Some of it perhaps seems more innocuous and it may be difficult to see how the attitudes being promoted could disadvantage someone else. Some of it is even presented with a veneer of apparent 'Christian' virtue. However, a thoughtful reflection on what undergirds all this quickly reveals that the 'self' has become so ubiquitous that we hardly even notice that so much of what is written under the guise of even well- meaning advice and encouragement is fundamentally, and by definition, 'selfish'.

'Selfishness' is the antithesis of the kind of character and behaviour that the Bible time and again exhorts disciples of the Lord Jesus to exemplify in their lives. We read, for example, in Romans 15:2 the clear and simple statement: *"Each of us is to please his neighbour for his good, to his edification."* James, in his letter, expresses it in his own typically forthright way: *"For where jealousy and selfish ambition exist, there is disorder and every evil thing."*[1] The apostle Paul again expressed this all- important virtue of unselfishly seeking to please others in this way:

"Do nothing from selfishness or empty conceit, but with humility of mind regard one another as more important than yourselves; do not merely look out for your own personal interests, but also for the interests of others."[2]

He then went on to describe the underlying reason why this attitude of unselfish care and concern for others is such a necessary characteristic of the believer:

"Have this attitude in yourselves which was also in Christ Jesus, who, although He existed in the form of God, ... emptied Himself, taking the form of a bond- servant, and being made in the likeness of men. Being

found in appearance as a man, He humbled Himself by becoming obedient to the point of death, even death on a cross."[3]

The Lord Jesus Christ is the supreme example of this beautiful and divinely inspired quality of unselfish humility that brings about absolute good to those who are on the receiving end. Such selflessness also demonstrates a heart that is willing to accept us all just as we are, with our differences in maturity levels, cultural backgrounds and even annoying tendencies, because it was *"while we were yet sinners, Christ died for us."*[4] Though we are the people who have cause to be profoundly pleased and delighted at what Christ has done, first and foremost it was for the pleasure and delight of His Father in heaven, as He declared: *"...for I always do the things that are pleasing to Him."*[5]

With such an example, then, as followers of Christ – and recipients of His mercy – together we are to emulate Him, accepting one another with all our varied characteristics and weaknesses, so that we will be able to unitedly bring praise and glory to God.[6] As Paul wrote his letter to the Romans, he expressed the desire that, *with one accord* [we] *"may with one voice glorify the God and Father of our Lord Jesus Christ."*[7] He didn't suggest that it would be easy; rather, that it would only come through God-given endurance, encouragement and a spirit of unity through following Christ. As we strive to exemplify Christ-like humility and unselfishness in our acceptance and preferment of others, we will find ourselves indeed being 'people- pleasers' – in all the best and most wholesome aspects of that expression. More importantly still, we will also find ourselves being those who are well-pleasing to the Lord.[8]

References:
[1]Jas.3:16 [2]Phil.2:3-4 [3]Phil.2:5-8 [4]Rom.5:8 [5]Jn 8:29 [6]Rom.15:7 [7]Rom.15:6 [8]Heb.13:20-21

Bible quotations from the NASB (1995).

Understanding the megachurches

David Pattison, Leigh, England

'Mega' churches, where rock star lookalike preachers deliver their optimistic messages, punctuated by a soundtrack of loud live music, to large congregations of mainly young people gathered together in an atmosphere which resembles a festival or rave far more than it does a conventional church service, are undeniably popular among their target audience. TV and Internet broaden the size of that audience, so that even those who practise more modest forms of worship might look at them with admiration and wonder why their own church can't be more like that.

At a point in history where church attendance in the Western world continues to fall, it is tempting to look at this phenomenon with more than a little envy, which of course would be a very unchristian thing to do! But a closer examination is in order, since there are facts that need to be learned which shine a different light. Far from adopting the tactics of the atheist trolls who would pour their venom on any church activity, this will be done the only way it should be done: from a Christian and Biblical standpoint.

The recent alliance of the Australian Hillsong movement and the US-based Bethel Church created a powerful united front that seems to have earned itself a free pass into a sizeable swathe of Christian media. Indeed, on that very front Trinity Broadcast Network (TBN) and United Christian Broadcasters (UCB) are now plugging each other's efforts with all the enthusiasm of a mutual admiration society.

So what, you might well ask? Aren't amalgamations and quid pro quo deals an established part of business practice? (Indeed they are, although that raises the question of which direction influence should travel between the business and Christian worlds). More to the point, turn on TBN these days, as many have done during pandemic lockdowns in search of a message of hope, and you will see – guess what? – an outside broadcast from a megachurch in action or a 30-minute monologue or interview with one of their representatives.

Messages of "unconditional love and unending hope" – terms used by the UK's Freeview guide as a one-line summary of Joel Osteen's regular TBN broadcast – are very persuasive, and whether the preacher appears suited and booted à la Osteen or with the T-shirted, tattoos-on-parade, just-been-to-the-gym look of the Hillsong UK speaker an hour or so later, it all looks very telegenic. But is it very biblical?

Well it certainly incorporates Bible readings, although these are selective and made to fit the programme makers' stance, which is one of addressing an audience of those considered to be fundamentally good people – as opposed to the sinners redeemed at Calvary that we should recognise ourselves as – whose prayers, whatever they may be, will be answered, and any failure to achieve the desired outcome is ascribed to individual weak faith rather than the wrong motives addressed in James chapters 1 or 4. Typically in the megachurch, there is nothing wrong in praying for more money for oneself as this keeps the church car park full of impressive vehicles, but remain poor afterwards and you obviously weren't listening to the speaker closely enough last time, were you?

Wealth orientation is a familiar theme in the world of the megachurch. Other more serious allegations exist around sexual abuse – which has stained the reputation of longer- established churches as well, it should be added, as Satan worms his way in – and even reports of attempts to raise the dead long after life has been pronounced extinct.

Those with long memories or an interest in history will remember similar events surrounding televangelists of the 1980s and 90s. That was seen at the time as an issue confined largely to the United States, where the take-up of the then-contemporary cable and satellite television markets that housed their pulpits was much greater than in the rest of the world. Nowadays, with the communication system of the 2020s, we are all potential prey to fraudsters and fake news messengers. We are explicitly warned (by Jude, John, Peter and Paul, for example) about false teaching.

Perhaps at the end of the day, we need to replace any desire to be 'mega', wrapping the pseudoscience of the life coach up in the hashtag of the week, with a prayer to be more majorly humble, compassionate and biblical truth-seeking.

God's desire

From Eden to Sinai

Andy Seddon, Swindon, England

Ancient Near Eastern people believed that they lived in a symbiotic relationship with their gods; mutually dependent on each other. Humans, through rituals and sacrifice, would provide for their gods' needs whilst the gods would return the favour and provide for humans. In stark contrast, the God of the Bible does not depend on anything or anyone for His existence or wellbeing.[1] Paul declares to the Athenians that God *"...does not live in temples made by man, nor is he served by human hands, as though he needed anything."*[2] It is staggering, then, that God has revealed a deep longing, not just to be associated with humans from a distance, but to dwell intimately with them, without compromising His eternal glory and holiness. This volitional desire of God's is evident from the opening pages of Genesis to the closing pages of Revelation. In this series of articles, we take a journey through the Scriptures to survey this desire of God's, and the first stage of our journey takes us from Eden to Bethel.

Eden

"And the LORD God planted a garden in Eden, in the east, and there he put the man whom he had formed."[3] Men and women were created in God's *own image,*[4] unspoiled by sin and endowed with the capacity to enjoy an intimate relationship with God. Soon after Adam's creation, we read of God planting a garden in a certain place, and putting Adam in it, before being joined by Eve as his *"helper."*[5] As a garden, this was a cultivated place of God's own planting, forming a beautiful backdrop to the humans' relationship with God and with each other. It contrasted with the uncultivated outside place from where Adam came – and to where he was returned after the Fall.[6] Even in Eden we can observe certain principles when God dwells with humans.

A place of revelation

God made Himself known to humans and enabled them to experience the awe and pleasure of His presence, as evidenced by God's *"walking in the garden in the cool of the day."*[7] How sad, of course, that sin had already entered by the time we read this, resulting in human shame and separation.

A place of reverence

Dwelling in Eden came with conditions. God gave directions to Adam that were to be obeyed out of a reverent fear of God.[8] The consequences of disobedience included expulsion from the garden, so that it became impossible for humans to return again on their own initiative.[9]

A place of responsibility

As a cultivated place, God delegated stewardship of it to the man, to *"work it and keep it"*,[10] indicating that neglect would result in its demise. So, from as early as Eden, one could say that principles of worship, fellowship, obedience and service are connected to God's dwelling with humans, and they remain so today in God's spiritual house.

Bethel

The first time we come across the term 'house of God' in the Bible is in relation to Jacob when he was fleeing for his life and travelling to his uncle Laban in Haran. We pick up the narrative in Genesis chapter 28:

"And he came to a certain place and stayed there that night... And he dreamed, and behold, there was a ladder set up on the earth, and the top of it reached to heaven. And behold, the angels of God were ascending and descending on it! And behold, the LORD stood above it... Then Jacob awoke from his sleep and said, "Surely the LORD is in this place, and I did not know it." And he was afraid and said, "How awesome is this place! This is none other than the house of God, and this is the gate of heaven."[11]

This unforgettable vision occurred at a very forgettable place called Luz.[12] We don't read of anything humanly impressive about this place; it was simply somewhere Jacob lay down to rest, no doubt haunted by his thoughts and fears. However, after Jacob awoke from his vision he was filled with awe and re-named the place Bethel, meaning 'house of God' in Hebrew.

'Jacob's ladder' has become a well-known expression. In reality the term could mean a flight of stairs which may have conjured up, in the mind of the ancient reader, an image resembling the stairs that would ascend the outside of a ziggurat (a large tower-like structure with a temple or shrine at the top). Some commentators think the Tower of Babel may have been such a structure, though that was a human initiative with vain and rebellious motives. In contrast to Babel, Bethel was of God's initiative, and God Himself *stood above it,*[11] portraying His ultimate authority there.

It was here that God reaffirmed His covenant with Jacob's grandfather, Abraham. He declares to Jacob: *"The land on which you lie I will give to you and to your offspring,"[11]* reflecting God's purpose to dwell among a collective people under His authority in the years to come. It is significant that the stairway was based on earth but reached to heaven. The angels *"ascending and descending"[11]* were a graphic picture of service towards God in heaven, carried out from earth. In Eden we had the first glimpse of God coming down to a certain place on earth to meet with humans; in Bethel we have the first glimpse of a certain place where humans can envisage approach to God in heaven itself. Jacob himself calls the place, *"the gate of heaven"*. As in Eden, we can see similar principles relating to God's dwelling place in Bethel.

A place of revelation

God reveals Himself to Jacob in a unique way at Bethel. As Jacob himself admits, he would never have known that God was there without the vision God brought about. The reiteration of God's covenant promises formed the basis of Jacob's relationship with God and his confidence in the Lord's faithfulness. To mark the place and the memory, Jacob turns a stone from a pillow into a pillar, as he anoints it with oil and calls it *"God's house".[13]* A single stone is hardly a house from a human perspective, but here marks the beginning of something bigger to come, especially as we discern the spiritual house of later revelation. Later, when Jacob was experiencing trouble with his uncle Laban, God again reveals Himself, but this time as the *"God of Bethel"*. So, for the first time, God's identity becomes associated with a place and not just with individuals. Years later when Jacob returns to Bethel, he further names it *"El-bethel"*,[14] literally 'the God of the house of God'.

A place of reverence

Given his vision, it is no wonder Jacob cried out, *"How awesome is this place!"* To everybody else Luz was as ordinary as before (except it had a new stone pillar), but not to Jacob. The realisation of God's presence made all the difference. Years later, after Jacob had acquired wives and children, God commands him specifically to return to Bethel to *"dwell there"*, and to *"make an altar"[15]*. In reverent response, Jacob has his household dispose of the multiple gods and idols associated with the polytheistic world in which they travelled.[16] For Jacob now there was one God, and a unique place for worship.

A place of responsibility

When God reiterates his covenant promises to Jacob at Bethel, Jacob responds with a vow on his part: *"The LORD shall be my God, and this stone, which I have set up for a pillar, shall be God's house. And of all that you give me I will give a full tenth to you."[17]*

Jacob's vow indicates commitment to one God, and his dedication to give back to God out of what God has given to him.

So, God's desire and design to dwell with humans is glimpsed at the beginning of our Bibles, paving the way for greater revelations to come, leading ultimately to the incarnation of God Himself when *"the Word became flesh and dwelt among us."[18]* Speaking to Nathanael of millennial glory, Jesus says, *"You will see heaven opened, and the angels of God ascending and descending on the Son of Man".[19]* Today it is through Christ, our great high priest, that we collectively draw near to the throne of grace. Christ also is *"faithful over God's house as a son. And we are his house, if indeed we hold fast our confidence and our boasting in our hope."[20]*

References:
[1]See Rom.11:34-36 [2]Acts 17:24-25 [3]Gen.2:8 [4]Gen.1:27 [5]Gen.2:18 [6]Gen.3:23 [7]Gen.3:8 [8]Gen.2:16-17 [9]Gen.3:24 [10]Gen.2:15 [11]Gen.28:11-17 [12]Gen.28:19 [13]Gen.28:22 [14]Gen.35:7 [15]Gen.35:1 [16]Gen.35:1-4 [17]Gen.28:21-22 [18]Jn 1:14 [19]Jn 1:51 [20]Heb.3:6
Bible quotations from the ESV.

Can you help me with this?

Emptied of what?

Geoff Hydon, Mount Forest, Canada

I have always loved Philippians 2:7 in its description of the humility of Christ, but more recently I've seen people saying that it means the Son of God left His divinity behind when He came to be a man. I've always been taught that Jesus was fully man, but fully God at the same time. Who is mistaken?

First, we should firmly state the truth that the Lord Jesus Christ was fully God even while He was a man on earth. That is so clearly stated in Colossians 2:8-9 we can do no better than simply quote it here:

"See to it that no one takes you captive by philosophy and empty deceit, according to human tradition, according to the elemental spirits of the world, and not according to Christ. For in him the whole fullness of deity dwells bodily, and you have been filled in him, who is the head of all rule and authority."

This statement follows on from chapter 1:15-20 concerning the Son's deity and humanity, which includes:

"For in him all the fullness of God was pleased to dwell, and through him to reconcile to himself all things, whether on earth or in heaven, making peace by the blood of his cross."

So how then are we to properly understand Philippians 2:5-8, which says:

*"Have this mind among yourselves, which is yours in Christ Jesus, who, though he was in the form of God, did not count equality with God a thing to be grasped, but **emptied** himself, by taking the form of a servant, being born in the likeness of men. And being found in human form, he humbled himself by becoming obedient to the point of death, even death on a cross."*

When Paul wrote 'emptied', he used the Greek *ekenosen*, the past tense of a verb meaning 'to empty' and *kenosis* meaning 'an emptying' is the word used by theologians to describe Christ's emptying of Himself. Note, Paul writes that the Son was already in the 'form of God'; He displayed that His essential substance was that of being God, and this necessarily means He always is God.[1]

Because of that He always is entitled to receive the service of all. That right to receive service stands in stark contrast to the fact that, as a man, He displayed Himself as a servant, whose obedience to God His Father was tested to the uttermost when He died on a cross rather than disobey.[2] But this was not something that was forced on Him: He humbled Himself; it was a voluntary humility. When, in order to meet the needs of others, He did not use the right to have everyone serve Him, that was the result of His decision, His mind, and His love,[3] not something that any external force could compel Him to do. This specific emptying (*kenosis*) was only possible because He is God; only He could deny Himself rights that others simply do not have. The focus is on His divine attitude, not on specifying what was given up (which would be beyond our understanding[4]).

This clear scriptural teaching about the deity and humanity of Christ was appreciated in the early New Testament churches and has been repeated in various creeds ever since. But, more recently, some have wrongly taught that the *kenosis* involved the Son giving up His essential divinity when He became a man. Perhaps they have been led astray by noting that, as a man, Jesus chose not to use all the power available to Himself as God. This is clearly displayed in His response to the Tempter's challenges.[5] It was also in evidence when He would not call on angelic assistance to avoid the cross;[6] He gave up a right of deity without giving up deity.

In its context, Paul in Philippians 2 was appealing to Christ's example of humility as the model for Christian behaviour. True humility is expressed when a lower place is taken than that to which one is entitled. Our responsibility is to count others as more significant than ourselves, instead of clinging to our rights. And for emphasis, in declaring Christ to be the highest possible example in this humility, Paul says that Christ *"did not count equality with God a thing to be grasped"* because that equality is always His, making his humility all the more amazing.

References:
[1]Ps.90:2; Jn 1:1-3 [2]Lk.22:42 [3]Phil.2:2 [4]Job 37:23 [5]Lk.4:1-13 [6]Matt.26:53-54
Bible quotations from the ESV.

Grace in action

An interview with Steve Peers, Aberkenfig, Wales

Looking back over my life, 'grace' is the word that best describes it. The grace of God has been evidenced time and again such that I hardly recognise the person I once was. I grew up in a rented council house, the middle one of three children, relatively poor, academically average. My first real contact with the Christian faith came when I was in the 6th form where one of my A-level Maths teachers would sometimes answer questions put to him about the Bible. Privately at home, I came to faith in Christ. I asked God to put me in a church like my Maths teacher's. Unknown to me, the Lord was also working with my sister (Ann Allport from the Church of God in Towyn) who had been saved and one day asked me to attend her baptism. At my sister's baptism, I discovered that she was joining the same church as my Maths teacher, who was our chauffeur for the night, and after the baptism I remember saying to myself, "That's it! My life will never be the same again." I was right. I was baptised three weeks later; my prayer of joining a church like my Maths teacher's was more than answered and, apart from an initial period of hesitation, I have found great joy in serving the Lord, firstly in the Church of God in Rhyl (now Towyn), four years in the Church of God in Barry and, since 1987, in the Church of God in Aberkenfig.

I went to work in retail management. This was the time when I had joined the church I mentioned above, the Church of God in Rhyl. I came to have doubts about my job where I was selling goods that were not honouring to the Lord. I then took my first holiday alone, which saw me spending a week in Scotland, at the home of beloved David and Margaret Gray. I'd never been completely immersed in a Christian home before and the wonderful experience that it proved to be, transformed me. I came home knowing that all I wanted to do was serve the Lord, and I had determined to give up my job; but I still had the problem of what to do next. My Maths teacher, now my Christian brother, suggested I should consider a teaching career. That sounded like a crazy idea, because I'd failed A-level Maths! I did have an interview in which I'm convinced I gave the wrong answer to every question, but I was accepted. In 1975, I began studying and discovered that the Lord had opened my mind and the once impossible Maths now seemed straightforward. I even came top in some exams, something which had never happened before. This was grace in action.

In 1979 I began teaching and in 1980 I married a wonderful Welsh girl from the Rhondda Valley, called Rose. By 1987, I was the Head of a Maths department and in 1990 a Deputy Head. I happily stayed in that post until January 2013, when I agreed to take on a Headteacher role until I retired in August 2016. I've always believed that the Lord took me into teaching to develop skills and qualities I needed for service amongst His people.

I wasn't capable before, but the Lord in His grace has slowly taken me forward and fitted me for His service. Those skills have enabled me to write blogs and produce videos, all of which go out on our Church Facebook site and YouTube channel.

I've discovered that it's through the hard times that God's grace has most been in evidence in my life. I began to experience signs of depression when I was 19, but it was at the age of 21, during my second year in college, that it hit me hard. For years, my wife was the only one who knew and she has been a great support, but it is the grace of God that has sustained me. Today I am open about my depression, since mental illness should be treated no differently to physical illness. It is not a lack of faith; in fact, it probably takes more faith to live with depression than without it. My family and friends have been wonderful and I'm so glad that I can be open with them. It's been a while since I had a bout of depression, but we all know that it may return at any time and God's grace will enable and sustain me. He has never failed me.

Rose and I also suffered the loss of our first child, Elizabeth: stillborn, suffering with anencephaly and no hope of survival. Those who have lost a child at any age will understand the pain, but we have always been thankful to the Lord that we have never doubted His love for us. We were privileged with a remarkable learning experience as we submitted to God's sovereign will and learned that the Judge of all the earth always does right.[1] We lost one child, but He has blessed us with two more, and four wonderful grandchildren who bring great joy to us.

Reference:

[1]Gen.18:25

Curses to blessings

Geralde Mag-usara, Uraya (Davao), Philippines

Life has been hard for many in this Covid-19 pandemic. The hardest thing was when our worship as well as our witnessing became restricted. Although **we** cannot control what is happening in our world, God is in control. When lockdown occurred, one family in Davao moved to a mountain area outside of Davao city to plant vegetables as a source of income. When the harvest came, the price suddenly dropped and transporting it to market would have been more expensive than its profit. Instead of waiting for the crop to decay, they decided to give it all away freely to their hungry neighbours. One curious neighbour was prompted to ask about their spiritual background. And so they came to hear the Good News, including about churches of God. We conducted Bible seminars every evening, and soon fifteen persons received the Saviour. These people were not deterred by the muddy hillside path or the darkness or even the rain: so eager were they to learn God's Word. One of them is a man who is illiterate. Every verse I gave during the talks, he would ask his daughter to take note of, and then to read it again later for him at home. Truly, you could sense the Holy Spirit working.

But we also encountered opposition. One local pastor spread a rumour among these people that we were connected to the New People's Army (a communist group). As a result, we faced religious persecution. We conducted a crusade in the next village. One hundred families live there, including the relatives of the new converts who had encouraged us to go there because of there being no Christian denomination already there.

But the following day, their tribal chieftains banned us. They worship spirits ('Panubaran') and hate Christians. Added to these challenges, was the risk of frequent fighting between rebels and government soldiers. However, under God's controlling hand, we continued to press on. In fact, when once we scheduled to baptize eight of them, we struggled for a week to find water in the forest because of the fighting there. So we travelled 40 km to Davao. They were successfully baptized and numbered in the Church of God at Uraya (Davao) in November 2020.

However, the following month, their tribal chieftains forbade them to come to Davao City due to a Covid-19 surge there. But thanks to the resolution that was circulated on behalf of the elders of Churches of

God, we were able to make a temporary Covid-19 company in Malabog. The eight plus five saints who were already established in Uraya (Davao) formed this company. And this proved to be a blessing in disguise.

The Covid curse turned into a blessing for us, as in the following months many were saved, baptized and found their place in this temporary company.

This work that started in September 2020 kept getting stronger. For seven months, these people had been walking for 2-3 kilometres each Sunday to gather. At that point, the group was composed of twelve families (31 individuals). Initially, none of them were able to handle ministering God's Word but were dependent on visiting brothers from Uraya. But for more than two months, they underwent training on how to preach, and now they can do this capably. Four men in particular have shown themselves capable. They love their Bibles, and study carefully. If they find difficult verses, they consult first. Two of them are now engaged in regular outreach work among their relatives. The same four also show leadership potential. Among the thirteen brothers, seven of them are regularly participating in thanksgiving and prayers. Two months ago, they moved their gathering to an expanded mission hut that is both central and accessible.

By God's grace, they were recognised as the Church of God in Malabog on September 12, 2021. Truly, God works all things together for good.[1] By His grace, these former spirit-worshipers are now obeying the form of doctrine that was delivered once for all[2] – and passing it on to their relatives in Alon, about 15 km from Malabog.

References:

[1]Rom.8:28 [2]Rom.6:17; Jude 1:3

From the Editors' desk

Issue 2 2022

If there's one word that seems to link nearly all the articles in this issue of NT, it is 'endurance'. You may want to bear that in mind as you read through the magazine, and see whether you reach the same conclusion. Christian disciples are encouraged to show endurance. Hebrews 12:1 tells us to *"run with endurance the race that is set before us."* Some versions use the term 'patience' or 'perseverance', and the obvious thought is to not give up when the going gets tough. Our example is the Lord Jesus Himself, of course, who endured the cross, evaluating the joy of heaven He left behind and the shame to be inflicted at the cross as realities that should not divert Him. Some of the articles in this issue point us to the very real sacrifices that faithful obedience to the will of God may bring our way, though our challenges pale in comparison to the endurance demanded of our divine Example.

No doubt to Paul and Barnabas' disappointment, John Mark seems to have left the race when he was challenged. Peter was to learn painfully that only Spirit-empowered endurance would meet this need. It seems the apostles especially had to endure injustice, provocation, disinformation and worse;[1] conquering by faith. How easy it would have been for them to give up, and how mentally, physically and spiritually demanding to endure the prolonged difficulty involved in successfully bringing the thoughts of their audiences into captivity to Christ. Today, we may face entrenched heresy, expressed by those who refuse to change their minds. We might wonder how Mary would feel regarding the errors taught about her, which by unduly exalting her demean the child she bore, who bears the only Name in which there is salvation. Throughout past centuries Christians have had to seek asylum from those who violently oppose them and their beliefs; and today's asylum seekers will know better than most what endurance means in practice, for the hurdles they face are immense. But like the two faithful spies, they may evaluate what must be endured and positively choose to go forward. When their aim is first to *"seek first His kingdom and His righteousness"* they, like the rest of all who walk in that path of faith, are assured that patient endurance and the encouragement from Scripture will yield hope.[2]

Now see if these comments tie in with what you read in this issue!

Geoff

References:
[1] 1 Cor.4:9-13 [2] Rom.15:4

The journey of faith

Tony Smith, Kirkintilloch, Scotland

Thousands of people every day are beginning a journey of faith that is the Christian life. It's a great adventure; a life of faith that depends on our obedient response to the revelation of the Lord Jesus Christ as our Saviour and to the truth of God.

What is faith?

Some may think that faith is a kind of passive intellectual acceptance of various spiritual truths, but faith really is acting on God's Word, combining it with simple trust. The focus of our faith is Christ Himself. What matters is not the strength of our personal faith so much as its direction; it must always be towards Christ.

Growing in faith

Faith is not a static thing; it should be living and growing. Twice in Matthew's Gospel Jesus spoke of 'great faith' shown even by Gentiles.[1] The question is: "Is your faith weak, little or great?" Not only are there degrees of faith, but there is also the matter of the **quality** of faith; it must be sincere.[2] The Bible describes some believers as excelling in faith[3] and others as becoming rich in faith.[4] Where do we stand?

A working faith

James is right to tell us that *faith without deeds is dead*.[5] We are not saved **by** works, of course, but **for** good works.[6] Dorcas demonstrated her faith by doing good and helping the poor.[7] We need to do the same, earning the right to speak to people and show them the outworking of our faith in Christ. A working faith grows deeper when we let it be known we are on the side of Christ.

Walking by faith

The Bible is clear how the Christian pilgrim should progress; it says, *we walk by faith, not by sight*.[8] Someone quipped, 'When Columbus set out, he didn't know where he was going. When he arrived, he didn't know where he was. And when he returned home, he didn't know where he'd been.'

Abraham was commended because, *He went out, not knowing where he was going*.[9] However, Abraham had his faith in God to lead him and *he did not waver through unbelief regarding the promise of God*[10] but was strong in his faith. Have we stepped out, trusting entirely in God?

Trial of faith

There is continual testing in the life of faith. What is your faith up against just now? The scripture says, *"for a little while you may have had to suffer grief in all kinds of trials. These have come so that your faith – of greater worth than gold, which perishes even though refined by fire – may be proved genuine and may result in praise, glory, and honour when Jesus Christ is revealed."*[11] Strong and steadfast believers prove the scripture, *"the testing of your faith produces perseverance."*[12]

The shield of faith[13]

In Numbers 13, when reason saw giants, it had an inferiority complex and said, *"We seemed like grasshoppers"*[14] but when two faithful men 'linked shields', their faith said, *"We are well able to overcome."*[15] Although reason and faith may at times go hand in hand, when reason can't take another step, faith keeps right on going. God is greater than our enemy. So don't let giants eat our grapes, live in our houses, or rob us of enjoying our rightful place.

Prayer of faith

Jesus said, *"If you have faith and do not doubt...you can say to this mountain, 'Go throw yourself into the sea,' and it will be done."*[16] What 'mountains' are overshadowing your Christian life? It may be failure, health problems, unemployment, relationships, exams or other pressures that loom large. God is bigger than your problem. Let us ask, nothing wavering, believing in our hearts that God is able.

Will the mountain be removed? Caleb, who said, *"Give me this mountain"*[17] did not, of course, ask for it to be removed, but he knew how to put mountains into perspective. With God's help he conquered that mountain. God answers prayer according to His will; even if the problems are still there at present, He gives us the grace to sustain us through our trials.

Come on pilgrims! It is time for God to work! Expect great things from God, position yourselves to receive them and start by building up your faith today.

References:
[1]Matt.8:10; 15:28 [2]1 Tim.1:5; 2 Tim.1:5 [3]2 Cor.8:7 [4]Jas.2:5 [5]Jas.2:26 [6]Eph.2:8-10 [7]Acts 9:36 [8]2 Cor.5:7 NKJV [9]Heb.11:8 ESV [10]Rom.4:20 [11]1 Pet.1:6-7 [12]Jas.1:3 [13]Eph.6:16 [14]Num.13:33 [15]Num.13:30 ESV [16]Matt.21:21 [17]Josh.14:12 NKJV
Bible quotations from the NIV (1984) unless stated otherwise.

Justice

Justice and the vulnerable

David Webster, Liverpool, England

The concept of social justice, that is meeting basic needs, the distribution of wealth and the opportunities for people in the way they live their lives, is very topical. Practising equality means not discriminating against some people and the vulnerable means those in need or at risk. Vulnerable people ought to be protected. God's word teaches us: *"Defend the weak and the fatherless; uphold the cause of the poor and the oppressed. Rescue the weak and the needy; deliver them from the hand of the wicked."*[1]

God's people Israel were instructed to uphold the principle of impartiality in respect of right and wrong. In practice, and that's where it counts of course, it meant providing for the poor, not taking away bare necessities and refusing to blame foreigners living among them for the things going wrong or denying justice to those who were powerless to do anything about it.[2] That's a familiar-sounding aspiration in our twenty-first century world, isn't it?

Justice – protecting the weak

Solomon wrote: *"Speak up for those who cannot speak for themselves, for the rights of all who are destitute. Speak up and judge fairly; defend the rights of the poor and needy".*[3] Isaiah drew attention to the attitude of those in the 8th century BC who couldn't understand why God was not happy with them. *"Why have we humbled ourselves, and you have not noticed?"* they asked God. The answer was stark: *"...on the day of your fasting, you do as you please and exploit all your workers... You cannot fast as you do today and expect your voice to be heard on high."*[4]

The lesson is obvious: the way we treat each other, and especially the vulnerable and weak, is as important to God as keeping the commandments. Later, when some of the people of Judah had returned to their land, the prophet Zechariah was caused to deal with this matter yet again: *"This is what the LORD Almighty said: 'Administer true justice; show mercy and compassion to one another. Do not oppress the widow or the fatherless, the foreigner or the poor. Do not plot evil against each other.'"*[5]

It is part of a church elder's work to look after the interests of those who are weak and vulnerable. It may be hard work sometimes. Paul, addressing the elders of the Church in Ephesus on the beach, referred to the attitude of the Lord Jesus:

"In everything I did, I showed you that by this kind of hard work we must help the weak, remembering the words the Lord Jesus himself said: 'It is more blessed to give than to receive.'"[6]

The Lord Jesus pointed out the seriousness of not looking out for the interests of vulnerable children: *"See that you do not despise one of these little ones. For I tell you that their angels in heaven always see the face of my Father in heaven"*;[7] and, later, John, widening this to include anyone who is in need, writes, *"If anyone has material possessions and sees a brother or sister in need but has no pity on them, how can the love of God be in that person? Dear children, let us not love with words or speech but with actions and in truth."*[8]

Some of us may also support food banks or sponsor a child in a developing country or make a donation to charities like Tearfund or the Relief arm of Churches of God. Others make a habit of calling on neighbours who live alone to see that they are safe or take a meal to an elderly person in their church. Those of us working with children or pastoring vulnerable adults must ensure that we have in place policies to ensure they are kept safe.

In a global world market, we may come to realise that some of the products available cheaply to consumers in the West come at the cost of exploitation of the workforce many thousands of miles away. In good conscience we may have to avoid buying into that injustice. That may mean doing without, or it may mean buying a more expensive alternative that has been produced fairly. Products that are fairly traded are sourced through a supply chain where small-scale farmers and producers are treated with dignity, respect, equality and fairness.

Justice – no discrimination

Discrimination is not always bad! We teach our children to discriminate between good and evil and we must learn to discriminate between those attitudes and actions that bring honour to God and those that don't. However, we should never discriminate on the grounds of someone being a foreigner[9] or poor or show favouritism to those we think are better than others. James goes right to the heart of the matter instancing an example of someone attending a church meeting and being disrespected for being poor.[10] Read that powerful rebuke! Sometimes we have to admit that a needy person may not be particularly welcome, neither might someone who presents unkempt or who is unable to communicate.

But we need to turn from such discriminatory thoughts and be ready to give a welcome to everyone. To do less is to be part of the injustice people meet day after day in seeking to access amenities or have their needs met. The Lord Jesus is a great example in meeting the needs of people irrespective of their gender or social or economic status.

Justice – hospitality and care

The condemnation by John and James of religious people who make pious sounding statements without actually doing anything about the situation is blunt.[11] James says that *"faith by itself, if it is not accompanied by action, is dead."*[12] In fact, an essential part of genuine Christianity is to be hospitable, caring and people of action. Hospitality, in this sense, is not having your favourite friends round for lunch! It's putting ourselves out and rolling up our sleeves to help those needy folks we meet. Peter linked hospitality and serving with love: *"Above all, love each other deeply, because love covers over a multitude of sins. Offer hospitality to one another without grumbling. Each of you should use whatever gift you have received to serve others, as faithful stewards of God's grace in its various forms. "*[13]

Paul instructed the disciples in Rome to share and practice hospitality,[14] a command repeated in the letter to the Hebrews.[15] The Greek word for 'hospitality' in each of these verses carries the thought of love of strangers. 'So Christian hospitality is not the begrudging performance of a duty but the glad act of a cheerful giver,' says HM Carson.[16]

Similarly we are to *"carry each other's burdens, and in this way you will fulfil the law of Christ"*[17] and the Lord Jesus makes the principle plain in His parable recorded in Matthew 25 that whatever we might have done *"for one of the least of these brothers and sisters of mine, you did for me."*[18] That puts a very different complexion on care and support given to a brother or sister in the church, doesn't it?

In the western world there are countless children and young people who are suffering neglect in not being introduced to the Bible or the gospel. We can give our time in preparation and then open our church buildings for Sunday schools and youth clubs. There are single parents struggling with their young children. Some of our churches have been able to offer parent and toddler groups as somewhere these people can find someone to talk to and a safe place for children to play. Care and hospitality costs us in time and resources. Maybe realising that it is really the King Himself who is being looked after would focus our minds.

Justice – remember and reflect

It is good to stop and reflect. Five times in Deuteronomy the Israelites were told to *"Remember that you were slaves in Egypt..."[19]* and that they were foreigners.[20] Why? So that they would have softened hearts of compassion for others in situations of hopelessness. And it is the same for us. We also need to remember the 'at one time' of our lives: *"All of us also lived among them at one time... Like the rest, we were by nature deserving of wrath. But because of his great love for us, God, who is rich in mercy, made us alive with Christ... For we are God's handiwork, created in Christ Jesus to do good works, which God prepared in advance for us to do. Therefore, remember..."[21]*

Let's remember what we were, what God has turned us into and how we can show care and compassion to those we come into contact with.

References:
[1]Ps.82:3-4 [2]e.g. Deut.16:19-20; 24:17-22 [3]Prov.31:8-9 [4]Isa.58:3-4 [5]Zech.7:9-10 [6]Acts 20:35 [7]Matt.18:10 [8]1 Jn 3:17-18 [9]See Lev.19:33-34 [10]See Jas.2:1-5 [11]1 Jn 3:17-18 [12]Jas.2:17 [13]1 Pet.4:8-10 [14]See Rom.12:13 [15]See Heb.13:1-2 [16]The New Bible Dictionary IVP, 1977, p.542 [17]Gal.6:2 [18]Matt.25:40 [19]e.g. Deut.5:15 [20]e.g. Lev.19:34 [21]Eph.2:3-5,10-11a
Bible quotations from the NIV (2011).

Preparing for the Lord's return

Provocation

Ira Williamson, Trinidad, USA

Provoke one another!

That's basically what it says in Hebrews 10:24 (AV & ASV) and might sound like unhelpful advice in building relationships in a church, especially considering that the only other New Testament usage of this Greek word (which is a noun in the original language) is found in Acts 15:39 and describes the sharp disagreement that arose between Paul and Barnabas. Very few of us would need training, or even encouragement, to provoke other people – it seems to come naturally enough to say sharp words that have sudden impact on the recipient.

'Sharp' and 'quick' are root ideas in this Greek word *paroxusmos*, which other Bible versions translate as spur, stimulate or stir. Proverbs 12:18 (NIV) warns against the careless use of sharp words: *"The words of the reckless pierce like swords, but the tongue of the wise brings healing."* Sharp words that come suddenly to mind and, once said, have an immediate, hurtful impact on their target, demonstrate the negative thought carried by this Greek word. But let's try to frame it in the positive setting of Hebrews 10:24-25 (ESV):

"And let us consider how to stir up one another to love and good works, not neglecting to meet together, as is the habit of some, but encouraging one another, and all the more as you see the Day drawing near."

You'll have already noticed that we don't just jump into spurring, provoking or stirring up in this verse. We are first commanded to consider, and this is a vital step – without it, we will fall to the negative consequences of this word. The Greek word translated 'consider' here may also mean to behold or to know and even to discover[1]– that is to view others with such careful, selfless perspective that we discover things about them that we might have missed at first glance. In other words to really get to know them. And who are they? The author uses the expression 'let us' a few times in and around these verses in Hebrews 10.

- verse 22 – *"let us draw near"*
- verse 23 – *"let us hold fast the confession of our hope"*; and
- verse 24 – *"let us consider ... one another."*

These are the people linked together in holy service to God; these are the people in our local church of God. Who do we see when we look around the occupied seats of our buildings? No doubt you could name them all, but could we honestly say we've considered them? Beheld them? Discovered who they are?

These are the sheep, known absolutely by the 'good shepherd'[2] These are the ones for whom Christ died.[3] They are the unnamed disciples of the Lord's prayer: *"I pray also for those who will believe in me through their word."*[4] Each one of us – known by our Shepherd, loved to death and considered by Him when all the weight of His death at Calvary was looming ahead.

What about us? Does our spurring – that sudden impactful jab – land with thoughtful precision to the encouragement of positive action from the recipient, or does it simply hurt and push someone away? We must not only be practised at prodding, but also willing to receive that provoking too. For this careful considering and precise prodding to be possible, we must be regularly in the setting of Hebrews 10:25. This short exhortation to not neglect meeting together is more broadly described in Acts 2:43 onwards. The early Church of God at Jerusalem didn't stop at verse 42. They carried on into each other's homes, meals and lives. They knew each other. They loved each other. They were mutually spurred on to love and good deeds.

In this series, we are intended to consider our actions in light of the imminent return of our Lord Jesus Christ to the air. The command to consider, stir up, gather together and encourage is given emphasis for us as we *see the Day drawing near*. It has never been nearer than now, and it has never been more important to spend time with the people God loves, to love them as He does and to be mutually spurred on to love and good deeds.

References:
[1]Acts 27:39 [2]Jn 10:14 [3]1 Cor.8:11 [4]Jn 17:20
Bible quotations from the ESV unless stated otherwise.

Paul's travel companions

Barnabas: the encourager

Martin Jones, Hamilton, Canada

According to Hesiod, he brought peace in place of violence; carefree, he loved to laugh out loud and was regarded as wise, fair, merciful and prudent.[1] If I've led you into confusing Barnabas with Zeus, you'll perhaps understand why the Lycaonians did the same;[2] happily, we needn't rely on Greek mythology to deduce Barnabas' conduct and character!

In the New Testament, we find Barnabas consistently displaying the grace of God that was experienced collectively across the churches post-Pentecost.[3] Like the sacrificial givers of the Macedonian churches,[4] he'd found grace as he first surrendered himself at the Master's feet then surrendered his money at the apostles' feet.[5] Just as the multitude brought their sick to the feet of Jesus,[6] total control was handed over to God's sovereign purposes; unlike Ananias and Sapphira,[7] there was no portion held back, and no pre-conditions – even if it meant that Barnabas now perhaps had to work for a living.[8]

Of course, Paul was not yet of those apostles – at his feet had only come Stephen's stoners to set down their coats[9] and, no doubt, the Christians as he dragged them off to prison.[10] But almost everything was to change near Damascus, again at the feet of the Lord. *"Of this gospel I was made a minister according to the gift of God's grace,"*[11] recounts Paul; from persecutor to preacher, but only Barnabas' vital vouching turned the disciples' understandable apprehension to unqualified acceptance.[12] Could God bring Paul into His purposes, despite his past hate? Not for the last time, Barnabas had discerned the grace of God in action, was glad[13] and determined a fitting response.

That pattern was repeated in pioneering and Cypriot- driven developments in Antioch, about which some in the Jerusalem church seem to have had concerns.[14] Could God bring the Gentiles into His purposes, despite their current heritage? A natural ambassador as well as a Cypriot native, Barnabas saw (like Peter earlier in Acts 11) the unmistakable but unexpected display of God's grace at work in the Gentiles, and knew what the situation required. So well-known were his exhortations that he was nicknamed 'Son of Encouragement' but, as John Miller, a Bible teacher of a past generation, once said, "If we stick only to exhortation, it's like trying to feed a horse with a whip, rather than the nose bag…"

Apprehending his gifts and the gifts of others, Barnabas knew a man with whom he could partner – Paul, clever, bold and determined, in tandem with the gentler Barnabas. After a 300-mile round-trip to track Paul down, twelve months of establishing teaching in Antioch were followed by an evangelistic tour of the region, including his home island.

As a Levite,[15] he would know all about being set apart for the service of the temple of God's glory; but now, he was being set apart for the service of the gospel of God's grace.

At Pisidian Antioch, it should come as no surprise that he and Paul urged Gentile converts to *"continue in the grace of God"[16]* before encountering repeated Jewish objections to the same gospel of grace.

Ultimately, this was to trigger the first of two sharp disputes.[17] In this case, he and Paul were on the same side as he vouched for the Gentile mission at the Jerusalem Conference of Acts 15. Once again, his testimony was critical. The second sharp dispute saw Barnabas vouching again, this time for John Mark.[18] Could God bring John Mark into His purposes despite his recent hiatus? Uncharacteristically, the testimony of the senior brother went unheeded this time; perhaps Paul had overlooked God's 'second-chance grace' granted to him? Without choosing sides, it might be that Paul's subsequent positive reference to John Mark[19] vindicates Barnabas' grasp of grace at work – regardless, what an encouragement for John Mark to have him in his corner!

God's grace often works in ways that we might not have considered possible and that take us out of our comfort zone. Are we ready and glad, like Barnabas was so consistently, to detect it in action and then work with it instead of against it?

References:
[1]Hesiod, Work and Days [2]Acts 14:12 [3]Acts 4:33 [4]2 Cor.8:5 [5]Acts 4:36-37 [6]Matt.15:30 [7]Acts 5:1-11 [8]1 Cor.9:6 [9]Acts 7:58 [10]Acts 8:3 [11]Eph.3:7 [12]Acts 9:27 [13]Acts 11:23 [14]Acts 11:20-22 [15]Acts 4:36 [16]Acts 13:43 [17]Acts 15:2 [18]Acts 15:37-39 [19]Col.4:10
Bible quotations from the ESV.

The Holy Spirit

Learning from Peter

Steve Seddon, Manchester, England

Great expectations

Simon Peter enters the scene as one whose attention had been arrested by the testimony of his brother Andrew, a disciple of John the Baptist. Andrew had pursued Jesus and spent a day with Him. The result: *The first thing Andrew did was to find his brother Simon and tell him, "We have found the Messiah."*[1]

No doubt Andrew's testimony would have included all that John the Baptist had said about Jesus: *the Lamb of God, who takes away the sin of the world*;[2] the one who *has a higher rank*;[3] the one *more powerful*;[4] and the one on whom the Spirit had come down from heaven;[5] the one who would *baptize with the Holy Spirit.*[6]

From the very beginning, the expectation is set in Peter's mind that the Holy Spirit would become an increasingly significant feature in the experience of followers of the Lord Jesus. But at this stage what would Peter have known about the Holy Spirit?

Core kingdom truth

Left with only the Old Testament Scriptures, our appreciation of the nature, character and work of the Holy Spirit would be very limited – which is how it was for Peter and the apostles at the beginning. A special insight was required so that what had hitherto been a concealed mystery, would become a precious revealed truth.

Dr Luke, in what some like to call 'the Acts of the Holy Spirit', describes how Christianity began with a teacher- student dynamic: the Lord Jesus speaking to His apostles and fielding their questions on the truths of the kingdom of God. It is evident that a central theme in this apostolic training for service was the person and work of the Holy Spirit. The Lord Jesus had already introduced the topic back in the upper room (a later article in this series), and He picks up the theme again as part of the apostles' pre-Pentecost 40-day training course.[7]

Author, power-source, divine, a person

That Peter had embraced this new, fuller revelation of the person and work of the Holy Spirit is evident in his leadership amongst the apostles even prior to the outpouring of the Holy Spirit at Pentecost.

Recognizing that Judas Iscariot must be replaced, Peter turns to Psalm 109 – attributing it first to the Holy Spirit, and then to King David, the author of the Psalm.[8] While there are some pointers in the Old Testament Scriptures to the work of the Holy Spirit in their production and conservation,[9] it wasn't until the times of the apostles that this truth was explicitly stated and understood – a truth that Peter was to further emphasize in his later letters.

At this point, a pause for reflection:

"We also have the prophetic message as something completely reliable, and you will do well to pay attention to it, as to a light shining in a dark place, until the day dawns and the morning star rises in your hearts. Above all, you must understand that no prophecy of Scripture came about by the prophet's own interpretation of things. For prophecy never had its origin in the human will, but prophets, though human, spoke from God as they were carried along by the Holy Spirit."[10]

Let's not be selective in our reading of the holy Scriptures, rather recognise their divine origin and therefore the important contribution the entire canon makes in the unfolding story of God's purposes and His love.

In his choice of Joel 2:28-32, Peter anchors his first public sermon to a prophecy pointing to a future role the Holy Spirit would have, one which was now finding its fulfilment. It would involve His divine agency with humanity – a blend of communication and conviction leading to salvation:

"...God says, I will pour out my Spirit on all people...even on my servants, both men and women, I will pour out my Spirit ... And everyone who calls on the name of the Lord will be saved."[11]

From here onwards the Holy Spirit would have a much more visible and expansive ministry than had been seen before.

In Peter's dealings with the deception of Ananias[12] he makes clear that the lie told to the Holy Spirit was indeed a lie told to God Himself – thus ascribing to the Spirit both deity and personality (someone who could be lied to). In the confrontation with Sapphira shortly after, Peter frames the accusation as a conspiracy to *"test the Spirit of the Lord"[13]* – underlining the truth of the deity of the Holy Spirit by attributing to Him Lordship.

While the Acts narrative provides glimpses of the truth Peter held dear, his epistles give a fuller insight into the depth of his appreciation of the person and work of the Holy Spirit.

One of three – distinct in person and in purpose

The terms used at the beginning of his first letter are rich in their description of the work of the Holy Spirit, and how His work complements that of God the Father and God the Son in the united community that is our triune God. Sublime mystery!

"To God's elect, exiles scattered ... who have been chosen according to the foreknowledge of God the Father, through the sanctifying work of the Spirit, to be obedient to Jesus Christ and sprinkled with his blood: Grace and peace be yours in abundance."[14]

Peter is addressing his epistle to a distinguished group – distinguished not on the basis of their own merit or worthiness, but rather as objects of a divine calling, pre- arranged by the united persons of the Godhead, each playing a distinctive role in the process:

- Chosen by God the Father – according to His eternal foreknowledge.

- By the sanctifying work of the Holy Spirit – God's agent on earth living within those chosen, thereby making them distinctive.

- For obedience to Jesus Christ and sprinkled with His blood – a nod back to the Old Testament principle of the collective consecration of God's chosen people in readiness for specially ordained divine privilege and service.[15]

Sanctified for service

The context is the collective obedience of 'God's elect' to Jesus Christ – symbolised by the sprinkling of blood. Peter reiterates this point later in his epistle:

"you also, like living stones, are being built into a spiritual house to be a holy priesthood, offering spiritual sacrifices acceptable to God through Jesus Christ. ... you are a chosen people, a royal priesthood, a holy nation, God's special possession, that you may declare the praises of him who called you out of darkness into his wonderful light."[16]

By the Spirit's sanctifying work the elect are chosen, fitted together, made royal, made holy, and become the possession of God – fit for spiritual service in a spiritual house! Peter himself is an example of how, by God's amazing grace, ordinary folk can be transformed into men and women made distinctive and fit for divine service. However, to stop there is to miss Peter's main point.

The sanctification brought about by the Spirit finds its full application in saints being called into collective service together; living stones being built into a spiritual house – the only biblical context in which priests serve collectively as a priesthood – thus fulfilling the purpose intended by the Spirit in bringing about their sanctification. The challenge comes to us from Peter a little later in his epistle:

> *"If anyone serves, they should do so with the strength God provides, so that in all things God may be praised through Jesus Christ. To him be the glory and the power for ever and ever. Amen."[17]*

Elsewhere in his writings, Peter delights to broaden our appreciation of the person of the Holy Spirit and His work, by referring to Him in terms not expressed elsewhere. His reference to *"the Spirit of Christ"*,[18] pointing Old Testament prophets to the suffering of Christ, shows a divine unity in the knowledge of how the Son must suffer.[19] Similarly, it was *"the Spirit of glory"*[20] who would rest upon those saints who, because of their service to God, would become objects of ridicule and persecution. His ministry was to point them to the glory that would follow.

Our worthy aspiration

At a personal level, Peter's divinely revealed appreciation of the person and work of the Holy Spirit was translated into experience. He boldly stepped forward into practical service – availing himself of the Spirit's glorious enabling. The outcome: an unschooled, ordinary man[21], included in God's elect, taking his place in the spiritual house; as a priest, engaging in holy and royal priesthood service – all bound together in a glorious experience he describes as 'participating in the divine nature',[22] to the glory of the Lord Jesus both now and forever.[23] Our worthy aspiration!

References:

[1]Jn 1:41 [2]Jn 1:29 [3]Jn 1:15 NASB (1995) [4]Matt.3:11 [5]Jn 1:32 [6]Jn 1:33 Peter specifically recollected this when speaking to the Jerusalem 'circumcision party', revealing his new found conviction that this same gift of the Holy Spirit was being given to the Gentiles (Acts 11:15-17), and that this was the same experience as they had, not a kind of 'second blessing' as some might call it. [7]Acts 1:3 [8]Acts 1:16,20 [9]e.g. 2 Sam.23:2 [10]2 Pet.1:19-21 [11]Acts 2:17-21 [12]Acts 5:1-11 [13]Acts 5:9 [14]1 Pet.1:1-2 [15]Ex.24:6-8 [16]1 Pet.2:5,9 [17]1 Pet.4:11 [18]1 Pet.1:11 [19]c.f. Heb.9:14 [20]1 Pet.4:14 [21]Acts 4:13 [22]2 Pet.1:4 [23]2 Pet.3:18 Bible quotations from the NIV (2011).

Jesus Christ

A model for sacrifice

Lindsay Woods, Belfast, N. Ireland

"Walk in the way of love, just as Christ loved us and gave himself up for us as a fragrant offering and sacrifice to God." (Eph.5:2)

It's been the eternal purpose and desire of God to live – or walk – in an intimate relationship with men and women[1] created in His own image.[2] He found delight walking with Adam and Eve before they sinned and, subsequently, with righteous men like Enoch, Noah and Job.

God told His redeemed people Israel, that He would dwell – or walk – with them only if they brought sin offerings and also fragrant offerings[3] as thanksgiving for all that He had done for them in His grace and mercy. These fragrant offerings would please Him if they were brought from obedient and humble hearts.

Humble obedience has always been key to God's pleasure.[4] His Son exemplified that in His sinless life on earth. No one walked with God as He did,[5] kept the Law like He did;[6] no one could be so obedient as to receive God's commendation: *"This is my Son, whom I love; with him I am well pleased."*[7]

Christ's delight was to do the will of His Father throughout His life.[8] His ultimate sacrifice was to give up that life to His Father at Calvary as a fragrant offering,[9] wholly consumed like the burnt offering on the altar.[10] Christ's sacrificial love, first in total obedience to His God and Father and then towards all men and women, His friends, neighbours, and even His enemies,[11] beautifully encapsulated what sacrificial love should look like for us as His disciples.

On that night before His death at Calvary, Christ wanted to show His disciples the full extent of His love by assuming the role of a servant and getting down to wash their feet. In doing so, He set them and us an example of humble, selfless service motivated by love for God and love for each other.[12] Peter must surely have had memories of that night when, some years later, he wrote, *"All of you, clothe yourselves with humility toward one another."*[13]

What Christ did that night speaks to us so powerfully of who He was, what He had come to earth to accomplish, and what would be so pleasing to His Father in all His sinless and obedient life.

He, though being equal to God, emptied Himself by 'pouring' Himself into becoming also a man, a servant, obediently humbling Himself to die on a cross.[14] He had come not to be served but to serve and to give Himself, His life, for many.[15]

The life of Christ contrasted so sharply with that of the religious leaders in Israel. Their self-love and desire for prominence, rather than love for God and neighbour, served as their primary motivation. What mattered to them was status, rank and reputation.[16]

It should not be so for us. Christ is our model of sacrifice. He has shown us how we should live in every situation, no matter what position we might attain to in life. The greatest leaders are humble servants. We must demonstrate to our self-centred and celebrity- obsessed world that we follow Christ's example – that humble service is what pleases God and brings reward.[17]

Walking suggests a way of life. In walking with God in a way that pleases Him, we must: *"Walk in the way of love, just as Christ loved us and gave himself up for us as a fragrant offering and sacrifice to God."*[18]

Paul urges us to do just that, by offering our bodies as living sacrifices, wholly acceptable to God.[19] For this to happen there will need to be the ongoing transformation of our minds by the Spirit, so that we have the mind and attitude of Christ.[20] Such a life will please God, just as Christ's did.

References:
[1]Rev.21:3 [2]Gen.1:26-27 [3]Lev.1-3 [4]Mic.6:8 [5]Jn 8:29 [6]Matt.5:17; Rom.10:4 [7]Matt.3:17; 17:5 [8]Heb.10:5-7; Ps.40:6-8 [9]Eph.5:2 [10]Heb.9:14 [11]Jn 15:13-14; Rom.5:8,10; Col.1:21-22; [12]Jn 13:1-17 [13]1 Pet.5:5-6 [14]Phil.2:5-11 [15]Matt.20:28 [16]Matt.23:1-12 [17]Eph.6:7-8 [18]Eph.5:2 [19]Rom.12:1-3 [20]Phil.2:1-5 Bible quotations from the NIV (2011).

Losing sight of reality?

Geoff Hydon, Mount Forest, Canada

The company that owns the world's largest social media platform is changing its business name to Meta. Although meta is a prefix long used in English, what it means and why it is used are not always the same. For instance, it can mean 'beyond', or 'behind', or 'after', or 'changed'. Really, it is what comes after the prefix that often helps us understand why it used in a particular context. Thus, metadata refers to large scale data sets that may reveal greater insights about trends and developing concerns that are not apparent when looking at the detailed data one by one. There seems little doubt that the decision by Facebook's owners to invest multi-billions of dollars in 'metaverse' projects indicates why they have chosen their new name. But what is the metaverse?

Metaverse is a combination of meta and universe. It is intended to describe how technology can enable people to experience interactions not possible in the real physical universe. One aspect of the metaverse is the use of virtual reality to engage in games, or even business communications. Instead of interacting by being physically with other people, an electronic substitute is used, often called an avatar. The avatar may be given abilities to compete or communicate that are beyond the restrictions of normal life. By virtual reality, it is implied that something is very nearly, but not quite, the same as the real thing. As long as we don't forget what the reality is, a close substitute can sometimes be very helpful. But often it seems the objective of virtual reality is to move a person into a completely unreal world, where they can be absorbed in experiences that can never be physically realized. And it also absorbs lots of time!

So much for the scene-setting, though we shall only be tackling here the unexpected hazards, not the potential upsides. The metaverse may be a surprising development for you or me, but it is no surprise to God! The idea of people wanting to escape from the drudgery and unwelcome limitations of real human existence is not new. For millennia there have been some who would even try to enter a spirit world, to gain experiences, information or insights that others would not possess. God condemned such exploits, which often masked the intent of the evil adversary of God, Satan.[1] In a diabolical twist he may now induce people to exchange the real world for an imaginary one, and he would deceive people into thinking evil is fun, whereas being in strong control of your thinking is made to appear boring. Check out 2 Tim.3:13 or Tit.3:3 or Col.2:18-23 for starters to verify these issues.

In this overall context, the increasing use of hallucinogenic drugs and absorbing fantasy games is to be expected, and the wrong use of the metaverse could become just another enabling mechanism for the unwary.

This magazine attempts to give a biblical perspective, a Christian viewpoint, that addresses real-life concerns and interests. So, we must draw attention to Bible instruction like Peter's words: *"Therefore, preparing your minds for action, and being sober-minded, set your hopefully on the grace that will be brought to you at the revelation of Jesus Christ."[2]* Or again: *"Be sober-minded; be watchful. Your adversary the devil prowls around like a roaring lion, seeking someone to devour."[3]* Or the words of the Lord Jesus: *"But watch yourselves lest your hearts be weighed down with dissipation and drunkenness and cares of this life, and that day come upon you suddenly like a trap."[4]*

The battle is for the mind, and if we allow our attention to be devoted to the unreal but attractive challenges of 'augmented' or 'virtual' reality, we may find our headsets are robbing our heads of their proper purpose! Christians are not immune to the drawing power of imagery, that can entangle them again in unprofitable pursuits.[5] Entertaining ourselves in a virtual world cannot improve our usefulness in the real world, the world of people who need a Saviour to deliver them from eternal loss, not just losing in a forgettable game. Paul summarizes the real battlefield:

"... we are not waging war according to the flesh. For the weapons of our warfare are not of the flesh but have divine power to destroy strongholds. We destroy arguments and every lofty opinion raised against the knowledge of God, and take every thought captive to obey Christ."[6]

And if we are to succeed in taking the thoughts of others captive, we must start by carefully managing our own! Many more examples could be cited, all indicating Christians need to be mentally alert, living in the expectation they will soon stand before their maker. That may not leave us much time to spend in the metaverse!

References:
[1]See Deut.18:9-14 [2]1 Pet.1:13 [3]1 Pet.5:8 [4]Lk.21:34 [5]2 Pet.2:20 [6]2 Cor.10:3-5
Bible quotations from the ESV.

God's desire

From Sinai to Babylon
Michael Johnston, Kirkintilloch, Scotland

Birth of a nation

The story of the House of God so far has centred on individuals, chiefly Adam and Jacob. However, with the events of the Exodus, God was forming a nation to be his worshippers[1] in the same way that those individuals had beforehand. This nation would bear the hallmarks of God's salvation relationships: redeemed from slavery; baptised in water; established in covenant with blood; preserved by His strength; and responding in obedience and worship.

Meeting place

One thing that was particularly obvious in all these activities was the presence of God. From the beginning of their escape from Egypt, the pillar of cloud and fire was with them as a guide and a defence.[2] However, He would not permanently accompany them in this manner. Rather, during those nation-forming events at Sinai, God laid out plans that He would dwell among them in a sanctuary we call the Tabernacle.[3] Thereafter, when the people were not travelling, the cloud would remain on the Tabernacle as the sign of the presence of God among His people.[4]

The Tabernacle was also referred to as the Tent of Meeting (as was its prototype): people went to it when they wished to seek God. This could be for worship through the various kinds of sacrifices made there, but they also went to make requests in prayer. Moses was the most noteworthy of the people who spent time in prayer there, having the closest bond with God and thus coming away from the experiences with a shining face.[5]

This double purpose of the Tent of Meeting would be continued even once it was replaced with the permanently-located Temple. We see this particularly in the reign of Hezekiah: not only did he consider it the place of communal worship and re-instituted the Passover there, but also considered the Temple the place he was to go when he was in distress and seeking God's will.[6]

And it's this requirement to congregate that we see in the New Testament pattern for God's house, made up of churches of God.

For both worship and prayer, we do the same as God's Old Testament people: meeting together at an agreed place to congregate with our fellows at an appointed time. What was: *"[they] shall appear before the LORD your God at the place that he will choose... They shall not appear before the LORD empty-handed"*[7] is now *"When you come together [as a church], each one has a hymn, a lesson, a revelation, a tongue, or an interpretation."*[8]

A throne for God

During the early history of the Israelites, the most notable artefact in the Tabernacle was the Ark of the Covenant, a chest gilded inside and out that acted as the store for objects that were a testimony to God's relationship with the Israelites.[9] As a lid to the chest was a separate piece known as the 'mercy seat', which had worked into it the figures of bowed cherubim – mighty creatures that were the mark of God's throne.[10]

"And when Moses went into the tent of meeting to speak with the LORD, he heard the voice speaking to him from above the mercy seat that was on the ark of the testimony."[11]

The Ark of the Covenant went before the people of Israel across the Jordan and around Jericho; a symbol of God leading them in otherwise perilous situations. It came to rest with the Tabernacle being set up in Shiloh,[12] a central location within the land that was being given to the Israelites as an inheritance. This was due to the eventually appointed place, the city of Jerusalem, not being captured until after the death of Joshua.[13]

Source of blessing

The Old Testament law, particularly when summarized in Deuteronomy, was balanced on the matter of *a blessing and a curse*,[14] the execution of which depended on their faithfulness to God as opposed to idols and their continued dedication to Him in the matter of tithing. Both these things centred on the place of worship of the people: only God was to be worshipped, and only at the place of the name;[15] and the tithe was to be dedicated at that same place.[16]

The blessing that was given to the people when they observed these things was prosperity in the land that they had just entered into: *"[the LORD] will give the rain for your land in its season, the early rain and the later rain, that you may gather in your grain and your wine and your oil. And he will give grass in your fields for your livestock, and you shall eat and be full."*[17]

It is worth fortifying the point that the material nature of this blessing was assured in specifically the Old Testament; today our benefits and aims are found in Christ, being content in every circumstance as we rejoice in the blessings that we have in the heavenly places, which are chiefly enjoyed as we cleave to God both by being faithful in worship and a life of service.

An exalted house

Some time later, God announced His decision to make David the person who would represent Him in an exceptional manner among Israel's leaders, identifying with him and his capital: *"I have chosen Jerusalem that my name may be there, and I have chosen David to be over my people Israel."*[18] God provided the design for a new house to be built for Himself, enhancing its dimensions and those elements that identified it, such as the cherubim.[19] Therefore David and his son Solomon took on the responsibilities of preparing and building a Temple for God in Jerusalem.

God Himself no longer considered the Tabernacle as His own, and withdrew His glory from it in this period.[20] However, with the completion of the Temple, the glory of God returned During the time that the Tabernacle had rested at Shiloh, Eli's sons misused the Ark of the Covenant for military purposes and it was captured by the Philistines. It was understood that once more to be among His people, and the Temple became the primary symbol of that.

Psalms 120-134, the Songs of Ascents, are a collection of psalms that particularly wonder at the phenomenon of God having His house on earth. Pilgrims to the festivals in Jerusalem would sing them to one another as they climbed up towards Jerusalem and its Temple, fixing this association in the cultural mindset of the people as having God's presence among them and bringing them blessings.[21]

Protection

This link between God's name and the people's protection was preserved in the minds of those pilgrims: *"Our help is in the name of the LORD, who made heaven and earth."*[22]

We've noted the pillar of cloud protecting the Israelites as they fled from Pharaoh, and the presence of the Ark at Jericho guaranteeing victory there, but the protection of the nation God dwelt with is most clearly stated in retrospect, when He brought them back out of their exile in Babylon because of the impression it made on the other nations.[23] Therefore the continued existence of a son of David on the throne in Jerusalem was the ongoing proof that God was able to protect and preserve his people. Similarly, our security in Christ is assured by the continued presence of the Holy Spirit in our hearts.[24]

Privilege revoked

However, in the last days of the independent kingdom of Judah, God spoke through Jeremiah and announced that, because of their idolatry, He was abandoning Jerusalem in the same way that He had left Shiloh before.[25] And indeed, once His presence left the city, it was quickly destroyed and its treasures ransacked,[26] proving the protection and blessing God's presence was guaranteeing until that point. As generations before had sung: *"Unless the LORD builds the house, those who build it labor in vain." "Unless the LORD watches over the city, the watchman stays awake in vain."*[27]

References:
[1]Ex.19:5-6 [2]Ex.13:21; 14:19-20 [3]Ex.25:8-9 [4]Ex.40:34-38 [5]Ex.33:11; Ex.34:30,34-35 [6]Isa.37:1 [7]Deut.16:16 [8]1 Cor.14:26 [9]Ex.25:16; Heb.9:4 [10]cf. 2 Sam.6:2; Ezek.1:26; Rev.4:6 [11]Num.7:89 [12]Josh.18:1 [13]Judg.1:8 [14]Deut.11:26 [15]Deut.12:5 [16]Deut.26:2 [17]Deut.11:14-15; c.f. Ps.128 and Mal.3:8-12 [18]2 Chron.6:6 [19]1 Chron.28:19; 1 Kgs.6:23-28 [20]1 Sam.4:21 [21]Ps.132:15 [22]Ps.124:8; see also Ps.125 [23]Ezek.36:20-21 [24]2 Cor.1:21-22 [25]Jer.7:14; 26:6 [26]2 Kgs.25:9,13-16 [27]Ps.127:1

Bible quotations from the ESV.

Can you help me with this?

Born of a virgin

Peter Hickling, Cromer, England

Have you heard the expressions 'the virgin birth' or 'the immaculate conception' recently? Some people might think that they describe more or less the same thing, but in fact they are fundamentally different. If we look for authoritative answers on any subject we must agree on the authority that we accept; in this case, editors of Needed Truth believe that the Bible is the Word of God, and hence accept that its statements are definitive. The 'virgin birth' describes the fact that Jesus, the Christ, had no human father in Matthew's gospel[1] and in Luke.[2] How did Mary become pregnant? Matthew writes,

"Now the birth of Jesus Christ took place in this way. When his mother Mary had been betrothed to Joseph, before they came together she was found to be with child from the Holy Spirit. And her husband Joseph,…as he considered these things, behold, an angel of the Lord appeared to him in a dream, saying, "Joseph, son of David, do not fear to take Mary as your wife, for that which is conceived in her is from the Holy Spirit. …" All this took place to fulfil what the Lord had spoken by the prophet: "Behold, the virgin shall conceive and bear a son, and they shall call his name Immanuel" (which means, God with us). When Joseph woke from sleep, he did as the angel of the Lord commanded him: he took his wife, but knew her not until she had given birth to a son."[3]

This is corroborated by Luke's account:

"The angel Gabriel was sent from God … to a virgin betrothed to a man whose name was Joseph, of the house of David. And the virgin's name was Mary. And he came to her and said, "Greetings, O favoured one, the Lord is with you!"… And the angel said to her, "Do not be afraid, Mary, for you have found favour with God. And behold, you will conceive in your womb and bear a son, and you shall call his name Jesus. He will be great and will be called the Son of the Most High. …" And Mary said to the angel, "How will this be, since I am a virgin?" And the angel answered her, "The Holy Spirit will come upon you, and the power of the Most High will overshadow you; therefore the child to be born will be called holy – the Son of God."[4]

Notice in both of these passages that Mary and Joseph were afraid that they might be charged with having an illegitimate child, and Scripture carefully inserts 'before they came together' – this really was the holy Son of God. The fact of the virgin birth of Christ is embedded in the consciousness of most Christians, and only a few challenge it, because it is clearly taught by Scripture.

What about the 'immaculate conception? What does this mean? It is the doctrine that God preserved the virgin Mary from the taint of original sin from the moment she was conceived; it was defined as a dogma of the Roman Catholic Church in 1854 by Pope Pius on 8th December 1854 and is one of the four Marian dogmas of the Catholic Church, meaning that it is held to be a divinely revealed truth whose denial is heresy. We can see that there is a conflict here between the sources of authority accepted by different believers. On the one hand, if you accept that the Bible is definitive you will only accept what can be proved by it – this is our stance. On the other hand, you might accept a statement of a leader as to what is essential to salvation.

Scripture does reveal some things about Mary and shows us that she was very highly honoured to be chosen to be the mother of the Lord, but it does not support the four Marian dogmas. Compare the dogmas with Scripture:

Assertions	What the Bible says
The immaculate conception	Mary *found favour with God.* He favoured her; there is no suggestion that He favoured her because of any special virtue of her own.
Mary, mother of God	*The child to be born will be called holy – the Son of God.* It was this child that Mary bore – not the Godhead.
The perpetual virginity of Mary	Reference to the fact that he (Joseph) *knew her not until she had given birth to a son,* even *her firstborn son*[5] and mention of Jesus' 'brothers and sisters'.[6]
The bodily assumption of Mary to heaven	Scripture says nothing about this: it was stated as a dogma of the Roman Catholic church by Pope Pius XII in 1950.

References:
[1]Matt.1:18 [2]Lk.1:34 [3]Matt.1:18-25 [4]Lk.1:26-35 [5]Lk.2:7 [6]Matt.12:46

Bible quotations from the ESV.

Prioritising God's kingdom

An interview with Oscar Soko, Bangwe, Malawi

Oscar, tell us something about your background, please?

I was born on 5 May 1985, into a poor Malawian family with 7 siblings. My father was a security guard and resided in the Ndirande township within the city of Blantyre. He was a devoted Christian in the Ndirande assembly of the churches of God. In early 2000, he became relocated to his home village at Solomon in Ntcheu District following staff retrenchment at work. There, he was to play a big role as a pioneer leading to the planting of the church of God in 2003 at Solomon Village. My father mentored me on various aspects of the churches of God. He always reminded me to be exemplary to other young boys within the village so that he should not be ashamed. It was during this period, in 2002, when I was 15 years of age, that I received salvation, and was later added to the church of God in Ndirande (that was our nearest assembly when Malawi still had only two churches of God). I married Mercy Saidi in 2010 and we have 3 daughters.

What is your education and work background?

In 2003, I was considered by the church of God through Mark Imoukhuede (visiting overseer from Nigeria) for inclusion on the list for an education bursary. The church paid my school fees at primary, secondary and tertiary levels. I graduated with a Diploma in Clinical Medicine at Malawi College of Health Sciences in 2013. I secured a job in a Government hospital as a clinical officer and was posted to Nkhotakota District Hospital in 2014. Following my father's pioneering example, while there I contributed to the start-up of the Ndalama group that recently became the church of God at Ndalama.

In 2017, I secured a job in Banja la Tsongolo (a Family Planning clinic) and was posted to Bangwe in Blantyre. The salary was higher and I was offered a two years contract. I completed that and was offered another. The second contract, however, had some unethical conditions unfavourable to Christian healthcare providers. My conscience before the Lord forced me to terminate it, and I was jobless for two months. That was a difficult time indeed, but by the grace of God, the way opened up for me to rejoin the government hospital and I was posted to

Blantyre where I am still working currently.

Can you tell us something now of your spiritual development?

I was appointed as an overseer in 2020, and I received this call with joy. I believe it is better to work for the Lord than serving the interests of the world where money is taken as the first priority. The Bible clearly says: *"But seek first the kingdom of God and his righteousness, and all these things will be added to you."*[1] So, I left a job with a better salary and took one where the salary is low, in order to please God.

I also accepted an invitation to become a member of the Malawian Outreach Committee. With my ambition to see the work of God in churches of God spreading to other parts of Malawi including the north, also neighbouring Tanzania and Zambia, I'm very grateful for the opportunity to be part of this committee to help spread the message of the Gospel.

Most recently, I have become the District Correspondent of the new SECA District (South East and Central Africa) of Churches of God. I have thought that God may have called me into His service for this purpose. I'm very grateful to serve the Lord as a communication officer within the growing SECA district. My primary responsibility is to ensure proper communication channels are followed in SECA, so as to reflect its increasing maturity as a Fellowship district.

Lastly, but most importantly, I want to glorify the Lord in these opportunities. It's not about my personal desires, but rather a desire to be useful for the Lord, in measure as the Bible says, *"Before I formed you in the womb I knew you, and before you were born I consecrated you; I appointed you..."*[2]

References:
[1]Matt.6:33 [2]Jer.1:5
Bible quotations from the ESV.

The nations on our doorstep

David Woods, Manchester, England

Government data shows that 44,190 people applied for asylum in the UK the year ending September 2021.[1,2] Many have made long and dangerous journeys fleeing humanitarian crises: war, deprivation and persecution. News reports frequently tell heart-breaking stories of the loss of life during such perilous journeys. People are desperately seeking safety and security.

The Lord has brought asylum seekers to the Church of God in Manchester in the past two years. Our basic Google maps listing has resulted in five young Christian men attending the church's gatherings, all originally from Eritrea (where Christians who aren't from state-approved denominations face extreme persecution[3]).

The first three had just recently arrived in the UK and were temporarily housed in a hotel four miles from the church hall. Taking two buses, they (Biniam, Sintayehu and Yohannes) came to observe the Remembrance and would join our 'Zoom' sessions during lockdowns. COVID restrictions meant that it was difficult to develop meaningful relationships with them, but it was our joy to interact with them when we could, even though communication was sometimes difficult due to the language barrier. Full of faith in God, thankful for His protection and care, they asked for nothing and refused almost all assistance, content with what God had provided them with in the UK. We gave them English Bibles and second- hand mobile phones to improve their ability to connect with us. They've since been relocated to other towns in the North West of England. Knowing something of what they have escaped from, we continue to pray that their applications for asylum will be favourably considered by the UK Government.

Soon afterwards, another young man – again from Eritrea attended and requested a Bible. He was keen to find a hard-copy Bible in Amharic, his mother-tongue. After three weeks of online searching, we eventually found stock of one Amharic Bible. By the time the Bible arrived, Benjamin had obtained one from another source. But we held on to the Bible in the hope that more Eritreans might come along. We were becoming accustomed to having Eritreans visit us!

Amazingly, Habtu arrived at the church hall two weeks later, having found our listing on Google. He'd recently been relocated to an area near our hall. We learned that at a young age he and his mother had fled the persecution of Christians in Eritrea to live in neighbouring Sudan. And he spoke Amharic! What an amazing work of God; he gladly took our Amharic Bible and an English one too.

A baptised believer, Habtu continued to attend Manchester on Lord's Days and on Tuesday evenings for the church prayers. He expressed his desire to join with us and, after hearing his testimony, we were delighted to receive him into church fellowship on 2 January this year. Praise God!

Habtu is waiting for the asylum process to take its (long) course, praying that he will be granted leave to remain and then able to bring his wife and children, and his mother (still in the Sudan), to the UK. Sadly, due to difficulties during his journey, Habtu has lost contact with his family; we're praying that God will make a way for him to be able to contact his family again. Despite all he has been through he repeatedly says, "God is good … Jesus is love … God knows … every day is a happy day because of God."

Asylum seekers are not permitted to take paid employment; they receive a small subsistence payment from the UK Government in addition to their basic housing. Some, like Habtu, take the opportunity to gain some education (provided by the UK Government) to help them increase their confidence in English and maths. With many at a loose-end most days, maybe there is an opportunity for us to proactively engage, helping with basic language skills, for example?

A friend in Northern Ireland works with an organisation reaching out to Muslim asylum seekers in Belfast and reports the remarkable grace of God at work. Brothers and sisters in Glasgow and Armagh have similar experiences to speak of. The Lord sent His apostles to go and make disciples of all nations.[4] Today our Western cities are considered safe havens for the displaced 'nations' in all of their need. We can 'go' without having to travel very far at all.

References:

[1]https://www.gov.uk/government/statistics/immigration-statistics-year-ending- september-2021/how-many-people-do-we-grant-asylum-or-protection-to [2]During the same period 13,210 were granted asylum, or other forms of protection and resettlement. [3]Eritrea is number 6 on the Open Doors 'World Watch List' https://www.opendoorsuk.org/persecution/world-watch-list/eritrea/?ref=wwmap [4]Matt.28:19-20

From the Editors' desk

Issue 3 2022

I left the house this morning carrying today's calendar verse with me – *"we look not at the things which are seen, but at the things which are not seen; for the things which are seen are temporal, but the things which are not seen are eternal"* (2 Cor.4:18). This is part of a flow of thought that runs through much of the letter, contrasting the New Covenant (which Paul described as 'the ministry of the Spirit') with the Old (which he describes as the 'ministry of death') – the Old passing away, the New glorious and eternal. The Lord the Spirit leads us into the kind of living quoted above in 2 Corinthians 4:18. As we move in step with the Spirit, we increasingly learn the value of the unseen in our lives.

The role of the Spirit and appreciation of the unseen underpins much of the content of NT in this issue, as in others. It is the Spirit who leads us into the peace and justice of the Kingdom, who brings power to the preaching of the word and grows the activity of the churches around the world, who guides earnest prayer, who enables real forgiveness, and who leads us to humility and the washing of one another's feet. All of this and more is covered in the pages that follow – as well a deep dive into the Holy Spirit as seen in John's writing – majoring on the abundance of life that comes through Him.

It is my prayer that as you explore the articles here, the Spirit will guide you into the preciousness of looking at the things which are not seen.

Stephen

Step by step

Oscar Soko, Bangwe, Malawi

Paul addressed his two letters to the Corinthians to *"the church of God that is in/at Corinth"* as seen in the opening verses of each epistle. We will discuss step by step the benefits and characteristics of this group of people described as the Church of God. In what follows we will illustrate how the same features of the first Church of God at Jerusalem were again to be seen in the Church of God at Corinth. Repetition like this plainly shows us that this is a pattern to be followed everywhere until now. In following the steps below, we will draw all our main references from Paul's first letter to Corinth.

Step 1: To begin with, Paul said, they were *sanctified in Christ Jesus*, which means the believers were set apart in a special relationship with

Christ Jesus: *"you were sanctified, you were justified in the name of the Lord Jesus."*[1] A believer's former way of life is to be changed from the time of his or her acceptance of the Lord Jesus as Saviour: the time of their 'receiving the word'.[2] The Corinthians had certainly received and believed the Gospel.[3] They were now to live out the truth that they were *"called to be saints,*[4] or were 'saints by calling', as those having been sanctified *in the truth."*[5]

Step 2: 1 Corinthians 1:12-17 shows clearly that all of the church were baptized. Paul is thankful that it was not he personally who had performed the baptizing, for fear that any should put his name on a higher plane than that of Christ. The believers obeyed the commandment of the Lord[6] and the example of Acts 2:41 was given effect.

Step 3: The Church of God in Corinth was a well- defined entity, with an inside and an outside. So Paul instructed that those who were behaving sinfully were to be put out of the church (disciplined),[7] with the object of causing them to seek repentance, before they could be added back into the church. The principle of adding believers to the church is another of the matters highlighted in Acts 2:41 and this was, of course, equally practiced by the Corinthian church.

Step 4: Another feature of this group of disciples was their steadfast adherence to the teaching of the Apostles.[8] Paul received what he was teaching to them through direct revelation from Jesus Christ.[9] The local church at Corinth continued steadfastly in that Apostles' teaching.[10]

Step 5: Paul encouraged the church to maintain unity and togetherness. For example, there was no point in a brother speaking at that time in a tongue without an interpreter, if the whole church could not understand what was being said.[11] This would bring disunity and spoil church fellowship.[12] Also Paul instructed members of the church to resolve their differences among themselves. No one should take a brother/sister to any court of law, but rather resolve it within the church itself.[13]

Step 6: Another important characteristic for the church of God is steadfastness in the Breaking of bread.[14] All numbered in the church at Corinth came together to function as a church for this ordinance. They were encouraged to wait on one another so as to perform the breaking of bread together.[15] And they were also to avoid fleshly appetites.[16]

Step 7: Collective prayers were practised by the church.[17] Here, by the principle of 1 Corinthians 11:2-16 women should have their heads covered; and only men, with uncovered heads, should speak audibly in the church prayer meeting (and in thanksgiving and praise). Women should remain silent.[18]

A summary of seven important principles of a biblical church of God, seen in the first church at Jerusalem, and also seen in the Church of God at Corinth, and so may be inferred as found in every New Testament church of God:

1. received the word
2. were baptized
3. were added to the existing church
4. continued steadfastly in the Apostles' teaching
5. continued steadfastly in the fellowship
6. continued steadfastly in the breaking of bread
7. continued steadfastly in the prayers

Congregations of believers throughout the denominations fail to recognize the fact that the Faith of the Lord Jesus Christ, expressed in the teaching of the Apostles, clearly defines the basis of gathering for His disciples during the whole period from the Pentecost mentioned in Acts chapter two. Not following this pattern is surely a serious departure from the Faith.

References:
[1] 1 Cor.6:11 [2] Acts 2:41 [3] 1 Cor.15:1-8 [4] 1 Cor.1:2 [5] Jn 17:17 [6] Matt.28:19 [7] 1 Cor.5:13 NKJV [8] see Acts 2:42 [9] Gal.1:12; see 1 Cor.11:23 [10] 1 Cor.3:10-11; 4:17; 7:17 [11] 1 Cor.14:5-9 [12] 1 Cor.1:9-10 [13] 1 Cor.6:5-8 [14] 1 Cor.11:23-26 [15] 1 Cor.11:33 [16] 1 Cor.11:21,27 [17] 1 Cor.11:4-5; 14:14-16 [18] 1 Cor.14:34 [19] Jude 1:3 Bible quotations from the ESV.

Justice

Justice and God's kingdom
Stephen Hickling, Birmingham, England

Justice and peace

The first article in this series drew attention to the link, in both Old and New Testaments, between the words for 'justice' and 'righteousness'; the Scriptures also reveal a close connection between the words for 'justice' and 'peace'. At times those terms are used interchangeably. Viewed in parallel to justice, peace is an active rather than a passive thing; peace is something to be pursued rather than something that simply happens. So, in Psalm 85:10, "*righteousness and peace kiss each other*"; they go hand-in-hand in the blessed life of God's covenant people on earth, as they mirror the loyal love and faithfulness of the covenant God in heaven.[1] In Isaiah 32:17, we learn that "*the work of righteousness will be peace*,"[2] which implies that peace is more than a resulting state of tranquillity. Rather, peace is a deep commitment to the 'work' of justice. Peace in action is the pursuit of wholeness (*shalom*) in community through rightly-ordered, just relationships, established on the bedrock of God's unchanging standard of righteousness.

Peace and the kingdom

'Wholeness in community' is a legitimate definition of 'shalom' because the baseline for our understanding of God's peace is our triune God Himself, eternally existing in the perfectly-ordered, supremely harmonious 'community' of Father, Son and Holy Spirit. God's kingdom is, then, an extension of the blessings of this divine community to God's creation – to men and women who, according to the riches of God's mercy, are called into fellowship with Him to experience and to express His *shalom*.

God's covenants provide the framework of law and love in which relational *shalom* can be pursued and, indeed, guaranteed. This is why God's covenant is sometimes characterised as a 'covenant of peace'.[3] It is through the covenants that God promises His peace to His people,[4] whom He has gathered to Himself and set apart for His own glory – relational wholeness with God and with one another that proclaims the excellencies of God's name. The glory of God dwelling among His people, manifested in the glory cloud under the old covenant, is a confirmatory witness to the presence of divinely- ordained *shalom*.[5]

That is why God's house, the locus of the *shekinah* glory, is regarded as the focal point of God's peace.[6] God's kingdom, another term associated with His covenant, is the realm in which God's peace is both enjoyed and pursued by His covenant people as they serve Him in His house. Peace, together with righteousness and joy, is the very substance of God's kingdom,[7] a way of life that sacrifices individual preference for the edification of the community, making *"every effort to do what leads to peace."*[8]

Justice and the kingdom

Given the overlap we have observed between peace and the work of justice, we should expect the themes of justice and God's kingdom to be linked in the Scriptures. And, frequently, they are! There's an interplay between the eschatological reality of God's *shalom* and justice, to be enjoyed in their fullness in the millennial and then the eternal kingdom, and the current work of God's holy people in giving expression to that reality in kingdom life today.

In Psalm 82, we are transported to the unseen realm, to the highest court of justice, to witness God judging the spiritual rulers to whom He had entrusted the administration of the nations. The reason for God's scathing judgment upon them is their perversion of justice, their favouritism of the wicked and their neglect of the vulnerable in the kingdoms that had been entrusted to their care.[9]The abuse of power and the sad plight of the oppressed is a depressingly consistent theme throughout the kingdoms of human history right up to the present day. As Augustine observed: 'Justice being taken away, then, what are kingdoms but great robberies?'[10]

The true God, who delights in exercising justice on earth, was zealous to reveal a better way and, to that end, He required a nation of His own special possession. Indeed, it was for the sake of justice that, following the Babel event, God called Abraham and promised to make from him a nation – a nation and a kingdom unlike any other and through which all other nations on earth would be blessed. God said: *"For I have chosen him, that he may command his children and his household after him to keep the way of the LORD by doing righteousness and justice, so that the LORD may bring to Abraham what he has promised him."*[11] God's choice was for the purpose of working God's justice in order that God's blessings might come to the whole earth. That's the defining concept of the holy nation. *"But seek first his kingdom and his righteousness, and all these things will be given to you as well."*[12]

The work of justice, then, is not an optional extra for the people of God, but their essential priority. The pursuit of the kingdom, a commitment to experience the rule of God in a community life which both expresses God's *shalom* within its borders and extends it to the nations, is bound up with a passion for righteousness and justice. The proclamation of the gospel of the kingdom must be supported by the evidence of a people who hunger and thirst for justice in all their relationships, especially on behalf of the quartet of the vulnerable so dear to God's heart: the widow, the orphan, the immigrant and the poor.[13]

Justice and the king

Historians tell us that in the ancient Near East, the concept of divine justice was inextricably linked to the edict of the king, since human kings were regarded either as divine or divinely appointed. Justice, for many in the ancient Near East, was inseparable from law, which was brought into effect by royal pronouncement. It isn't hard to imagine how those invested with such power could abuse their position. The witness of the Old Testament stands in contrast to the customs of the ancient Near East in that the measure of righteousness for Israel was not the word of the king but the word of God, spoken through His prophets. Nonetheless, Israel's king would be central to the administration of justice among God's people in accordance with God's revealed standard of lawfulness.

A millennium after Abraham, the covenantal promise of blessing was refocused from the nation as a whole to one of the nation's great kings, to Solomon, in particular.14 Attributed to Solomon, Psalm 72 is a prayer for the king to be endowed with divine ability to judge righteously. The psalmist anticipates the blessings of prosperity and peace that flow from such a righteous rule, in which the oppressed are defended and the oppressor is crushed.

To some extent, the psalm may be descriptive of Solomon's reign. For, following her investigation of Solomon's splendour and glory, the Queen of Sheba praised Israel's God, saying: *"Because of the LORD's eternal love for Israel, he has made you king to maintain justice and righteousness".*[15] Surely, though, the Psalmist looked forward, as indeed the prophets did, to one far greater than Solomon, *"a King who will reign wisely and do what is right and just in the land"*,[16] a King who would reign on David's throne eternally, *"establishing and upholding it with justice and righteousness from that time on and forever."*[17] In this context, the title 'Prince of Peace'[18] should perhaps be understood as the 'Bringer of Justice'. Since the sceptre of His kingdom is a sceptre of justice,[19] there will be no end to the greatness of His kingdom and to the peace that accompanies the return of the King to this earth.[20]

The Lord Jesus Christ is the figure described in Isaiah 11:1-5, who will inaugurate His millennial kingdom, a just and peaceable kingdom in which *"the wolf will live with the lamb."*[21] After that 1,000-year reign, the curse of sin will be fully and finally removed, death itself will be thrown into the lake of fire, and the restoration of God's *shalom* will be complete. Though the King has already ascended the throne, we long for the day when His enemies will be made a footstool for His feet, the brokenness of injustice will be done away with, and abiding peace will reign in righteousness.[22] *"In keeping with his promise we are looking forward to a new heaven and a new earth, where righteousness dwells."*[23]

References:
[1]Ps.85:10-12; Matt.6:10 [2]Isa.32:17 NASB [3]Num.25:12; Ezek.34:25; 37:26 [4]Ps.85:8; Ps.29:11 [5]Ps.85:8-9 [6]Hag.2:7-9 [7]Rom.14:17 [8]Rom.14:19 [9]Ps.82:2-4 [10]Augustine of Hippo. 'The City of God', chapter 4. [11]Gen.18:19 ESV [12]Matt.6:33 [13]Zech.7:9-10 [14]Ps.72:17 [15]1 Kgs.10:9 [16]Jer.23:5 [17]Isa.9:7 [18]Isa.9:6 [19]Ps.45:6-7; 99:4; Heb.1:8-9 [20]Isa.9:7 [21]Isa.11:6 [22]Isa.60:17 [23]2 Pet.3:13
Bible quotations from the NIV (2011) unless otherwise stated.

Preparing for the Lord's return

Preach the word

Gareth Andrews, Belfast, N.Ireland

The last Bible letter that Paul wrote, imprisoned in chains and possibly shortly before his martyrdom in Rome, was written not to a church or churches but to his apprentice and protégé Timothy. The conclusion to Timothy, the culmination of his writings and encouragement and example to his beloved, true child in the faith[1] was this: ***preach the word***.

"I charge you in the presence of God and of Christ Jesus, who is to judge the living and the dead, and by his appearing and his kingdom: preach the word; be ready in season and out of season; reprove, rebuke, and exhort, with complete patience and teaching. For the time is coming when people will not endure sound teaching, but having itching ears they will accumulate for themselves teachers to suit their own passions..."[2]

Paul's solemn charge to Timothy was not merely a suggestion but the entrusting of a sincere, serious and urgent command, made in the presence of God and in anticipation and preparation for the Lord's return. This would entail working with fellow overseers in faithfully implementing Paul's counsel.

After spending years working in Ephesus himself, Paul had then asked Timothy to serve in the church of God in Ephesus, and charged him to address problems and divisiveness there by confronting and correcting certain teachers; those making confident but incorrect assertions. His first letter was to help equip Timothy and the church to aim for *"love that issues from a pure heart and a good conscience and a sincere faith."*[3] Paul encourages Timothy that the way to achieve this aim is to command and teach the words of faith and good doctrine, to set an example, and to devote himself to *"the public reading of scripture, to exhortation, to teaching."*[4] He is to immerse himself in these things. This second letter, probably written a few years later, continues to address these ongoing problems in the local church and the solution is still the same – preach the word.

Strengthened by the grace that is in Christ Jesus, Timothy is called by Paul not to be ashamed of the gospel, or his chains, but to look on the duty, dedication and diligence of the soldier, the athlete and the farmer, and ultimately to remember Jesus Christ as preached in Paul's gospel.

For His sake Paul may be suffering and bound in chains, but the word of God is not bound![5] Paul knew that from childhood Timothy was acquainted with the Word of God available at the time, the sacred writings of the Old Testament, *"able to make you wise for salvation through faith in Christ Jesus"*, and Paul goes on to say: *"All scripture is breathed out by God and profitable for teaching, for reproof, for correction, and for training in righteousness, that the man of God may be complete, equipped for every good work."*[6]

So, it's clear to see that the importance and efficacy of God's Word is fundamental and runs throughout the core of Paul's divinely-breathed advice to his dear child in the faith – and by extension also to each one of us today.

The context of the external and internal pressures that the Ephesian church was facing is similar to the pressures we face today. Paul said, *"understand this, that in the last days there will come times of difficulty,"*[7] and the ensuing list of traits is increasingly visible and evident. Those around us seem ever less willing to understand Scripture as the divinely inspired Word of God, and less tolerant of those who would preach it.

What about us, and our brothers and sisters? Do we still have the appetite to 'endure' and enjoy sound teaching for our hearts,[8] or do our ears itch for things that are more palatable, even if more insubstantial, lightweight and fleeting?

The solemn charge to preach the word is as important and urgent for us today as it was for Timothy nearly 2,000 years ago – to be immersed in it, to be prepared for the good times and the tough times; for scheduled meetings and unscheduled opportunities, to publicly proclaim the word boldly and unashamedly, not just repeating or conveying information but discerning and diagnosing the need for reproving, rebuking or exhorting, with complete patience and teaching.

References:
[1] 1 Tim.1:2, 2 Tim.1:2 [2] 2 Tim.4:1-3 [3] 1 Tim1:3-7 [4] 1 Tim.4:6,11,13 [5] 2 Tim.2:1-9 [6] 2 Tim.3:15-17 [7] 2 Tim.3:1 [8] Jer.15:16
Bible quotations from the ESV.

Paul's travel companions

Epaphras: the wrestler

Ross Osborne, Glasgow, Scotland

The Apostle Paul describes Epaphras as a *"beloved fellow servant ... a faithful minister of Christ"*[1] and *"a servant of Christ Jesus."*[2] Although Epaphras is only mentioned three times in the Bible, these glowing commendations mark him out as someone whose example Christians should follow.

When writing to the Colossians, Paul refers to Epaphras as *"one of you,"*[2] which indicates he was a resident of Colossae. Earlier in the letter, when Paul says that believers have a hope laid up for them in heaven,[3] he mentions that the Colossians learned this good news, which he calls the *"word of the truth"*, from Epaphras.[4] It's possible then that Epaphras was the one who first shared the gospel with people in Colossae and had a hand in planting the church there. Christians often have a great fondness and respect for the person who led them to put their faith in the Lord Jesus; this is how the Colossians must have felt about Epaphras.

Paul recognises that since that day when they first heard the message, the gospel had been *"bearing fruit and increasing."*[5] This growth and vibrancy in the Colossian church would have been due in part to the hard work of Epaphras as we see in Colossians 4:12. Epaphras was an encourager! He was someone who had grasped the truths of the Word of God, delighted in them and spent his time sharing them with others. He was concerned – in a good way – for the growth of disciples of the Lord Jesus. I'm very grateful that there have been many people who have sought to encourage me as a Christian. I trust you've had people who have done the same for you. The challenge comes, though, not only to recognise and appreciate the helpful encouragement of these men and women, but to also be such a person for others!

Epaphras' positive concern for these Christians was also expressed in his persistent prayers for them. In this, he is said to have worked hard[6] for the Colossians. Paul commended him for always struggling, or wrestling, on their behalf in his prayers.[2] The original Greek word used here can mean 'striving in warfare'. This shows just how earnest Epaphras was as he prayed for them. We sometimes describe people who respond to every situation with devoted prayer as 'prayer warriors'; Epaphras certainly would have to be considered to be one of those!

This striving in prayer that he exemplified seems to be exactly what Jesus taught His disciples to do when He *"told them a parable to the effect that they ought always to pray and not lose heart."*[7] Do we work hard in prayer for fellow believers?

In verse 13 we read that Epaphras not only prayed for those in his home church, but also for those in two neighbouring churches – he had concern for their spiritual growth too. Isn't it great that in our time, through prayer-mail and social media, we can have before us prayer requests from around the world! As well as praying for the needs and activities of our own church, we can pray for those of other churches and individuals. This has mutual benefit. It means people going through difficult times or carrying out some work for the Lord can feel uplifted by the knowledge that many people in many places are praying for them. It also results in those praying being reminded that we are part of a worldwide community, and that these really are our brothers and sisters in Christ, even though we are physically far apart.

But it wasn't just the quantity or range of Epaphras' prayers that was commended; it was also their quality. He prays *"that you may stand mature and fully assured in all the will of God."*[2] Often we feel we ought to pray for someone, but we don't know how. Praying that they would know and desire God's will is something we can always do, no matter the situation.

Epaphras' few mentions are linked with the success of the Colossian church; they show the power of thoughtful encouragement and earnest prayer, that we should strive in prayer and not lose heart.

References:

[1]Col.1:7 [2]Col.4:12 [3]Col.1:5 [4]Col.1:7 [5]Col.1:6 [6]Col.4:13 [7]Lk.18:1

Bible quotations from the ESV.

The Holy Spirit

Learning from John

James Needham, Birmingham, England

Of all new the New Testament writers, John is perhaps the most explicit in declaring the reasons for which he writes. His gospel account was written *"so that you may believe that Jesus is the Christ, the Son of God, and that by believing you may have life in his name"*;[1] his first epistle *"that you may know that you have eternal life"*;[2] and Revelation *"to show to his* (that is, the Lord Jesus') *servants the things that must soon take place."*[3] Underpinning each of these purposes is a desire to ensure John's readers enjoy the fullness that comes from assurance in the truth, and as we explore what John has to tell us about the person and work of the Holy Spirit, we find these three purposes repeated, for it is by the Spirit that we receive **the assurance of life**, the **abundance of life** and the heavenly **appeal to look forward** to the consummation of all things in God.

The assurance of life

The first reference to the Holy Spirit in John's writings is found in the account of the baptism of the Lord Jesus in the Jordan.[4] The significance of the Lord's baptism, and of the Spirit's appearance descending as a dove upon Him, is emphasised by its place in all four gospel accounts. *"This is he who came by water and blood,* John writes; *not by the water only but by the water and the blood. And the Spirit is the one who testifies."*[5] Here, John seems to look both to the beginning and the end of the Lord's earthly ministry—to His baptism in water and to the work of the cross. His baptism was the moment He was revealed to Israel as God's beloved Son[6] and the Lamb who had appeared to take away the sin of the world.[7] Submerged beneath the waters in a baptism of repentance, the sinless Saviour took the sinner's place and confirmed His unwavering commitment to fulfil at Calvary that eternal purpose of which His baptism was just a symbol – that He should suffer the waters of divine judgment, bearing the penalty for the sin of the world.

And so His unveiling was by water, but the fulfilment of His purpose required blood, for the commitment to death He made at the Jordan must be answered in the blood of Calvary's cross. The testimony of the Spirit that day in the river was in His descending from heaven as a dove to remain upon the Lord. The dove reminds us of the two birds Noah released from the ark as the floods abated. Initially, the dove returned to the ark, for she *"found no place to set her foot."*[8]

Unlike the raven, which would light on carrion, the dove would only rest where there was life. As the heavens parted and the Spirit descended, He found at last a man on whom He could remain, for *"in him was life, and the life was the light of men."*[9]

As the Spirit testified of the water, He testifies of the blood too. That testimony is universal, since it was *"through the eternal Spirit"* that the Lord Jesus offered Himself to God,[10] and *"in the Spirit"* that He was made alive in resurrection,[11] the powerful confirmation of His deity.[12] But it is intensely personal too, and it is that personal witness of the Spirit which the Lord described to Nicodemus in John 3. By physical birth, Nicodemus had received mortal life, but to enter God's kingdom required a spiritual rebirth into a new and eternal life.

Nicodemus had witnessed the signs the Lord Jesus had performed, but an intellectual appreciation of His power had to be answered in a heartfelt recognition of His person and His purpose, and that could only be accomplished through *"water and the Spirit."*[13] Here, as elsewhere in the New Testament, water may speak of the Word of God,[14] by which the Holy Spirit works in the heart of the sinner, bringing conviction of sin, righteousness and judgment,[15] and then, through the working of faith, rebirth to new life *"by the washing of regeneration and renewal of the Holy Spirit."*[16] And so, above all else, it's in the heart of the repentant sinner that the Spirit testifies to the blood, and to the power of its working in us who, according to grace, believe.

The abundance of life

This eternal life, received by means of the new birth, is an unlimited life, because the Spirit – who gives us both its assurance and its abundance – can be given without measure.[17] Twice in his gospel – in the scenes at Sychar's well and at the feast of tabernacles[18] – John records the Lord Jesus' promise to give living water to all who come to Him in faith, and that this water would well up within them and overflow, pouring out of their hearts in ceaseless supply. *"This he said about the Spirit,"*[18] John confirms, the image of the river drawing from the Psalms the assurance of abundant delight for those who drink from the waters of God.[19]

The essence of this abundant life is developed in John's first epistle. In chapter 2, he explains that God anoints with the Holy Spirit all who believe on the Lord Jesus at the time of their new birth.[20] It is an anointing for knowledge, an enablement to discern between that which is of God and that which denies Him, so that by the pure word of God abiding in us, we might know and obey the truth and so *"abide in the Son and in the Father"* in full enjoyment of the eternal life we have received.[21]

Abiding in God through obedience to His Word is transformative, because it is answered by His abiding in us,[22] and if God truly abides in us He will change us to bear the image of His Son.

Christ-likeness is demonstrable, of course, displayed in selfless love outworked in deed and in truth.[23] This transformation of the believer's heart is the lifelong work of the Spirit[24] who assures us of God's abiding presence by the development and outflowing of His gracious character in us.[25] So the abundance of eternal life wells up within us by the work of the Spirit, overflowing the limits of our mortal lives.

To those gathered in Jerusalem to remember Israel's abiding in makeshift booths,[26] the Lord spoke of an abundant satisfaction sourced from a far greater abiding; and to the Samaritan at the well, the promise of perpetual fulfilment developed into a description of a life of true worship, uncoupled from earthly identity and geography, a fulness flowing upwards in spirit and truth.[27] All of this is the Spirit's work, for *"it is the Spirit who gives life; the flesh is no help at all."*[28]

The appeal of the Spirit

At the end of our Bibles, although we find John exiled on Patmos on account of his testimony of Jesus,[29] we find the Spirit there too, still at work in the old man's heart. It is the Spirit who reveals to him the glory of the exalted Christ,[30] who carries him into heaven and extends his vision to witness things which must still come to pass.[31] Here He is the seven-fold Spirit before the throne,[32] which many associate with the profundity of His person described in Isaiah 11:2. In that fullness he bears witness to the churches, both of the here and now and of what still lies ahead. Of the present, because the Spirit knows our every circumstance, and He appeals to us to overcome error, stand fast for the truth and look to the reward.[33] And of the future, because He groans within us longing for the day when the sufferings of this present time are over and the sons of God are finally revealed.[34] Then at last His current work in us will be complete, as we reflect the Saviour whose image the Spirit yearns to form within us.[35] So John closes God's Word with his heart's desire in echo of the Spirit's glorious appeal: *"The Spirit and the Bride say, "Come" ... Amen. Come, Lord Jesus!"*[36]

References:
[1]Jn 20:31 [2]1 Jn 5:13 [3]Rev.1:1[4]Jn 1:29-34 [5]1 Jn 5:6 [6]Jn 1:31,34; Matt.3:17 [7]Jn 1:29 [8]Gen.8:9 [9]Jn 1:4; 1 Jn 1:1-2 [10]Heb.9:14 [11]1 Pet.3:18 NIV; Rom. 8:11[12]Rom.1:4 [13]Jn 3:5 [14]Eph.5:26 [15]Jn 16:8-11 [16]Tit.3:5 [17]Jn 3:34 [18]Jn 4:13-14; 7:37-39 [19]Ps.36:7-9; 65:9 [20]1 Jn 2:20-27; 2 Cor.1:21-22 [21]1 Jn 2:24-25 [22]1 Jn 3:24 [23]1 Jn 3:16-18 [24]2 Cor.3:18 [25]1 Jn 3:24; 4:12-13 [26]Lev.23:42-43; Jn 7:2,37 [27]Jn 4:23-24 [28]Jn 6:63 [29]Rev.1:9 [30]Rev.1:10-18 (for the purpose of this article we adopt the well-accepted view that Gk *pneuma* in these references means the Holy Spirit) [31]Rev.4:2; 17:3; 21:10 [32]Rev.4:5 [33]Rev.2:7,11,17,29; 3:6,13,22 [34]Rom.8:18-23 [35]1 Jn 3:2 [36]Rev.22:17,20
Bible quotations from the ESV unless stated otherwise.

Jesus Christ

A model for forgiveness
Stephen McCabe, Belfast, N.Ireland

The latter part of Ephesians 4 provides us with one of the clearest passages in the New Testament on spiritual transformation to Christlikeness. Paul first outlines the characteristics of the mind which turns in on itself (verses 17-19) – ultimately flowing from a hard heart[1] which consistently rejects the rule of God, and leads to a callousness that embraces sensuality and the practice of *every kind of impurity with greediness.*[2] What is being described is the outworking of a mind that is subordinate to the desires of the flesh or sinful nature. This leads to the shipwrecking of spiritual lives. Paul says: *You did not learn Christ in this way.*[3]

'Learning Christ' disrupts the darkened picture that Paul paints from verses 17-19, re- ordering lives under God. The spirit of the mind, instead of being darkened,1 is renewed,[4] so that the old self can be laid aside,[5] and the new self put on – a new self which, *"in the likeness of God, has been created in righteousness and holiness of the truth."*[6] Paul sets out what this looks like in practice from verses 25-32: speaking truth to one another, not letting anger lead us into sin, working with integrity so that we can share what we have if someone is in need, speaking in ways that will build others up, and not grieving the Holy Spirit of God through any callous behaviours. As the chapter closes, Paul focuses in on relational issues – the jettisoning of bitterness, wrath, anger, slander and malice from our lives.[7] These negative things are to be replaced by what Paul describes in the culmination of the passage: *"Be kind to one another, tender-hearted,* **forgiving each other, just as God in Christ has forgiven you.***"*[8]

This is Paul's climactic statement in Ephesians on what it is to 'learn Christ'. Paul had not invented this teaching – he had received it from the Lord Jesus. Paul's passage signposts us to the Lord's own teaching in Matthew 5-7 (a prime location for learning Christ). Here, anger and contempt – emotions that we may naturally tend toward when someone wrongs us, or indeed when we wrong someone else – are to be jettisoned, and replaced by an attitude that seeks reconciliation.[9] Consider too the Lord's model prayer, in which He teaches us to say to the Father, *"forgive us our debts, as we also have forgiven our debtors".*[10] The Lord is actively seeking to develop this attitude in us as His students – that, as we have been forgiven by God, we forgive others.

As we pray the Lord's model prayer, we are committing ourselves in prayer to being the kind of people who forgive debts of all kinds – not holding on to the bitterness of the past, or to old debts, or offences against us.

The Lord also describes a community of asking, seeking, and knocking, which is met by receiving, finding, and opening.[11] The culmination of this teaching is what we sometimes call 'the Golden Rule' – *"in everything, therefore, treat people the same way you want them to treat you."*[12] In this reciprocal community of love (with God at its centre), the matter of forgiving one another sits firmly under the 'everything' that the Lord Jesus speaks about.

Paul's command, by the Spirit, is to *"forgive one another– just as God in Christ has forgiven you."*[8] How has God, in Christ, forgiven me? On the basis of repentance, He has forgiven me out of His infinite stores of love.[13] He has forgiven me through Christ giving Himself up for me.[14] He has forgiven me because He was completely satisfied by Christ's sacrifice.[14] He has forgiven me, in Christ, because I am now *"in Christ"*, and there is no condemnation there.[15]

As we deal with one another, and **crucially flowing out of the radical transformation of character** outlined by Paul in the preceding verses, and by the Lord throughout the Sermon on the Mount, we are to forgive in the same way that God does – out of a mature character of Godly love, in the knowledge that the Lord's work at Calvary is complete and that God is completely satisfied, and knowing that we are united with our brother or sister *in Christ* where there is no condemnation.

The Lord's teaching on forgiveness led to Peter's question: *"How often shall my brother sin against me and I forgive him? Up to seven times?"*[16] The Lord's answer is astounding, and the revolutionary counterpoint to Lamech's ancient boast of vengeance.[17] *"I do not say to you, up to seven times, but up to seventy times seven."*[18] The legalist in us may proclaim that on the 491st time we should not forgive. Of course, that would be a wilful misinterpretation of the real teaching – that, just as Lamech stood in constant readiness to retaliate, so we are to be in a constant disposition to forgive our repentant brothers and sisters, just as God in Christ has forgiven us.

References:
[1]Eph.4:18 [2]Eph.4:19 [3]Eph.4:20 [4]Eph.4:23 [5]Eph.4:22 [6]Eph.4:24 [7]Eph.4:31 [8]Eph.4:32 [9]Matt.5:21-24 [10]Matt.6:12 [11]Matt.7:7-11 [12]Matt.7:12 [13]Eph.5:1-2 [14]Eph. 5:2 [15]Rom.8:1 [16]Matt.18:21 [17]Gen.4:24 [18]Matt.18:22
Bible quotations from the NASB.

An abundance of caution

Martin Jones, Hamilton, Canada

Isn't it fascinating how language develops? 'Social distancing' is now burned into our consciousness (thanks, COVID-19!), but other phrases become embedded without us really noticing. How about 'out of an abundance of caution'? It seems I'm tripping over it regularly as a justification for a certain course of action, by no means all COVID-related.

We used to refer to 'erring on the side of caution' – implying a slightly more conservative approach to something was regrettable but prudent, and tacitly acknowledging it might be proven wrong. But now we have a veritable plenitude of caution at our disposal, why not use it? The Canadian government at one point mandated that we social distance by 2 metres; why didn't I personally, out of an abundance of caution, triple it? Why not quadruple it?

There are a few good reasons why not:

1. it might imply we know better than the rule- makers,
2. it can paralyze us and make life unnecessarily difficult – caution isn't cost-free,
3. it's probably not any more effective in dealing with the reason for the rule,
4. it could distract us from focusing on more worthwhile actions,
5. it could belie a culture of fear, even a lack of faith and
6. where else do we draw the line if not at where the facts indicate?

I suspect our new catch-phrase would have been a favourite of the Pharisees, who not only took God's rules and added their own layers and interpretations onto them, but then imposed that heavy, even paralyzing, burden on others. Worse, this burden of outward righteousness merely concealed inward sin and took away focus from the weightier matters that were God's priority – including doing good on the Sabbath. Jesus condemned them and offered the people His yoke that was easy and a burden that was light, so they could live in freedom and not fear.[1]

A futile pharisaical kind of mindset is always a risk. Paul warned the Colossians,

"why...do you submit to [this world's] *rules: "Do not handle! Do not taste! Do not touch!"? These rules, which have to do with things that*

are all destined to perish with use, are based on merely human commands and teachings. Such regulations indeed have an appearance of wisdom...but they lack any value in restraining sensual indulgence."[2]

We should beware of an abundance of caution that has merely the appearance of wisdom and replaces walking by the Spirit, especially when we try to impose that caution on others.

However, don't walk away from this article thinking we can completely throw caution to the wind. A sign of a mature disciple is discerning what is just the right amount of caution in any situation; not an unmeasured abundance – more a measured allocation.

Paul warned the Ephesians, "*Be very careful, then, how you live – not as unwise but as wise.*"[3] The thought here is about gaining exact information with the highest level of accuracy and in strict adherence to the facts. The same word is used to describe the Magi's search for the baby Jesus[4] and Luke's research into Jesus' life[5] – in both cases, caution was called for to ensure something of vital importance wasn't carelessly missed. Indeed, any careful study of God's Word will highlight many things about which we need to exercise caution. The first epistle by John warns about false teaching: "*do not believe every spirit, but test the spirits to see whether they are from God, because many false prophets have gone out into the world.*"[6]

The false will appear in different culturally relevant guises across NT's global readership, some obvious and others much more subtle. Some purport to be of a religious origin[7] and others not,[8] but careful investigation and strict adherence to the facts of the Bible, rather than our emotions and what feels good, will help us to avoid being blown about by every wind of teaching.[9] Take, for example, the underlying teaching and practices of movements such as Hillsong and Bethel, the publishers of many of today's well-loved Christian songs, about which some Christian commentators have expressed concerns. Caution – careful listener investigation is advised!

References:
[1]Mk.3:1-6; Matt.23:23; 11:25-30 [2]Col.2:20-23 [3]Eph.5:15 [4]Matt.2:8 [5]Lk.1:3 [6]1 Jn 4:1 [7]Heb.13:9 [8]Col.2:8 [9]Eph.4:14
Bible quotations from the NIV (2011).

God's desire

From exile to the cross
Sam Jones, Aberkenfig, Wales

Throughout this series we have been considering the remarkable fact that one of God's desires is to dwell amongst His people. Perhaps even more remarkable is the fact that He has made the fulfilment of His desire dependent on His people's behaviour. If His people choose to live in obedience to His commandments, God's desire can be fulfilled;[1,2] if not, God, in His holiness, will forego the desire He has to dwell amongst them.

God's earthly dwelling destroyed

It is in those circumstances that we pick up from the previous article in this series. Disobedience and idolatry have led to the destruction of Jerusalem and Solomon's Temple at the hands of Nebuchadnezzar.[3] God's people have been exiled into Babylon, losing the opportunity of having Him dwell amongst them, along with the privilege of serving Him collectively.

The importance of obedience is something that we still need to be mindful of today. Although our salvation is assured,[4] our service within His house is conditional. The writer to the Hebrews tells us that "we *are His house **if** indeed we hold fast our confidence and our boasting in our hope.*"[5] The hope referred to here is the 'better hope' of Christ's high priestly ministry[6], which offers us access to God in the inner sanctuary.[7] It is a hope we are instructed to hold fast to[8] and not doing so could result in our position as God's house being lost.

God's earthly dwelling restored

Sadly, we often fail to hold fast. However, in such times we can remind ourselves that we have a gracious and loving God who is always willing to restore us if we repent. For the people of Israel, even before their disobedience led to destruction of Jerusalem, Jeremiah wrote: *"For thus says the LORD: When seventy years are completed for Babylon, I will visit you, and I will fulfill to you my promise and bring you back to this place."*[9]

God keeps His promises. After the Babylonian empire had fallen to Cyrus, king of Persia, a decree to allow God's people to return and *build Him a house at Jerusalem* was made.[10] The geographical location of this house is important to God – it was not to be built in Babylon.

Instead, a remnant of God's people obediently returned to Jerusalem to rebuild it in the exact location chosen for Solomon's temple,[11] using its foundations as a starting point.[12,13]Their obedience meant that God could once again make His desire to dwell among them a reality, and His people could again take up the collective service of His house. The priests were restored to their duties,[14] the people re- taught the Law of the Lord,[15,16] and the sacrificial system was re-established.[17]

Laying the foundation for the transition from a physical to a spiritual house

Although the restoration of service in the reconstructed temple was an important milestone in the history of His people, it was never God's long-term plan. When the Lord Jesus spoke to the woman at the well, He mentioned that there was to be a transition from worshiping in a particular place to worshipping *"in spirit and truth."*[18]

Our sinful nature had previously made 'true' worship impossible – the blood of animal sacrifices, offered by priests on the people's behalf, could only temporarily cover sin.[19] However, the blood of Christ's sacrifice on the cross cleanses those who put their faith In Him from all sin.[20] This opens up the way for us to have both a direct, personal relationship with God, who can now dwell within our cleansed bodies as the person of the Holy Spirit,[21] and to be involved in His collective service, being built together, as living stones aligned to the Lord Jesus as the chief cornerstone, into a spiritual house with the purpose of offering spiritual sacrifices.[22,23]

It was not long after meeting the woman that the Lord Jesus left the temple in Jerusalem for the final time. As He left He declared, *"your house is left to you desolate."*[24] The presence of God had left His physical house and, a few days later, as the Lord Jesus died on the cross, the veil of the temple, that was the means of access to its Most Holy Place where God had dwelt, was torn in two,[25] revealing the absence of God. The way into God's heavenly presence had now been opened up, the ground-work for this transition into a spiritual house laid.

References:
[1]Lev.26:3-12 [2]Ex.40:33-35 [3]2 Kgs.25:8-12 [4]Jn 10:28 [5]Heb.3:6 [6]Heb.7:19 [7]Heb.6:19- 20 [8]Heb.10:19-23 [9]Jer.29:10 [10]Ezra 1:2 [11]2 Sam.24:18,21 [12]Ezra 3:3 [13]Ezra 6:15 [14]Ezra 6:18 [15]Ezra 7:10 [16]Neh.8:1-8 [17]Neh.10:32-33 [18]Jn 4:21-23 [19]Heb.10:1-4 [20]1 Jn 1:7 [21]1 Cor.3:16-17 [22]Eph.2:18-22 [23]1 Pet.2:4-5 [24]Matt.23:38 [25]Matt.27:50-51
Bible quotations from the ESV.

Psalm 121

Pilgrims' progress
Colin Brooks, Wishaw, Scotland

This beautiful 121st psalm is found among the fifteen psalms (120-134) entitled Songs of Ascents. Pilgrims might sing them on their journey to Jerusalem. Three times in the year, all the males in Israel would appear before the Lord, accompanied on occasion by family members. We have the record of Elkanah with his wives, Hannah and Peninnah, accompanying him on such an occasion when the Tabernacle was at Shiloh.[1] We read of Joseph with Mary and the boy Jesus going up to the feast of the Passover with many others *"in the company."*[2]

This word 'ascent' has also been translated as 'degrees' or 'steps'. The pilgrims were going up to the great City, but it has also been suggested that the construction of each song itself is in the form of an ascent or increasing by degrees. Psalm 121 is an excellent example of this. There is a progression of thought within it.

The psalm was, without doubt, intended to be sung by pilgrims as they neared their destination after a long and arduous journey beset with dangers and trials. With all this behind them, the next psalm (122) gives us a flavour of just what it meant to the pilgrims to find themselves standing within the gates of Jerusalem, the City of Zion!

We, too, take our own spiritual journey as pilgrims, being reminded of those who seek another city that God has prepared for them.[3] The Psalm is also a confirmation of the unfailing care and protection of God for His people in every vicissitude of life.

I lift up my eyes to the hills (v.1). The hills, in stark contrast to the valley experiences, convey that sense of enduring strength and timelessness that might be considered a metaphor for the psalmist's own Almighty God.

My help comes from the LORD (v.2). Earthly sources of hope and comfort may fail, but our God cannot. Did David, like the psalmist here, have times of doubt and fear? He surely did, as we all do, but in each of his own psalms, whether they be of lament or near despair, he concluded with confidence in God's ability to meet his need and restore his joy.

He will not let your foot be moved (v.3). We imagine that pilgrims would pick their steps carefully on stony paths. This serves also as a figure of speech, as when the psalmist wrote: *But as for me, my feet were almost gone; my steps had well-nigh slipped.[4]*

What assurance the believer can have in the providential care of our heavenly Father who protects us from the Adversary and from our own weaknesses.

He who keeps Israel will neither slumber nor sleep (v.4). We can appreciate that, tired after the day's journey, the pilgrims would lie down to sleep as night fell, but not without first ensuring watchmen were in place to guard them from marauding thieves. However, even watchmen might fall asleep. The Lord does not promise us immunity from life's problems, but He does promise to keep us from stumbling.[5]

The LORD is your keeper (v.5) and ***the LORD will keep you*** (v.7). He protects the people from both the sun by day and the moon by night. Did He not do this for Israel as they journeyed to Canaan? The cloud by day and the fire by night to guide, but more than that, to provide shade from the scorching sun by day and at night the pillar of fire to give heat and warmth under the desert air of a cold moonlit night. What providential care by God for this apparently ill-equipped people as they left Egypt.

The LORD will keep your going out and your coming in (v.8). The Hebrew word that is used for 'keep' means 'guard'. The apostle Paul was persuaded that nothing in all creation *will be able to separate us from the love of God in Christ Jesus our Lord.[6]*

References:
[1]1 Sam.1:2-3 [2]Lk.2:41-44 RV [3]Heb.11:14-16 [4]Ps.73:2-3 RV [5]Jude 1:24
[6]Rom.8:38-39
Bible quotations from the ESV, unless stated otherwise.

Can you help me with this?

Washing feet

Geoff Hydon, Mount Forest, Canada

Are we supposed to wash each other's feet? Isn't that what the Lord Jesus commanded when He said: *"If I then, your Lord and Teacher, have washed your feet, you also ought to wash one another's feet."*[1]

Perhaps the briefest answer is to say that if we only kept that command using soap and water, we would have missed the point! It is helpful to note that the Lord Jesus went on to say: *"For I have given you an example, that you also should do just as I have done to you."*[2] Two key words in this last sentence may help us: 'example' and 'as'. Jesus was providing an illustration that is not limited to His one act. More broadly speaking, what the Lord Jesus did for His disciples was just one example of His amazing humility. The spotless Son of God from the throne of heaven knelt at their feet and washed off the dirt. Whatever their need for cleaner feet was, it pales in comparison to their need for more humility. Humility is an expression of meekness.

Some think that meekness is equivalent to weakness, but that is an error, for meekness is often best expressed by people in powerful positions when they refuse to exert their authority for their own advantage and instead exercise patient self-control for the benefit of others.

William Pitt, the British Prime Minister in the 18th century is reported to have said, "Unlimited power is apt to corrupt the minds of those who possess it".[3] Perhaps this statement led to the more familiar: 'Power tends to corrupt and absolute power corrupts absolutely.'[4] We may all have a tendency to let power go to our heads. We need to keep such urges under careful control. Of course, the Lord Jesus Christ had no such urge to use His power for selfish means, but as the perfect Man with absolute power He used it for the benefit of others. That was meekness indeed, and Paul therefore could do no better than to make his appeal to Corinthian Christians *"by the meekness and gentleness of Christ."*[5] So, we must do 'as' the Lord Jesus did; there should be a likeness between our attitude and His; we should follow His example of humility.

It is important to be clear that some commands of the Lord Jesus do require us to simply do what He did, not just do 'as' He did. For instance, when He took a loaf and then a cup of wine and told the disciples gathered with Him to in future, *"Do this ... in remembrance of Me"*[6] we can only truly keep that command by also breaking a loaf and taking a cup. He did not tell us His action was an example of a general principle that would permit wide variation in practice. Hence, we find the first church of God in Jerusalem faithfully followed His command; they *devoted themselves ... to the breaking of bread,*[7] and the Church of God in Troas did so too.[8]

Likewise, when Christ told the disciples to forgive those who repent, He really meant it, and our forgiveness must not be withheld according to our whim or displeasure; it must be whole- hearted and unceasing,[9] not just formal words. Paul clearly understood that command when he restated it to those in the Church of God in Ephesus.[10] The Lord's commands are not a menu to choose from, or vary according to our personal preference or cultural expectation. It is worth re-reading Mark 7:1-13 to see how easy, yet dangerous, it is to substitute what we want to do instead of what God intends and may indeed require. We must certainly have a reputation of being ready to do what is menial, and 1 Timothy 5:10 shows how commendable menial service to others is to the Lord. But are there people for whom we would find washing their feet easier than forgiving them for an offence? Let us not evade our responsibilities in either matter!

Some Christian groups do practise foot washing as a church ritual. It is not our aim here to condemn them for doing so. Rather, we would simply point out that following Christ's example is not satisfied by just the physical act of washing feet. We must look behind the action of the Lord Jesus to His attitude, and then ensure we do 'as' He did, constantly adopting a genuine attitude of humility without constraining the observance of His words by merely a sometimes inappropriate formality.

References:
[1]Jn 13:14 [2]Jn 13:15 [3]speech, House of Lords, 9 January 1770 [4]letter from Lord Acton to Bishop Mandell Creighton in 1887 [5]2 Cor.10:1 [6]1 Cor.11:24-25 [7]Acts 2:42 [8]Acts 20:5-7 [9]Matt.6:14-15; 18:21-35 [10]Eph.4:32-5:2
Bible quotations from the ESV.

God is faithful

An interview with Neville Coomer, Buckhaven, Scotland

Neville, would you share something of your background with our readers?

My father was a poultry farmer, breeding turkeys and chickens, guinea fowl, egg- collecting, haymaking and had a donkey for pulling a cart. He also kept 80 hives of bees and sold honey. At 18 years of age I was called up for National Service and went into the army's medical corps. I was sent to Hamburg in Germany and saw the devastation of wartime bombing of cities – no buildings standing and old people gathering scraps out of garbage bins.

One day I decided to go to a 'Garrison Church' in Altona. As the Germans came out of the building, we went in. We were worshipping the same God, but as soldiers we were fighting each other. Was the world mad? Nothing made sense. A few months later, I was de-mobbed, came home, and went to Sparsholt near Winchester for agricultural training. I met a girl at the Farm Institute and she told me about some gospel meetings. I cycled seven miles each way to hear the message. It was all too clear. I was a sinner[1] and needed to be saved. Unforgiven sinners would be punished. I had to believe that Jesus died for my sins, then all my sins would be forgiven.[2] I returned home one night, having trusted in Christ as my saviour. I was 21 years old.

After my studies were completed, I went to the Stoke Mandeville experimental poultry farm where later on I met my future wife, Helen, the resident veterinary surgeon. In due course, I accepted the post of poultry advisor for the whole of Scotland and this involved a great deal of travelling.

After nine years, I resigned in order to start my own poultry farm. This involved rearing chickens from a day old to what we called 'point of lay' and then selling them in various numbers to people from all over Scotland and the Outer Isles. By 1970, we were rearing 40,000 birds each year.

That's mostly so positive. Have you known difficulties too?

Yes, indeed. We experienced the disastrous effect of the 'notifiable disease' known as fowl pest. At first, there were only a few dead birds; but by the end of that same week, hundreds of birds were dying. The Ministry vet said that the laboratory would need to confirm it, but he knew it was fowl pest. That weekend the BBC interviewed us for their news slot.

We were instructed to kill all our birds. Saturday was the day. Grandpa Archibald took our three children to the 'District Gathering' (an event organised by the Churches of God featuring Bible talks, singing, quizzes, etc.) at Edinburgh, while my wife Helen and I set about the unenviable task of having to kill all our own birds, with these being, of course, our livelihood. By 4:00 pm we needed a break.

Suddenly, we both noticed that a calm came over us as we had a cup of tea. When Grandpa Archibald returned, he told us it was at that exact time that they'd had a wonderful prayer meeting on our behalf at Edinburgh. With our livelihood gone, things were going to have to change. We sold our Mark 9 Jaguar and replaced it with an old Morris Minor.

In what sense did you know God's help at that difficult time?

We had newly started up another regular event organised by the Churches of God in East Scotland known as the East Scotland District Class. Jim Johnston and I launched it about that time. It was Jim's idea to look at the book of Ruth, from which was drawn the message: 'stay in the land'. This had a tremendous effect on me. Before hearing this, we'd been thinking of moving to New Zealand. Friends also told us to stay, and we did. On reflection, it was the correct decision. We depended on God, took up a new line of business, and proved once again that God is faithful. When I look back 52 years, I can still see the grave of all those birds. This was our pandemic.

References:

[1]Rom.3:23 [2]Acts 16:30-31

100 years celebration

Eric Sampou, Port Harcourt, Nigeria

On the 26th December 2021 the Church of God in Badagry, Lagos, Nigeria was planted with sixteen saints comprising eleven sisters and five brothers. On Good Friday, 15 April 2022, 500 people joined in celebrating the 100 years of the churches of God in Africa (1921-2021), the celebrations being a year delayed due to Covid restrictions. 100 young people stayed on for a youth forum. 120 children were in a session with Ann Dada and her team.

Badagry planting

At the conference, Eric Sampou looked back over the Fellowship history of the Lord's work in Africa. He traced the early days of brethren in Africa, making reference to why the faithful and godly men separated from the Open Brethren. We stand today on the shoulders of these giants.

Tom Wallace set foot on African soil. See what God can do with a man! Then followed men and women who were prepared to die for Jesus Christ to bring His Gospel to Africans. We glance today at the success story through radio work reaching Liberia, Ghana, Malawi, Kenya, Mozambique, and Zimbabwe. There are 500 million Christ- followers in Africa, and our joint prayer is for the elect to be drawn to the Fellowship of Churches of God. Through Christ's cross and atoning death, God has blessed the elect with reconciliation, redemption, forgiveness, salvation and freedom. Some of the redeemed have been sanctified and brought into the house of God.

We recalled a remarkable century of service in Africa. We placed on record our gratitude to our gracious and merciful heavenly Father. Thankful too for the pioneering missionaries who gave their all as an offering to God. To all who supported by way of prayers and material gifts in the UK we give thanks. 100 years of help received from the Fellowship, is appreciated by Africans.

To our review of missionaries to Africa already published in the pages of this magazine over the preceding two years, we would now like to come to those whom we might style– for the purposes of this present report – as being 'the last UK 5.' We remember George Horne who made his first trip to Nigeria in 1930; and Rice Horne who made his first visit in 1949. These were followed in more recent times by Malcolm Macdonald, Alan Toms and Phil Brennan.

At the celebratory conference, Anthony Nemi also gave an address. His was entitled: 'Let us arise to advance our godly heritage' and was aimed at looking forward in the Lord's work in Africa. He asked: "What is the way forward?" After reading Haggai 2:1-9, Tony explored God's dealings with Israel in the days of Ezra and Zerubbabel.

The highlights he drew out were: the need to depend on the power of the Holy Spirit, to contend for the faith, and for prayer, fasting, repentance and confession; the requirement to obey and evangelize; the use of modern media for outreach; the training of youth and ministry to children; the financing of the work of the Kingdom.

We were all delighted to have John Black among us. Now over eighty, yet his thoughts and heart are always in Africa. He brought encouragement and goodwill messages from the Fellowship of Churches of God. He stressed the need for effective soul- winning to secure the future, the hope for the future invested in our youth, and the Spirit's need for 'clean vessels'.

Like Israel, there are still very large areas of the land to be possessed.

From the Editors' desk

Issue 4 2022

When you picked up this magazine, knowing that it was the principal printed organ of the Churches of God, what did you expect? Long or elaborate essays on little-known and obscure points of doctrine? If that's what you expected you would be disappointed. As you read you will see scriptural teaching, and also articles about current issues in the world today, and often reports about the establishment of new churches in India, Zimbabwe, the Philippines, Malawi and Mozambique. The Lord Jesus Himself instructed His disciples to *"Go therefore and make disciples of all nations, baptizing them in the name of the Father and of the Son and of the Holy Spirit, teaching them to observe all that I have commanded you. And behold, I am with you always, to the end of the age"[1]* and these are examples of what is happening now.

We are very grateful to see practical results, and it encourages us to see photographs of churches that we are unlikely to see in the flesh, but we look at what welds us all together: Paul wrote, *"So now faith, hope, and love abide, these three; but the greatest of these is love."[2]* A common faith means that we believe the same things, a common hope means that we share the same prospects, and a common attitude means that we value each other as all joined together 'in Christ'. The opposite is destructive: I have seen churches destroyed by the inability of their members to get on with each other. The Lord Jesus prayed, *"that they may all be one,"[3]* and it is our duty to seek for that in our lifetime.
Peter

References:
[1]Matt.28:19-20 [2]1 Cor.13:13 [3]Jn 17:21 ESV

Greater than Noah

Steve Peers, Aberkenfig, Wales

Noah lived when the world was extremely wicked: *"every inclination of the thoughts of the human heart was only evil all the time"*,[1] but not his. God was grieved that He had made the human race, but Noah walked faithfully with Him and he found favour. His life was to be spared when God flooded the earth in judgement. Through the building of an ark and faithfulness to God's word, Noah and his immediate family were saved when the floodwaters came. Water from above and below flooded the earth rapidly until all the high mountains were covered. For 40 consecutive days the ark was tossed to and fro by the ever-increasing flood.

At a much later time Peter and other disciples of Jesus were in a boat with a sleeping Lord during a storm. That storm was so violent that the experienced fishermen were convinced their lives were in danger. So how must Noah and his family have felt during the flood? What thoughts may have passed through their minds as they perhaps imagined friends and neighbours dying and were now floating in the flood waters? How did they cope with the constant battering of the waves and the fear it created? Even though they knew that the deluge part of their suffering was limited to 40 days and nights,[2] how would they know when one day ended and another began?

When the rain stopped and the waters subsided, Noah set foot on a new world. He was one of only eight people alive and his responsibilities were great. He needed to continue to live a faithful life before God – and before his own family so that they could follow his example; but, on a sad day, Noah became inebriated, was seen by his son Ham, and in this way contributed to the development once again of an evil world.

At another time when the world was wicked, there lived the Lord Jesus Christ, Son of God and Saviour. Noah was so named because his father anticipated that *"he will comfort us in the labour and painful toil of our hands caused by the ground the LORD has cursed."*[3] Another reading is that Noah would be the one to bring rest.[4] Through the Lord Jesus, who was much greater than Noah, those of us who are weary and burdened are given rest as we take on His yoke.[5]

He grew in wisdom and stature and found favour with God and man,[6] favour like that which had been bestowed on Noah all those years before.

As the Roman Empire spread its ugly tentacles, the world the Lord Jesus inhabited was cruel and He lived in it blamelessly, in a way that was satisfying to God His Father who at one time said, *"This is my Son, whom I love; with him I am well pleased."[7]* How could God not be pleased? This was both the perfect Son and perfect servant who delighted to do God's holy will. He once said, *"My food ... is to do the will of him who sent me and to finish his work."[8]*

The Lord Jesus was never asked to build an ark. There was no need to because of God's rainbow-signed promise that He would never again flood the earth. Instead of an ark, there was to be a cross upon which the Lord Jesus would hang, to bring life and salvation to all who follow Him. If he had not been in the protection of the ark, it could have been said by Noah that he had *"come into the deep waters; the floods engulf me[9]* and *all your waves and breakers have swept over me."[10]*

However, those scriptures find their true fulfilment in the death of the Saviour who passed through the billows of the storm of God's wrath. He had no ark to protect Him as that wrath was poured upon Him in all its ferociousness. He had no companions for all had forsaken Him. He had no rest as He faced God's wrath and the Satanic onslaught that came upon Him. Noah's 40 days and 40 nights in the ark in the worst of the deluge, however awful, were nothing compared to those few hours on the cross when the sinless Son of God was made to be the sin offering on our behalf.

The newness that came after the flood – the new world, the new beginning – was sadly spoiled, but in the Lord Jesus we have a newness that can never be spoiled: a new life that continues endlessly in the presence of the one who loved us and gave Himself for us.

References:
[1]Gen.6:5 [2]Gen.7:4 [3]Gen.5:29 [4]NASB95 [5]Matt.11:29 [6]Lk.2:52 [7]Matt.3:17 [8]Jn 4:34 [9]Ps.69:2 [10]Ps.42:7
Bible quotations from the NIV.

Justice

Justice and the love of God

David Woods, Manchester, England

Love is love?

For many in our world, love is the ultimate fix-all concept. The mantra 'Love is love' essentially means we're to love everyone regardless of race, gender, religion, behaviour and lifestyle. Loving tolerance is considered the great cure for humanity's ills. Yet those who repeat this great-sounding ideology will, at the same time, demand justice in an evil world where others act in destructive ways, especially when such damaging behaviour affects them personally. The notion of an all-accepting love quickly vanishes to be replaced by vengeful hatred in the pursuit of justice at all costs. It seems it's either love or justice, doesn't it? Fallen human ideologies that leave God out of the equation will always fail to achieve optimal outcomes. Such improperly defined human 'love' and human 'justice' are doomed to failure.

God is love and God is a righteous judge

When we stop to consider the real love and justice that are intrinsic aspects of God's essential being, we learn how it is possible for love and justice to co-exist in perfection. Unlike humans, God is the fullness of all His glorious attributes all the time. One aspect of God's character cannot, and does not, overwhelm another; He is infinitely perfect in all His eternal qualities. For God to lack any characteristic of His being, or to compromise His perfections, would be a denial of His own unique holiness.

The Bible tells us that *"God is love"*[1] while at the same time revealing Him as *"God is a righteous judge."*[2] As we read Scripture, we see the perfection of divine love operating fully and concurrently with the perfection of divine justice.

The waiting God

Let's explore this further by starting with a text from Isaiah:

"Therefore the LORD longs [lit. waits] *to be gracious to you, And therefore He waits on high to have compassion on you. For the LORD is a God of justice; How blessed are all those who long* [lit. wait] *for him."*[3]

God was speaking through the prophet Isaiah to the people of Jerusalem who were facing the approaching violence of the Assyrian army in the late 8th Century BC, during the time of Hezekiah's reign.

Despite Israel's history being littered with miraculous deliverances, the people of this generation were making an alliance with Egypt in the hope that they could stand together against the immense Assyrian threat; they were refusing to trust in 'the LORD' who had proven Himself repeatedly in the past. In patient mercy God invited Israel to renew their trust in Him, *"In repentance and rest you will be saved, In quietness and trust is your strength,"[4]* and Isaiah observed their response: *But you were not willing.[5]*

Such sinful rebellion requires God to intervene in judgment; He must uphold the honour of His own name. Yet, God will always remain faithful to His declared promises to rescue His people! He will wait for the right time to bring judgment and redemption, to reveal His love and justice.

Isaiah was reminding the rebels of God's patient compassion and their opportunity to repent and trust. We hear God's revelation of Himself to Moses at Sinai, *"The LORD, the LORD God, compassionate and merciful, slow to anger, and abounding in faithfulness and truth,"[6]* quoted by Jonah, earlier in the 8th Century BC, when he was disgusted at Yahweh's mercy towards the barbaric Assyrians! God is patient, and even the most wicked of people can repent and be saved. The rebels of Israel were likewise guilty, and needed to repent and trust!

Isaiah was also reminding the minority who did trust in God that He was waiting for His time when it would be appropriate to reveal His love and justice. The trusting minority were suffering deprivation because of the majority's rejection of God. Surely God must intervene soon, to remove the unbelievers and bring about His promises of peaceful prosperity? That's what they hoped for, but they were told to wait patiently for the waiting God, who would act according to His own sovereign purpose and will, in His own time.

God's redemption timetable

Throughout Scripture, in the salvation and redemption of His people, God acts according to His own purpose and timescale. We're told,

"...when the fullness of the time came, God sent His Son, born of a woman... so that he might redeem,[7] that while we were still helpless, at the right time Christ died for the ungodly[8] and that the man Christ Jesus who gave Himself as a ransom for all, the testimony given at the proper

time."[9]

You can't hurry love, especially when God is at work. God had an appointed time when His perfect justice and His eternal love would be displayed in the sending and giving of His Son. Jesus Christ lived to God's timetable, progressing towards 'His hour',[10] the eternal appointment when He would give Himself on the cross to be the Saviour of His people.

God's perfect justice and love proclaimed at the cross

God brought His holy judgment against believers' sin down on Jesus. He was the perfect man who never sinned and who now offered Himself as a substitute to bear His people's sin. As perfect man He voluntarily took the sin of others, since He had no sin of His own for which He must be judged. As the eternal Son of God, He was able to bear the infinite wrath of God against sin. He is therefore the only Saviour![11]

Paul writes about this in Romans 3:24-26, where he says,

"...the redemption which is in Christ Jesus, whom God displayed publicly as a propitiation in His blood through faith. This was to demonstrate His righteousness, because in God's merciful restraint He let the sins previously committed go unpunished; for the demonstration, that is, of His righteousness at the present time, so that He would be just and the justifier of the one who has faith in Jesus."

And all of this is because of the eternal love of God towards His people, chosen in Christ before the foundation of the world.[12] The death of Christ on the cross was the single greatest act of self-sacrificing love which, at the same time, satisfied God's wrath against His people's sin. God's love and justice co-exist at the cross, to be enjoyed by all who believe. Only through the cross is God able to forgive guilty sinners and bring them into the fullness of His love.

The judgement to come

For sinners who continue to rebel against God, eternal punitive justice awaits: *it is destined for people to die once, and after this comes judgement.*[13] Yet God waits patiently:

"God is now proclaiming to mankind that all people everywhere are to repent, because He has set a day on which He will judge the world in righteousness through a Man whom He has appointed."[14]

It is the responsibility of believers to speak of both God's love and God's justice so that some will be saved. To minimise God's justice and His judgement against sin in our conversations and preaching is to erode the Gospel of its power. Many happily speak about 'God is love' today, and only give one side of the story of the cross – "a wonderful act of sacrifice" – that denies the full reason for which Christ died.

Let's be careful to speak of *"righteousness, self-control, and the judgement to come"*[15] and take people to the cross where saving love is revealed in all of its eternal glory.

Leave room for the wrath of God

For His eternally-loved people, God will bring about a new heaven and new earth in which righteousness dwells, where there is no longer any sin – a place of eternal safety from all evil.[16] What a consummate and unending act of love!

Until then, the redeemed of the Lord are to continue to wait for Him, trusting that His promises of ultimate justice and love are certainly coming. There is a day when the evil that affects so many believers – through persecution, oppression and hardship – will be judged by the one with all power and authority. He will also usher into existence a whole new world order. As Isaiah said, *How blessed are all those who long* [lit. wait] *for Him.*[17]

Paul exhorted the believers in Rome: *Never repay evil for evil to anyone… Never take your own revenge, beloved, but leave room for the wrath of God, for it is written, 'VENGEANCE IS MINE, I WILL REPAY,' says the Lord.*[18] In the face of suffering and persecution we continue to trust in the God of love and justice *who works all things in accordance with the plan of His will,*[19] looking forward to final justice being served and the eternal presence of God being among His redeemed people in the new creation for eternity. Perfect justice and perfect love await!

References:
[1] 1 Jn 4:8 [2] Ps.7:11 [3] Isa.30:18 [4] Isa.30:15a [5] Isa.30:15b [6] Ex.34:6 [7] Gal.4:4-5 [8] Rom.5:6 [9] 1 Tim.2:5-6 [10] see Jn 2:4; 7:6,8,30; 8:20 [11] see Isa.53:4-12; 1 Pet.2:24; 1 Cor.15:3; Heb.9:28 [12] Eph.1:4 [13] Heb.9:27 [14] Acts 17:30-31 [15] see Acts 24:24-25 [16] 2 Pet.3:13; Rev.21-22 [17] Isa. 30:18d [18] Rom.12:17,19 [19] Eph.1:11 Bible quotations from the NASB (2020).

Preparing for the Lord's return

Live as citizens of heaven

Martin Jones, Hamilton, Canada

"our citizenship is in heaven, and from it we await a Saviour, the Lord Jesus Christ..." (Phil.3:20)

"Oh, they're too heavenly minded to be of any earthly use!" You might have heard this accusation against a Christian who's viewed as having their 'head in the clouds' and detached from the gritty reality of daily life. Assuming we're not talking about mere sanctimony,[1] you won't find a scripture that warns such an outcome could be a real possibility. But there's plenty said about the reverse – being too earthly minded to be of any heavenly use! Paul vividly describes believers like that: *"many ... walk as enemies of the cross of Christ. Their end is destruction, their god is their belly, and they glory in their shame, with minds set on earthly things."*[2] We don't know exactly what Paul was referring to, but evidently a preoccupation with worldly passions and pursuits was so totally destroying their useful earthly service that they were anti-ambassadors for the gospel.

The Apostle Peter warned about the same passions: *"Beloved, I urge you as sojourners and exiles to abstain from the passions of the flesh, which wage war against your soul."*[3] He was writing to stateless emigrants fleeing persecution; they knew first-hand about being 'sojourners' and 'exiles' – non-citizens dwelling temporarily in a foreign land they didn't belong to and were simply passing through. But they were now being urged to consider themselves to be spiritual sojourners and exiles too – passing through this foreign world to somewhere better and to where they truly belonged. They needed that heavenly mindset both to keep them heaven-bound in their outlook, not earth-bound, and to be of earthly use to God.

Abraham had the same heavenly mindset as a stranger and exile on the earth[4] – which is remarkable considering he was dwelling with his wife Sarah in a land God had promised to him and his descendants as an inheritance. Sarah finally passed away at the ripe old age of 127[5] so there had presumably been plenty of time for Abraham to purchase a burial plot. Curiously, he left it until the last minute to acquire one in

Machpelah.

Far from this being careless, disorganized or a mark of disrespect, he was simply not in the business of acquiring property or putting down roots - he lived in tents, after all - because (as Hebrews insightfully reveals to us) he was just passing through this foreign land to a homeland, a better country, a heavenly one.[6] His sense of heavenly citizenship couldn't help but impact his earthly actions.

Paul reminded the Philippians that their citizenship (Greek: *politeuma*) was in heaven.[7] Although living as a citizen of the Roman colony of Philippi brought great rights and benefits (ranging from imperial protection to tax breaks) the saints had to resist the temptation to mentally put down roots there and immerse themselves in its social, political and economic life, especially in view of the soon expected return of the Lord and the transformation of their earthly bodies to heavenly ones. Their heavenly citizenship entitled them to many spiritual benefits in the world they were merely passing through, as well as some important responsibilities for earthly usefulness.

Paul commanded the Philippians: *"let your manner of life [politeuomai – life as a citizen] be worthy of the gospel of Christ."*[8] A high and heavenly standard was and is expected, and we're back to the thought of an ambassador called to impeccably represent both their monarch and homeland abroad. Paul testified before the Jewish Council that he had met the standard: *"Brothers, I have lived my life [politeuomai – life as a citizen] before God in all good conscience up to this day."*[9] This was why he could confidently say, *"Brothers, join in imitating me, and keep your eyes on those who walk according to the example you have in us."*[10] To successfully do this we must, by faith like Abraham, *"look not to the things that are seen but to the things that are unseen. For the things that are seen are transient, but the things that are unseen are eternal."*[11]

References:
[1]the action or practice of acting as if one were morally superior to other people
[2]Phil.3:18-19 [3]1 Pet.2:11 [4]Heb.11:13 [5]Gen.23:1, 4 [6]Heb.11:9-10, 14,16
[7]Phil.3:20 [8]Phil.1:27 [9]Acts 23:1 [10]Phil.3:17 [11]2 Cor.4:18

Bible quotations from the ESV.

Paul's travel companions

Demas: the forsaker

Ben Jones, Hamilton, Canada

There are three occasions in Scripture that we hear about Demas, one of Paul's companions: once in Colossians, once in Philemon, and once in 2 Timothy. When writing to the Colossians, Demas was recognized by Paul as one of his co-workers, along with Luke, serving together. From Colossians 4:18, we learn that Paul is imprisoned at this point, and he appears to greatly appreciate the company and support of those who are with him – including Demas. Similar thoughts are expressed in Philemon, probably written around the same time. At this point it appears that Demas is a valued friend and supporter of Paul in his imprisonment.

In his epistle to Timothy, Paul tells us that he is bound in chains once more,[1] and both tradition and scholarly interpretation leads us to conclude that this is a different, later imprisonment. Now though, many of Paul's companions have left him, leaving only Luke.[2] Paul's comment that Demas is *"in love with this present world"* indicates that Demas left against Paul's wishes, and had not been sent to Thessalonica as part of his service. While this could be taken to mean that he abandoned the Gospel, it is perhaps more likely that, when faced again with imprisonment and possible torture and death, Demas had prioritised his comfort and own safety over his service with Paul and his work for the Gospel.

If we assume that Demas simply wanted to avoid imprisonment and death, then Paul's condemnation seems to be very severe. Paul himself admits that not everyone is called to the same level of sacrifice for the Gospel as he. When instructing the Corinthians, Paul revealed that he wished that all could be unmarried as he was, and therefore more able to devote their time to the spread of the Gospel.[3] However, he acknowledged that *"each has his own gift from God, one of one kind and one of another."*

Similarly, Paul reveals that the qualifications for both deacons and overseers are not conditional on them being celibate, but that they are able to manage their households and families well,[4] demonstrating the importance and value of those who manage households and bring up children in the Lord's teaching.

Despite this, Paul felt that this departure was worthy of note. Based on his earlier testimony, it appears that Demas was aligned with Paul in his commitment to the work of the Gospel – facing imprisonment alongside him and committing to be by the apostle's side. However, by the time of his second imprisonment, Demas is not just leaving Paul behind, but he is abandoning his previous commitments and promises.

We can certainly picture scenarios where we might forgive Demas for his decision, but the fact remains that he reneged on his commitments to the apostle. This desertion is contrary to the Lord Jesus' own teachings about the importance of staying true to our word[5] and so, regardless of the justification, Demas' abandonment is still perceived negatively, and ultimately tarnishes the reputation of one who had previously been listed among the faithful fellow-workers.

We can speculate as to the damage that Demas' departure had on those who had been taught, encouraged, or even corrected by him during his service with Paul. Imagine hearing that the man who had taught you about the Saviour had abandoned Paul in his time of need? What kind of damage would that do to the faith and confidence of a new believer? In deserting Paul, Demas tarnished not only his future witness, but his prior witness.

The inclusion of Demas in the Scriptures reveals to us the importance of our continual witness and service. Moments of weakness or lapses in judgment can be very damaging to a disciple's witness. We are called not just to run a leg of a relay race, but to run a full race,[6] and we must be aware that stumbles along the way may not just trip ourselves but others around us as well. As disciples we have not been called to an easy life – in fact, the Lord Jesus explicitly warns His disciples that they will be hated by the world.[7] As a result, our support for, and commitments to, one another must be taken very seriously. To do otherwise is to jeopardize the integrity of our witness and service.

References:
[1]2 Tim.2:9 [2]2 Tim.4:10-11 [3]1 Cor.7:7-8 [4]1 Tim.3:4-6 [5]Matt.5:37 [6]Heb.12:1-2 [7]Jn 15:18-19
Bible quotations from the ESV.

The Holy Spirit

Learning from Jesus

Richard Hutchinson, Vancouver, Canada

Most of what the Lord Jesus said to His disciples about the Holy Spirit is found in chapters 14-16 of John's gospel, after Jesus has washed the feet of the disciples in the 'upper room'. The Cross is looming large in the mind of Jesus and yet, despite Jesus speaking quite frankly about it, the disciples remain resolutely ignorant of what the next 24 hours is going to bring. As Judas melts into the night on his dark purpose, Jesus speaks to the remaining disciples about how He is only with them a little longer,[1] and is going somewhere they cannot follow.

Chapter 14 begins with the reassurance, *"Let not your hearts be troubled. Believe in God, believe also in me."*[2] Jesus is concerned about His little flock, knowing what lies ahead, knowing He has to leave them – and so along with the promise that He will come back to take them to be with Him, the 'good shepherd' also promises that another 'Helper' will come from the Father[3] – a *parakletos*, one called to stand beside them.[4]

Over the next couple of chapters in John's gospel Jesus encourages His disciples that in His absence they must abide in Him,[5] keep His commandments,[6] love one another,[7] all while expecting trouble from the world and enduring through it.[8] It is into this context that Jesus repeats the encouragement of the Father sending the Holy Spirit to be all that He Himself has been to them and more. All of those instructions would require the Spirit's help.

The disciples had been following Jesus for between two and three years, drinking in His wisdom and teaching, witnessing miracles of healing and creative power, seeing firsthand a life lived in holy, loving grace and compassion towards others. The experience must have been absolutely thrilling, but now this singular person was going away from them. Jesus understood that the revelation had meant *"sorrow has filled your heart, "*[9] but He insists that His leaving and the Spirit's coming in His place is to their advantage.[10] Dare we ask, how so?

First of all, the Holy Spirit would be with them forever. With Jesus having just broken the news that He Himself had to go, there was comfort here for His followers. The Spirit of truth was there to stay,[11] and what's more He was no stranger to them: *"You know him, for he dwells with you and will be in you."*[12]

The Spirit had been interacting with them during their time with Jesus, opening them up spiritually to understand His teaching and revealing truth to them, which we see when Peter identifies Jesus as *"the Christ, the Son of the Living God"* and Jesus tells him, *"flesh and blood has not revealed this to you, but my Father who is in heaven."*[13]

The Spirit had convicted Peter, revealing heavenly truth to him, and how much more would Peter and his fellow disciples understand when that same Spirit soon dwelt within them.

What's more, the benefit was not just that the Spirit Himself would be present with them, but that through His abiding in them, they would perceive the ongoing presence of Christ with them also. *"Yet a little while and the world sees me no more, but you see me."*[14] Many translations for readability render the verb 'see' as future tense – 'will see' – but the verb is present tense in Greek. Jesus wasn't speaking of them seeing Him at His return to the earth, but rather He is telling them they will continue to see Him and that He would manifest Himself to those who love Him.[15] Judas (not Iscariot) understandably questions how Jesus would manifest Himself to them but not to the world, and Jesus says that for those who love Him and keep His commandments, *"we* [Jesus and His Father] *will come to him and make our home with him."*[16] This is a beautiful example of the intimacy of the triune God, that when we are indwelt by the Holy Spirit, the Father and Son are both abiding there also.

Beyond conveying the continued presence of their Lord, the Holy Spirit would also continue to teach the disciples, bringing all the words of Jesus to their minds again, teaching them *"all things"*.[17] In Jesus' absence there would be no deficit in what they could learn of God; in fact, the indwelling of the Spirit would only enhance their capability to grasp the deepest truths of God's eternal counsels, as Paul identifies in 1 Corinthians 2:10-16.

Jesus had more to teach them than He'd had time to in the few years they'd followed Him. *"I still have many things to say to you, but you cannot bear them now. When the Spirit of truth comes He will guide you into all the truth."*[18] The Holy Spirit was coming to continue the work of Jesus in speaking truth into their hearts, and He would teach them 'all things', guide them into 'all truth'. The disciples weren't being disadvantaged in any way.

In all of this, the Spirit would ultimately glorify Jesus in their hearts, continually seeking to generate the reverential awe that comes from those who behold the Lord. The Spirit takes what belongs to Christ and declares it to His disciples,[19] and Jesus clarifies *"all that the Father has is mine."*[20]

This is not about declaring Jesus' teaching any more, but proclaiming to us His exalted position, the radiance of His very being as He is seated at God's right hand. All authority and power is His by His Father's will, and the Spirit wants us to know the fullness of the glory of our risen and exalted Lord.

Throughout this article the focus has been on the Spirit coming to the disciples after Jesus left, but of course the encouragement they drew from the Lord's promise of another helper should be all the more precious to us who did not see the Lord face to face. By the Lord's own words we are not disadvantaged, because the Lord the Spirit has indwelt us also and blessed us in the same way – revealing Christ to us in the Word, teaching us all things, filling our hearts with the presence of the Lord, testifying to the glory of the exalted Jesus, and fulfilling His convicting work through us.[21]

Small wonder, then, to hear the Lord describe the bountiful nature of the Spirit's presence within human hearts: *"If anyone thirsts, let him come to me and drink. Whoever believes in me, as the Scripture has said, 'Out of his heart will flow rivers of living water.'" Now this he said about the Spirit, whom those who believed in him were to receive.*[23] How thankful we should be that we have received such a Helper.

References:
[1]Jn 13:33 [2]Jn 14:1 [3]Jn 14:16 [4]W. Mounce: "one called or sent for to assist another; an advocate, one who pleads the cause of another; one present to render various beneficial service". The Greek word appears five times in NT - four times referring to the Holy Spirit in John 14-16, and once in 1 Jn 2:1 in reference to the ascended Lord Jesus. See https://www.billmounce.com/greek-dictionary/parakletos [5]Jn 15:1-11 [6]Jn 15:10,14 [7]Jn 15:12-17 [8]Jn 15:18-25 [9]Jn 16:6 [10]Jn 16:7 [11]Jn 14:16 [12]Jn 14:17 [13]Matt.16:16-17 [14]Jn 14:19 - Beroean Literal Translation [15]Jn 14:21 [16]Jn 14:23 [17]Jn 14:26 [18]Jn 16:12-13 [19]Jn 16:14 [20]Jn 16:15 [21]Jn 16:8 [22] Jn 7:37-39
Bible quotations from the ESV.

Jesus Christ

A model for love

Phil Brennan, Buxton, England

"Husbands, love your wives, just as Christ also loved the church ..."
(Eph.5:25)

The words, 'just as Christ' have a deeply stirring effect on disciples of
the Lord Jesus. This is the fourth article in a series on characteristics of
Christ, looking at Bible references that tell of the unfathomable depth of
His perfect righteousness and of what is required of us as His disciples.

Our present text is found within the context of Christian relationships
and in particular the relationship of husband and wife. But within that
context of practical teaching, we find the most wonderful, exalted
statement about the relationship between the Lord Jesus and His church.

The love of Christ ought always to astound us. Scripture clearly teaches
that we did not deserve such love. It was while we were sinners that
Christ showed His love in dying for us.[1] The sinner-state, abhorrent in
the sight of God, is graphically described in Ezekiel[2] which, though
being a description of Israel, is applicable to us when we were unsaved.
We were not loved because we were lovable – He loved the unlovely.

In a depraved world that has debased the concept of 'love', it is
necessary to ask what its true nature is. The answer is found in i) the
distinction of the word used in Ephesians 5:25, and ii) the
demonstration of Christ's love for the church.

The word used is *agapao* in the original Greek text. Here it is used of
the love of God: His unmitigated love for us, and the outworking of that
in the lives of those who have been born again to love as they could
never love before. Over and above what is possible to the natural man,
there comes the love of God, described by Paul in 1 Corinthians 13[3] and
available to us through the indwelling Spirit of God.[4]

It is often pointed out that among the several Classical Greek words
for 'love', the following three are prominent:
- *eros* (not found in the New Testament) describes an attraction of
  the flesh often characterised by selfishness.
- *phileo* means 'to be fond of' and describes deep friendship, seen
  in the showing of affection, hospitality, etc.
- Though *phileo* is used of God,[5] *agapao* is the word chosen when

the essential character of God is being described.[6]

In the life of the disciple of Jesus, note how such love takes control of the first (*eros*). Recognising natural attraction, it keeps it firmly in place: it embellishes the second (*phileo*), recognising the importance of fondness that cements the bond formed by similar interests, etc. Then, 'the fuller element comes in: and it lifts up the other two, it sanctifies them, it gives a glory to them, it gives a splendour to them.'[7]

How is such love demonstrated? Our text says, *"Christ ... loved the church and gave Himself up for her."* This is the complete antithesis of selfish self-seeking; it is the epitome of selflessness, and it is sacrificial. Matthew's Gospel may give a beautiful picture of Christ's love for the church[8] if the merchant seeking beautiful pearls is viewed as a picture of Christ. In that parable, the merchant gives all he has in order to purchase the pearl. Just as the Father *"did not spare His own Son, but delivered Him over for us all,"*[9] so the Son gave Himself... *"having loved His own ... He loved them unto the uttermost."*[10]

The context sets the standard for Christian marriage. Little wonder then that the requirements of an overseer include the stipulation, *husband of one wife.*[11] If a man is being considered for leadership among God's people, it is reasonable to ask how he treats his wife. But the application is surely wider. This is how we who are the church the body of Christ are loved; therefore we ought to love God and one another with the same selfless, sacrificial love.[12] This is the splendid summary of the commandments and teaching given to the people of God.[13]

References:
[1]Rom.5:8 [2]Ezek.16:1-5 [3]1 Cor.13:4-8 [4]Gal.5:22 [5]Jn 5:20 [6]1 Jn 4:8-10,16 [7]D. M. Lloyd-Jones, Life in the Spirit, p.137, Banner of Truth [8]Matt.13:45-46 [9]Rom.8:32 [10]Jn 13:1 (RV margin) [11]1 Tim.3:2 [12]1 Jn 4:11,19; 1 Pet.1:22 [13]Matt.22:34-40
Bible quotations from the NASB (2020).

Perspectives on climate change

Stephen McCabe, Belfast, N.Ireland

Wildfires in the United Kingdom. Oscillating between drought and flooding. Melting of Arctic ice. Unusual weather patterns across the globe. Extreme weather events appear to be more common now. Climate change, referring to long-term statistical shifts in weather patterns, is real, and may account for much of what we are seeing. But as disciples of the Lord Jesus Christ, what are we to make of it all? Are calls to action compatible with what we believe?

Science and culture

While the dominant narrative around 'science' is that it objectively transcends culture, the reality is that science takes place necessarily in a cultural context and cannot be divorced from that. We approach it with a critical mind, then, aware that data can be taken and manipulated by different groups for different ends. From large scale multinational energy companies, to the pursuit of research grants, there are vested interests crowding around the issue of climate change. The consensus among scientists at present is that the weather patterns and temperatures we see are in part caused by carbon emissions from human activity. Numerical climate models developed in the 1970s have since won awards for their accuracy,[1] though there is inherent uncertainty in computer simulations and some models appear to project 'implausibly fast' warming.[2] Computer models have been useful in helping us to understand more about the complexity of the earth and atmospheric system.

Climate change and greed

Climate change may be seen as a systemic consequence of human greed. Many of us have, perhaps unquestioningly, bought into a very Western way of thinking – that of consumerism. Consumerism is a way of life that encourages us to pursue the acquisition of ever-increasing amounts of goods and services. The story goes that such an approach is good because it drives our economy ever onwards and upwards, so that society attains greater and greater levels of prosperity. This growth has gone hand-in-hand with, and has been fuelled by, the fossil fuel industry (the burning of coal, oil and gas), and associated increased carbon emissions.

Common sense says that there can be no infinite ascent of prosperity in a world of limited resources, and that the vulnerable will find themselves continually out- competed. It is common to hear developmental non- governmental organizations, or NGOs, calling for people to live more within our means. Living more frugally, being less driven by consumerism, is certainly something that sits comfortably with Paul's teaching in the New Testament. Paul wrote to the Philippian church that he had learned the secret of being content in every circumstance – having abundance or suffering need.[3] The thought is echoed by the writer to the Hebrews who urges believers to be *free from the love of money, being content with what you have.*[4]

Climate change and the vulnerable

Whatever the drivers, climate change is having an impact on society – especially in developing nations which may lack the infrastructural investment to deal with or adapt to extreme events. They are likely to face more food security issues as shifts in weather patterns impact on agricultural practices. Even within so-called developed countries, vulnerable groups are more likely to suffer hardship – for example, the elderly and very young are particularly vulnerable to prolonged heatwaves, and those with little choice of where to live may often find themselves in areas of flood risk.

It is in the heart of Yahweh to stand with the vulnerable, as He so often did through the word of Old Testament prophets. Today, as disciples of the Lord Jesus, compassion for the vulnerable should motivate action. We can be thankful that we have the ability to do this collectively in churches of God through initiatives of the Fellowship Relief Committee, for instance.

We trust the sovereign God

We do have a biblical basis for having confidence in the stability of the global atmospheric system. After the Flood, God promised: *"While the earth remains, seedtime and harvest, cold and heat, summer and winter, and day and night shall not cease"*[5] (albeit this looks different in different parts of the world), but 'climate disruption' is evident, and the consequences are very real for many – we might conceive of this as part of the groaning of creation, yearning in hope for the revealing of the sons of God.[6]

We know that God is Sovereign, and He is good. The Bible, in many places, records weather events that God ordained as judgment or blessing on people (for example, Joseph's seven years of plenty and seven years of famine in Egypt[7]). Under the Mosaic Law, Israel's idolatry invited crop failures.[8] In the end-time, certain judgements appear to involve climatic effects.[9]

Ultimately, we can be sure that God always remains in control of His creation.

References:
[1]https://www.nationalgeographic.com/ environment/article/how-climate-models-got-so- accurate-they-earned-a-nobel-prize;
[2]https://www.science.org/content/article/un-climate-panel-confronts-implausibly-hot- forecasts-future-warming [3]Phil.4:12; [4]Heb.13:5; [5]Gen.8:22; [6]Rom.8:19-22; [7]Gen.41; [8]Lev.26:20; [9]Rev.16:8-9
Bible quotations from the NASB 2020.

God's desire

From Pentecost onwards

Karl Smith, Kirkintilloch, Scotland

God still desires to live in a house on earth, corresponding to something that's in heaven. But where is it to be found? The Lord Jesus said that the time was coming when His worshippers wouldn't worship on Mount Gerizim, where the Samaritans worshipped, nor at the temple in Jerusalem, so we can rule these out. He contrasted these physical locations with the spiritual reality:

"But the hour is coming, and is now here, when the true worshipers will worship the Father in spirit and truth, for the Father is seeking such people to worship him."[1]

Spirit and truth are crucial if we are to understand how and where God wishes to live in the worship of His people.

The Holy Spirit came down on the Day of Pentecost. We know that He lives inside each individual believer from the moment he or she is saved.[2] This fact allows God to live inside us collectively also as we allow ourselves to be built into His structure. A key passage in understanding this is given in Ephesians 2:19-22. Note especially the final sentence:

"So then you are no longer strangers and aliens, but you are fellow citizens with the saints and members of the household [or 'house'] *of God, built on the foundation of the apostles and prophets, Christ Jesus himself being the cornerstone, in whom the whole structure, being joined together, grows into a holy temple in the Lord. In him you also are being built together into a dwelling place for God by the Spirit."*

This new spiritual house for God, like the physical Old Testament one, has a God-given structure. It is built on the person of the Lord Jesus Christ, who is central to the whole thing. His apostles to whom He had 'given commands' through the same 'Holy Spirit' as He spoke to them *"about the kingdom of God"*[3] formed the basis of this house, aligning their teaching with His. The 'prophets', who also worked in these early days, providing messages from the Lord until the New Testament was complete, joined them at the beginning of this age. Therefore the house must be built on the person of Christ as revealed by the Spirit in the New Testament. In this way *"the church of the living God"* will be *"a pillar and buttress of the truth "*,[4] a spiritual house exemplifying spiritual truth in its very structure. Only in such a place will God feel at home.

To the cornerstone of Christ are added individual believers, called, in the graphic language of the Bible, 'living stones', in contrast to the lifeless stones that formed the physical house in Old Testament days. Peter explains:

"As you come to him, a living stone rejected by men but in the sight of God chosen and precious, you yourselves like living stones are being built up as a spiritual house, to be a holy priesthood, to offer spiritual sacrifices acceptable to God through Jesus Christ. "[5]

The structural aspect of the house is also very important. This stands to reason. The truth is objective and coherent and the house that stands for it should be too. The Ephesians passage stresses the integrity of a house formed of several parts in divine architectural arrangement: *"the whole structure, being joined together, grows into a holy temple in the Lord."*[6] The Revised Version gave *"each several building, fitly framed together, groweth into a holy temple in the Lord"* and this may be preferable. The Greek word *pasa* can apparently bear either meaning, but in context 'each several building' seems to make more sense.

The Old Testament temple was made of stones used to construct buildings that together made up the temple. Referring to the reconstructed temple, the disciples said when they saw it: *"Look, Teacher! What wonderful stones and what wonderful buildings!"*[7] Characteristically, the Lord Jesus responded by pointing to the end of this mode of God's house.[8] A new and better way was approaching!

The Church of God in Corinth was told *"you are God's building. "*[9] It was part of a house composed of many such 'buildings'. The Bible not only gives instruction about the relationship between individual believers (stones) within a single church (building), but also about how these churches should relate to each other to form a united house. Believers were baptised and added to the numbers of those already gathered in a local church as we see in Acts 2:41. These are called churches of God and act in relation to other churches of God. Standing for truth, the churches were united in a God-given architectural pattern. To cite an example that is still a point of division for some today, Paul could say of churches divided by geographical borders and vast cultural differences: *"If anyone is inclined to be contentious, we have no such practice"* [as permitting women to pray in church with their heads uncovered], *"nor do the churches of God. "*[10]

In the same letter, he could say on other topics: *"This is my rule in all the churches"[11]* and that something should be done *as in all the churches of the saints.[12]* This verse also gives the reason: *"For God is not a God of confusion but of peace."*

These churches were no more left to form their own local policy than the buildings of the temple were allowed to be built by different architects on different principles. In New Testament times there was no thought in God's mind of 'independent' churches, as we sometimes hear about, and there is no thought about it today. God desires to live in a house, not a series of unconnected buildings.

How did the original churches achieve this unity of teaching and practice across a world as diverse and varied as our own? We get a good example in Acts 15 and 16. There, as people from non-Jewish backgrounds began to be saved and added to the churches, some believers from a Jewish background felt that their non- Jewish brothers and sisters should obey the laws of Moses, especially circumcising their men and sons. Instead of leaving each area to form its own policy (which would have led to disastrous divisions) they sent elders from Syria to Jerusalem where they discussed the issue with the elders there.

The discussion is captured in Acts 15 where we see open debate, analysing practical testimony with the Word of God,[13] which they viewed as authoritative on the subject. Finally they reached their conclusion, saying, *"it has seemed good to us, having come to one accord and it has seemed good to the Holy Spirit and to us."[14]* Again the house is built according to spirit and truth. Paul and Silas and others from Jerusalem then took the decision back to the churches where the issue had arisen.[15] Missionaries Paul and Silas continued by visiting the newest churches so that the decision applied to all the churches globally at that time:

"As they went on their way through the cities, they delivered to them for observance the decisions that had been reached by the apostles and elders who were in Jerusalem. So the churches were strengthened in the faith, and they increased in numbers daily."[16]

This is the pattern by which we operate today in the Churches of God. We see the practice of the early churches as a normative command of God. Those who are added to one of our churches are added to all of them and, conversely, if they have to be removed because of sin, or leave by choice, they are removed from all of them. Each church has its own elders, but when potentially divisive issues arise, they seek the fellowship of the community of elders as a whole so that the same truth is taught and practised everywhere.

The elders come together every eighteen months or so to make sure we are still operating in unity at the leading of the Holy Spirit and any issues that could divide us are raised and discussed.

Because we are human beings, our conferences are by no means perfect, but we see this as part of the architectural pattern by which the house God desires so very much to live in is held together and we want to put it into practice. He has taken the trouble to reveal it in His word and so we try to obey it.

References:
[1]Jn 4:21-24 [2]2 Tim.1:14 [3]Acts 1:2-3 [4]1 Tim.3:15 [5]1 Pet.2:4-5 [6]Eph.2:21
[7]Mk.13:1 [8]Mk.13:2 [9]1 Cor.3:9 [10]1 Cor.11:16 [11]1 Cor.7:17 [12]1 Cor.14:33
[13]Acts 15:15-18 [14]Acts 15:25,28 [15]Acts 15:22-35 [16]Acts 16:4-5
Bible quotations from the ESV.

Can you help me with this?

The inspiration of Scripture

Tony Smith, Kirkintilloch, Scotland

The English word 'inspiration' has wide and varied use in common speech. It can be applied to talented artists, song writers, musicians and poets, for example. However, when applied to the Bible, it has to do with the very origin of Scripture itself. How is it that fallible men were used in the production of the sacred writings that are described as 'The Word of God'? The Bible gives account of itself and its divine origin:

"All scripture is given by inspiration of God, and is profitable for doctrine, for reproof, for correction, for instruction in righteousness, that the man of God may be complete, thoroughly equipped for every good work."[1]

A more precise rendering of the first part of this verse is translated in the New International Version of the Bible as, *"All scripture is God-breathed"*. The original Greek word used here is *theopneustos* which is a compound word: *Theos* meaning 'God', and *pneo* which means to breathe out. The Scriptures are the product of the creative breath of God. Remember how God breathed into man and he became a living being?[2] This demonstrated the amazing power of the breath of God. However, it is not the case that the Scriptures were written and then God breathed into them. Isaiah says, *"The mouth of the LORD has spoken."*[3] They owe their origin to the activity of God the Holy Spirit. They were spoken directly by the Spirit of God to and through men so they could be described as issuing from Almighty God.[4]

A passage of profound importance sheds further light on this. *"For prophecy never had its origin in the human will, but prophets, though human, spoke from God as they were carried along by the Holy Spirit."*[5] So, the message did not originate with the writer, nor did the writers put their own construction or interpretation on what they wrote. They were moved by the Spirit of God. The Greek word used here is: *pherō* – borne along.

In the Acts of the Apostles the same Greek word is used to describe the movement of a ship in a storm. *"The ship was caught by the storm and could not head into the wind; so we gave way to it and were driven along"* [Greek: *pherō*].[6]

The direction of the ship was not determined by human initiative but by the wind. In the inspiration of Scripture, God was guiding and leading the human writers. They were being 'borne along' by the Spirit of God.

This is as far as Scripture goes in defining how the Spirit of God operated in those human writers. The divine and human were blended in a way we are unable to fathom, but one thing is clear: it was not usually done by mechanical dictation and did not lead to the obliteration of the personalities of the writers. Their minds and personalities were fully employed and their natural talents sanctified by the leading of the Holy Spirit. They were preserved from error and their writings were authoritative.

The Bible consists of 66 books penned by men of different types such as shepherds, kings, poets and fishermen, under the leading of the Spirit of God. There is no uniform style, yet there is a great unity of theme that has the stamp of the authority of God.

The writer of Hebrews begins by saying that, *"In the past God spoke ... through the prophets,"*[7] and in Peter's second letter he writes, *"prophets ... spoke from God."*[8] This is not a contradiction, as the words written by these men were in every sense God's word. The faculties of 40 writers over some fifteen centuries were fully used, yet the Bible claims only one author.

What we have today are translations of the original Hebrew and Greek texts, but clearly the doctrine of the inspiration of Scripture refers to the very words of the original text of the sacred writings, not the ideas behind the words (as some modern critics assert). The words are the vehicle of thought and upon their exact meaning depends the discovery of the divine mind.

The Bible is a supernatural book, transforming lives and able to speak powerfully and relevantly to us almost 2000 years since its completion. Its authority extends to all matters about which it speaks. It is the supreme source of our knowledge of God and of the salvation provided through His Son, the Lord Jesus Christ. It is the believer's indispensable resource for daily living.

References:
[1]2 Tim.3:16-17 NKJV [2]Gen.2:7 [3]Isa.1:20; 40:5; 58:14 [4]see e.g., 2 Sam.23:2; Isa.51:16; Jer.1:9 [5]2 Pet.1:21 [6]Acts 27:15 [7]Heb.1:1 [8]2 Pet.1:21
Bible quotations from the NIV (2011), unless stated otherwise.

Riveting revelation

An interview with Vidya Kiran, Mandapeta, India,
recently recognised as a full-time Lord's Servant

What is your family and study background?

I have a wonderful Christian family. My family consists of five members. I have one elder brother and one younger brother. I am the middle one. My father's name is B. Samuel Raju and he is a medical officer by profession. My mother's name is Lalitha and she is a housewife. My Grandpa has been a great influence on my life, edifying me and leading me into the Churches of God. He frequently teaches me more and more about the divine pattern of worship. He has guided me in connection with recognizing the call of God and His service. Recently I got married to Mounika Vardhani.

Regarding my studies, I completed my theological studies (BTh) in Bangalore and also I completed my masters in English (MA English). Now I am doing God's work along with the Fellowship of the Churches of God which is where I found the truth and the knowledge of God. The Church of God is the place where I have grown up.

Would you please describe your salvation experience?

At the age of seven, while sitting in a Sunday school class, I accepted Jesus as my Saviour and Lord. I became aware that I was a sinner and deserved the lake of fire as punishment for my sin. I came to the point of knowledge that Jesus was the Son of God and sent by God to pay the price for all our sins. On the authority of the Word of God, I know that I put my faith upon Jesus at that time for salvation. When I was reading the Bible, my finger stopped at John 3:16 finding the unconditional love and also John 1:12 that tells about my security and guarantee in Him. After some years, I realized that Jesus not only came to save us, but to give us an understanding that we may know Him that is true, and we are in Him who is true, and also He is *the true God and eternal life*.[1]

What is your appreciation of the house of God?

This is the one of my favourite subjects and is a revelation of God. Mr. John Miller wrote about the House of God in Needed Truth volume 42, 1935 on page 147. He brought out many helpful truths from the life of David, particularly in his relationship with the house of God, and exhorted us, and especially younger ones, to be steadfast. There is nothing worth contending for here below unless it is found to answer to the heavenly pattern.

Also brother A.F. Toms wrote about the house of God which is the church of the living God, the pillar and ground of the truth.[2] When I was seeing all these things, I was very surprised at how much He loves us and wants to dwell among us even though we are not worthy of it.

When I think about the house of God, I don't see this as just a topic to preach about, but it also shows me the heart of God and His divine pattern. This revelation is declared in Jacob's vision. 'A bad boy had a good dream' in a place that was revealed as the gate of heaven.

How did the new church at Mandapeta come about?

This ministry started in 2017 with one family. The mighty hand of God led us to show His love towards many others. In the midst of many trials, problems and shames, God showed His love to strengthen us. God Himself brought the people to church gatherings. The planting was in 2019 and the text was *"Fear not, little flock."*[3] Now we have 35 members.

What is your vision for the future?

My future vision is to do the ministry in Churches of God and establish many churches in India, preaching the Gospel and teaching the divine pattern of worship. Also, I have a great desire to equip the young people for the coming generations. God willing, I want to start Bible class programs as well as edifying the church saints to mature as disciples.

References:

[1] 1 Jn 5:20 [2] 1 Tim.3:15 NKJV [3] Lk.12:32 ESV

More than a golden opportunity

Gilbert Grierson, Armagh, N.Ireland

One of my favourite books of the Bible to read through is the Acts of the Apostles. It is so exciting to see how the Gospel spread out from Jerusalem, and the methods that were employed in proclaiming its life-giving and soul- saving truths.

The Apostle Paul adapted his presentation of the unchanging message to the audience or individuals with whom he came into contact as he fulfilled his calling. He travelled wherever he and his companions were led by the Spirit of God, seeking out his Jewish kinsmen first in the many towns and cities he visited, then turning to preach to Gentile audiences, as he'd been commissioned. He used a different approach in witnessing to Gentiles with no knowledge of the Old Testament Scriptures (for example in Athens), in contrast to Jews in synagogues where the Old Testament was read daily.

What situation do we find ourselves in today in the UK? Knowledge of the Scriptures has been largely lost, especially among the younger generation.

Consequently, writers of Gospel leaflets look around for some subject that will be familiar to possible recipients and will likely attract their attention and encourage them to read the leaflet. Different leaflets attract different people, so Hayes Press publish a variety.

Recently, the Platinum Jubilee of Queen Elizabeth II – Queen of the United Kingdom and fourteen other Commonwealth realms – provided an opportunity. Throughout her 70 year-long reign, Queen Elizabeth has consistently witnessed to her fundamental belief in God, the Bible and the person of the Lord Jesus as undergirding her life and service. Seizing the opportunity, a leaflet incorporating some truths of the Gospel was written by a sister in a church of God. Hayes Press, the publishing arm of the Churches of God, printed this for distribution. Here are a few accounts of how these were used around the UK:

London: "I gradually gave out a few tracts here and there locally, at the beginning of Jubilee week…. It was quite easy to say to people 'Can I give you a leaflet about the Queen?' … I took the remainder up to St.

James' Park and the Mall [in Central London]… there were a lot of bored-looking security guards along the route and most of them were happy to take one."

Leicester: "One or two people in the Leicester church use leaflets on a personal basis when opportunity presents itself rather than blanket distribution…. We used the Jubilee leaflets recently at our tea meeting and coffee morning… We have a selection of Hayes Press tracts and other publications on permanent display on our church bookstall in the foyer which people in the church, as well as visitors, are free to take."

Leigh: "In Leigh a few of us take gospel leaflets out every couple of months. With the recent Jubilee tract, many in the church took a handful of the leaflets to share with friends and relatives. About 700 leaflets were distributed in the locality of our church meeting hall. People took them willingly.

"Often when we've distributed gospel tracts we will have had visitors to the Remembrance. A label on the back points recipients to our hall address, our website, our Facebook page and gives a telephone contact. Occasionally a phone call comes for chat or enquiry."

Buckhaven: "Karl and I gave out 500 Jubilee tracts in Buckhaven recently. As a direct result of this, a man named Mohammad contacted Martin Jones via the Churches of God website asking for a Bible. Martin forwarded the email to Neville and me. Neville met with him at the hall and gave him a Bible…"

Whitehills: The Queen's Platinum Jubilee was a fine excuse to revisit and carry the Gospel to each home in Whitehills and some in nearby Banff. Two called out "Thank you!" as I left their gardens …John had had an accident at work and fell several metres into liquid cement. He saw a bright light come towards him; he thought the end had come, before his colleagues pulled him out and cleared his airways. "It has made me think," he said. I left him with the tract, 'Peace with God'."

As one contributor wrote, "We will only know the full extent of our labours in this field when we get home to glory."

Be encouraged: keep sowing brothers and sisters!